THE PENGUIN SM

Nicholas Humphrey is a partner with Deacons, and practices corporate law, specialising in mergers and aquisitions and private equity. He has practised as a lawyer for over 13 years and worked with major law firms in Sydney and London. He has a Bachelor of Commerce and a Bachelor of Laws from the University of New South Wales, and a Postgraduate Diploma in Applied Finance and Investment from the Financial Services Institute of Australia (FINSIA).

He is a member of FINSIA, the Australian Venture Capital Association, the Law Society of New South Wales, the Australian Institute of Company Directors and the American Bar Association (ABA). Nicholas has been acknowledged as a leading lawyer in private equity in the *Asia Pacific Legal 500* and the Guide to the *World's Leading Private Equity Lawyers*.

He has advised on a wide range of corporate transactions including acquisitions and disposals of private companies, management buy-outs, initial public offerings and joint ventures. He acts for some of Australia's leading private equity funds.

Nicholas is the author of a number of bestselling books including *The Business Startup Guide* and *The Penguin Australian Home Buyer's Guide*. He has been on the board of several private companies.

He is a regular contributer to media discussions on business and has had numerous articles and commentaries published in the *Sydney Morning Herald*, the *Daily Telegraph*, the *Securities Institute Journal* and the *Australian Venture Capital Journal*.

Nicholas lives in Sydney with his wife, Victoria, and their three children, Thomas, Megan and Angus.

PUBLICATION/EMBARGO DATE

JUN 2007

PENGUIN GROUP (AUSTRALIA)

To my loving wife, Victoria

THE PENGUIN

Small
Business
Guide

The complete reference handbook
for small to medium enterprises

NICHOLAS HUMPHREY

Penguin Books

Penguin Books

Published by the Penguin Group
Penguin Group (Australia)
250 Camberwell Road, Camberwell, Victoria 3124, Australia
(a division of Pearson Australia Group Pty Ltd)
Penguin Group (USA) Inc.
375 Hudson Street, New York, New York 10014, USA
Penguin Group (Canada)
90 Eglinton Avenue East, Suite 700, Toronto, Canada ON M4P 2Y3
(a division of Pearson Penguin Canada Inc.)
Penguin Books Ltd
80 Strand, London WC2R 0RL England
Penguin Ireland
25 St Stephen's Green, Dublin 2, Ireland
(a division of Penguin Books Ltd)
Penguin Books India Pvt Ltd
11 Community Centre, Panchsheel Park, New Delhi – 110 017, India
Penguin Group (NZ)
67 Apollo Drive, Rosedale, North Shore 0632, New Zealand
(a division of Pearson New Zealand Ltd)
Penguin Books (South Africa) (Pty) Ltd
24 Sturdee Avenue, Rosebank, Johannesburg 2196, South Africa

Penguin Books Ltd, Registered Offices: 80 Strand, London, WC2R 0RL, England

First published by Penguin Books Australia Ltd, 2004
This revised edition published by Penguin Group (Australia), 2007

10 9 8 7 6 5 4 3 2 1

Text copyright © Nicholas Humphrey 2007

Cover and text design by Karen Trump © Penguin Group (Australia)
Typeset in Stone Sans and Granjon by Post Pre-press Group, Brisbane, Queensland
Printed in Australia by McPherson's Printing Group, Maryborough, Victoria

National Library of Australia
Cataloguing-in-Publication data:

Humphrey, Nicholas, 1971–.
    The Penguin small business guide.

    2nd ed.
    Includes index.
    ISBN 9780143005520.
    ISBN 0 14 300552 9.

    1. Small business – Handbooks, manuals, etc. 2. Business –
    Australia. I. Title.

338.642

www.penguin.com.au

CONTENTS

ACKNOWLEDGEMENTS

Primary contributors

Many thanks to:

Fiona Wallwork from Deacons for the contribution of chapter twenty-one.

James Stewart from Deacons for reviewing chapter six.

Peter Norman from Deacons for reviewing chapters seven and eight.

Sally Woodward from Deacons for reviewing chapter ten.

IP Australia for contributing to chapter sixteen.

Dean Newlan from McGrath Nicol Forensic for the contribution of chapter twenty-two.

Sydney Business Enterprise Centre and the NSW Department of State and Regional Development for preparing the glossary of business terms.

Contributors

Further thanks to:

Austrade for the provision of research materials for chapter twenty.

Joseph Najem from Accenture for reviewing chapters three and four.

Neil Cooke and **Grant Layland** from Grant Thornton for reviewing chapters eleven and twelve.

Ken Lee from ANZ for preparing many of the case studies.

Nick Abrahams from Deacons for reviewing chapter sixteen.

Chris Allen from Deacons for reviewing chapters seventeen and eighteen.

Michael French from Deacons for reviewing chapter nine.

Joe Dowd for reviewing chapter five.

Australian Securities and Investments Commission for the provision of materials on directors' duties for chapter six.

Paul Moorcroft from AON Risk Services for reviewing chapter fifteen.

Contributors to previous editions of this book

This book has been a major undertaking over the last five years and there have been many other people who have contributed including: Andrew Cochineas, Georgina Rich, Arabella Mayne, Shane Hodson, Frank Sharkey, Pascal Gautheron, Rowan Macdonald, Derek Tennent, Malcolm Ramsay and Jim Kuiper.

INTRODUCTION

The Penguin Small Business Guide is a complete reference manual for small and medium enterprises. It provides practical and up-to-date advice on a broad range of issues affecting Australian businesses, including legal, financial, tax, marketing, workplace relations, strategy, accounting and business planning.

It will be useful if you are considering starting your own business, buying a business or franchise, growing an existing business or launching your products into overseas markets. The book aims to help your business at any stage of its life cycle, whether you are a small startup operation run from a garage or a multimillion-dollar operation with hundreds of staff and offices around the world.

Inspirational case studies of successful Australian and international businesspeople like Richard Branson, Dick Smith and Gerry Harvey are scattered throughout. The book is intended to be a 'one stop shop' and contains checklists, practical examples, useful phone numbers and web sites. Many chapters contain tips on how and where to get (free) advice or financial assistance (including government schemes and industry awards/grants).

It provides step-by-step instructions on the following topics, among others:

- effective business planning and strategy
- structuring your business from a risk and tax perspective
- maximising your chances of raising debt and equity finance (including from business angels and venture capitalists)
- understanding your legal obligations

- recent changes to the tax system and GST
- launching successful marketing strategies
- complying with your regulatory and licensing obligations
- making the most of e-commerce and the Internet
- understanding your financial statements and forecasts
- strategies for finding, hiring and retaining staff.

It is important to learn as much as possible about business and know when to get professionals, such as lawyers and accountants, involved. This guide covers a broad range of issues relating to establishing and growing a business. Not all topics considered will be relevant to your business, as much depends on the size of the business and your specific industry. Some issues will only become relevant to your business as it grows through its life cycle.

Challenges facing small and medium businesses

Running a small business presents unique and complex challenges for entrepreneurs. You will be required to master a broad range of technical skills such as strategic planning, financial accounting, sales and marketing techniques, negotiation skills and corporate law – skill sets which in larger companies would be spread amongst a number of specialist managers.

The competitive environment is unstable, unpredictable and hostile. New well-funded entrants may launch at any time. Similarly, new products and substitutes may appear, making your business obsolete. You must be agile enough to change your strategic direction and reinvent your business to respond to these factors. Existing players will not take kindly to a new entrant and will use whatever means necessary to remove you as a threat.

You will need extraordinary management, leadership and organisational skills if you are to build a robust business. You will need a quasi-evangelical personality to convince key stakeholders to back your high-risk idea – not only is demand for your product or business untested, it requires significant capital expenditure to build and is likely to run at a loss for quite a long time. You must compete for scarce resources – staff, capital and services – against other established businesses who can show their stakeholders a track record and proven business model.

This book attempts to examine the peculiar challenges facing small or medium enterprises, and to provide you with some of the skills to manage those challenges.

SOME RECENT TRENDS

The last few years have seen some fundamental changes in the Australian business environment. In order to successfully operate a business in such a dynamic climate you need to understand the key trends affecting business in Australia.

e-commerce

The forecast growth of the Internet, both in Australia and globally, represents a major opportunity for existing businesses to expand and capture market share by becoming e-commerce enabled. It also represents a continued opportunity for new businesses to be formed to utilise the technology in previously unthought of ways. Yahoo, Google, eBay and Amazon are now household names with billion-dollar market capitalisations, yet the businesses were unheard of five or so years ago.

Taxation regime

In recent times the Australian tax regime has gone through some fundamental restructuring including the introduction of the GST, introduction of share-to-share rollover relief, tax consolidation for corporate groups, and a 50 per cent exemption from capital gains tax for assets held longer than twelve months. Before adopting your corporate structure you must obtain advice from an experienced tax adviser. An inappropriate structure can result in adverse tax consequences at a time when your business cannot afford it. On the other hand, avoid adopting an overly complex or unusual tax structure as it may turn future investors off your company or jeopardise your long-term commercial objectives or exit strategies.

Globalisation

The geographical boundaries for business have blurred. Your competitors now include well-funded and aggressive foreign corporations looking to expand into new markets. The flip side of this of course is that your business has the opportunity to be 'born global' and service not only the Australian market but also the global market. You need to consider globalisation when setting up your business in order to understand the dynamics of doing business overseas.

Other trends

There are a number of other important trends which continue to shape business in Australia:

- Product life cycles have become shorter due to inbuilt obsolescence or rapid development programs.
- There is a high level of regulatory complexity facing small businesses in Australia (which has worsened with the introduction of the business activity statement).
- The government has committed a high level of support for small businesses, and will promote innovation through

a mix of tax concessions, government grants and free information/consulting services.

- Businesses are focusing on their core activities, with any non-core activities (such as human resources or IT services) being outsourced to third-party providers.

CRITICAL SUCCESS FACTORS

Critical success factors of small to medium businesses are:

- deciding the market entry strategy – the mixture of subsidiary sales offices and distributors
- managing the 'extent issue' – deciding what won't be done
- maintaining alliances with large nationals and multinationals, which can be the key to world markets, especially knowledge of overseas markets
- deciding the business model and plan, including exit strategies for investors
- establishing competitive pricing and margin models
- investing in market research
- finding customers who are risk takers, i.e. early adopters with technical expertise.

There are a number of other factors that are critical to the success of any business, including understanding your legal obligations, cultivating your best asset (your staff), understanding your market, gaining access to funds and understanding your competitors. All of these topics are dealt with in more detail throughout *The Penguin Small Business Guide*.

1. THE CONCEPT FOR YOUR BUSINESS

- **Degree of innovation**
- **Generating a business concept**
- **Assessing your business concept**

This chapter considers a number of methods to assist you in generating an innovative business idea or concept. It also considers a disciplined process for assessing and rejecting ideas to ensure you don't waste valuable time and money trying to launch a dead-end business.

DEGREE OF INNOVATION

INNOVATION QUADRANT

	Low	Market Diversification	High
High			
	Product/Service Diversification (1)		New Market (2)
Product/Service Innovation			
	Market Penetration (3)		Market Diversification (4)
Low	Low	Business System Innovation	High

The table above classifies new business ideas according to the level of innovation in the product/services offered and the level of innovation in the business systems used or the amount of market diversification. When thinking of innovation, people normally think of revolutionary new products. However innovation in business systems (such as manufacturing, distribution or marketing) is equally as important. Dell revolutionised PC Sales using a new form of direct distribution, where a PC is only produced after it is ordered.

Ideas can be classified as follows:

1. **Product/service diversification** – developing a new product or service and selling it to an existing market, using existing business systems. Ranges from minor improvements to radically new products.

2. **New market** – selling a new product or service to a new market and/or business system innovations. This is the highest risk/return part of the innovation quadrant. Australian inventors are prolific and innovative but not generally good businesspeople. Only 1 out of every 1000 inventors actually gets a product to market. Some well-known Australian products include Triton work benches, Hills Hoist rotary clothes lines and Kambrook multi-outlet power boards.

3. **Market penetration** – selling an existing product or service to an existing market. This is typically the lowest risk/return part of innovation quadrant. It involves trying to capture market share of an existing industry. The key drivers will be the level of competition and will often result in lower prices for that product or service.

4. **Market diversification** – selling an existing product or service to a new market (such as finding a new use for a product, new target segment or new geographical region), or using innovative business systems. A recent example is repacking wine and marketing to an under-thirties female demographic.

Some experts will tell you that to be successful you must have a groundbreaking innovation. In fact, the reverse may be true. A concept that attempts to offer a new product or service to an untested market is a gamble and, therefore, has a lower probability of success.

Another common misconception is that an innovative idea or invention will be guaranteed overnight success. Unfortunately, your unique concept must compete against a thousand other 'unique' ideas for consumers' interest, investors' wallets and suppliers' trust. In short, you must be able to execute the vision well.

GENERATING A BUSINESS CONCEPT

This section considers three methods for generating new business concepts:

- spotting a gap in the market
- copying a successful concept
- merging two existing concepts.

It is important to note that these methods do not guarantee that you will discover a truly novel business idea. The truth is that most good ideas will come to you when you least expect them (like on the bus or in the shower) – the important thing is to know a good business idea when you see it.

CASE STUDY:
Fred Smith – Federal Express (FedEx)

Fred Smith, founder of Federal Express, compiled a fortune by enabling the world of business to deliver its goods quickly, anywhere in the world.

FedEx was developed in two stages. The first stage began in Smith's undergraduate days at Yale when he wrote an economics paper about his observation that, as society became more automated, companies like IBM and Xerox that sold early computer devices needed to make sure that their products were dependable. It would be vital for them to be able to supply replacement parts or additions in a totally reliable way. Without this reliability, businesses which employed computers would come to a standstill. What was required was a delivery system that facilitated immediate replacement or repair. The postal system would be inadequate, as it was not sufficiently fast, dependable or far-reaching. The second stage – actually launching a business to fill this need – only occurred years later.

Smith graduated from Yale in 1966, joined the Marine Corps and was sent to Vietnam, serving as a platoon commander and pilot. During his tour of duty, he gained insight into the logistics system for the military which was an inventory-intensive supply–push system similar to the one he would later develop at FedEx. When Smith returned to USA in 1971, the predictions made in his Yale economics paper had come true. Computers were replacing human functions, but the dependability of those products and the delivery systems for repairs were not up to par.

Smith set about finding a solution to the problems by creating a delivery system that operated in the same way as a bank's clearing house. All points on a network were connected through a central hub. The rationale seemed absurd when narrowed down to each individual transaction because it meant making a minimum of one extra stop. However, if you were able to step back and analyse the network as a whole, it was an efficient way to create an enormous number of connections. For example, if you wanted to connect 100 markets with one another and you used direct point-to-point deliveries, it would take 100 times 99, or 9900, direct deliveries. If, however, you used a single clearing system, it would only take a maximum of 100 deliveries. Such a system would be about 100 times as efficient. This same idea was subsequently employed in the airline industry.

Smith recognised that it was feasible to run small, high-value-added computer parts through the delivery network connected at the central hub. His other display of entrepreneurial flair was the decision to combine planes and trucks within the same delivery system. At the age of 27, he started putting his theoretical system into practice.

The problem with starting FedEx was that it required a large quantity of seed funding – the nature of the business was such that you could not start small and expand, as you could with most businesses. He had to accept the risk and build an entire network upfront. In order to win potential clients, Smith had to have a complete network to sell. He reasoned that even though it was front-end loaded, once the network was up and running and the business achieved a break-even point, the incremental profits were exceedingly powerful.

Smith invested his own and his family's money to begin setting up a 25-city network. He leased some planes to test the system. For two weeks he flew empty boxes back and forth throughout the country and, on 17 April 1973, FedEx went live.

To keep the network growing beyond the original 25 cities, Smith raised a large amount of venture capital. While he was asking for significant amounts (about US$90 million), he had several things going for him. First, he had his own money in the venture and second, the business was demonstrating each day its ability to meet a growing need (many independent marketing studies backed this up). The underlying concept of the business was also very simple so people found it easy to understand. Once the demand for the service was established, there were no problems with obtaining the required investor funds.

While it was obvious how well FedEx would do once it achieved the break-even point, it took 26 months and losses of US$29 million before this occurred. While the venture capitalists remained nervous, Smith was absolutely convinced that he was right about the viability and immense profit potential of his business.

Smith believes that there were several keys to FedEx's success. The business model was truly different and sustainable. It was able to establish itself as the brand of choice and hold on to that market position. It started with a conservative business plan that was detailed and achievable with all the necessary buffers built in.

The key to inspiring the best in others, according to Smith, is communication and feedback – in particular, letting people know when they've done a good job. Workers want to know what's expected of them and how they're doing. They also want to know what's in it for them, so FedEx implemented award programs, profit sharing and internal promotions. You also need to communicate with your workers to ensure they understand that their work has purpose and meaning. FedEx tells its employees that they are delivering the most important commerce in the history of the world – someone's pacemaker, chemotherapy treatment for cancer, the part that keeps the F-18s flying or the legal brief that decides the case.

Spotting a gap in the market

'There is nothing in the world as powerful as an idea whose time has come.'   Victor Hugo

Spotting a gap in the market means identifying a need of a segment of the market that is currently not being serviced. In some instances the gap arises because of a change in the spending habits of a population, a new technological innovation or simply because of an event, such as the Olympic Games or the millennium bug.

You can find a gap by attempting to predict changes in the market. To do this you must understand socio-demographic and economic trends. The Australian Bureau of Statistics produces reams of data and statistics about the changing trends in Australia, such as instances of home ownership, usage rates of the Internet and the number of people with facsimiles (see their web site **www.abs.gov.au**). Newspapers and current affairs programs also report on current trends. Below are some important trends in Australia at present and the impact these may have on the future marketplace.

RECENT TRENDS IN AUSTRALIA

Trend	Impact
The proportion of people over 55 years of age is increasing.	There will be an increased need for health-care services and retirement villages.
There are over 450 000 students currently in higher education.	Highly educated people are more sophisticated in their buying decisions.
The proportion of women in the workforce has increased dramatically in the last ten years.	There will be a greater need for child-care facilities.
People are more prepared to take control of tasks traditionally outsourced, such as doing their tax return and renovations.	There will be a greater demand for magazines and books to help this do-it-yourself culture.

Once you have identified a trend, assess what needs that trend has created and then analyse what new business ideas will satisfy that need.

Copying a successful concept

Another way of generating new ideas is to analyse those businesses that are currently successful or have spotted a gap in the market. The market may be able to support a number of players, or you may be able to improve upon the quality of the product or service already provided.

There are a number of potential places you can search to find newly launched businesses:

- IP Australia's patents office (see chapter sixteen)
- business incubators (see chapter seventeen)
- trade associations
- trade expos
- trade journals and magazines.

You can also search for a suitable business idea when travelling overseas. A number of newly launched Australian businesses are merely copies of successful US and European models.

Merging two existing concepts

You may be able to combine aspects of different existing businesses to produce a new concept. Different industries and technologies are rapidly converging, creating opportunities for fast movers. For example, interactive television is an obvious example of merging existing ideas – Internet and TV.

CASE STUDY:
Dick Smith

Dick Smith has become an Australian business icon. He sold his first business, Dick Smith Electronics, to Woolworths for $25 million at age 38.

Dick unashamedly admits that his success has come from copying the successes of others. He would always seek out the best advice or observe what worked with others and duplicate these things in his own business. He believes that more small businesses would survive if they only knew how to ask for advice from people already in business. People love to help if only you ask them.

He started his first business with virtually no money and ran operations out of his home. When he had saved just enough to move out to his own premises, he found a small place, paid himself a meagre salary and continued to live at home and hitchhike to work. He emphasises the principle of spending within your means and keeping overheads as low as possible in order to limit your risk. All profits were put back into the business. His advice to startups is to minimise borrowings and only build the business with profits generated by the business.

A hallmark of Dick's business style was the importance of belief in the product being sold. He would only allow his salespeople to sell a product if they believed in it as much as he did. Another factor contributing to his success was that while he made many mistakes, he never made a mistake more than once.

When pressed, Dick states that good service is the key to his success. It is service that differentiates one business from another and failure in this area is what brings most small businesses undone. In order to ensure good service, he devised incentive schemes to enthuse his staff to go to work each day and align their personal goals with the goals of the business.

Another factor that Dick believes is important is to put your name to the business. If you are prepared to stake the credibility of your name on the business, customers are more comfortable in dealing with you. This belief was well rewarded when, in 1986, Woolworths acquired Dick Smith Electronics. A large part of the value of the company was attributable to the fact that the name and the trademark face had become so well known.

Dick believes that the more publicity you can get for yourself and the business, the better it will be for sales, which explains his constant presence in the media with various stunts and attention-grabbing statements.

After the electronics business, Dick went into publishing, which also proved lucrative. *Australian Geographic* was sold to John Fairfax in 1988 for $40 million.

His current business venture is Dick Smith Foods, where he has been tapping into the national consciousness with his calls to buy Australian products and keep jobs for Australian kids. This message has successfully drawn market share from the multinationals. His successful copycat methods have been evident in products such as TT's chocolate biscuits, Dick's Nutra-Bites and Dickheads matches to compete alongside established products Tim Tam biscuits, Nutri-Grain cereal and Redheads matches. In the first nine months, the food business made close to $28 million in retail sales, with $920 000 expended on marketing and trademark publicity stunts.

Even the media have found it difficult to strike him down with his nationalistic chord and large contribution of profits to charity.

Dick loves growing small businesses into large ones. However, once they become big businesses, he gets bored. If a business's staff cannot all fit on the same bus, then the business has become too big for him!

ASSESSING YOUR BUSINESS CONCEPT

The ability to evaluate new business concepts quickly is critical for entrepreneurs. Much time and money is wasted on concepts that will never be launched. Astute entrepreneurs and investors are able to quickly scrutinise the viability of a business idea and assess whether it can profitably compete and survive.

Unfortunately, the financial analytical frameworks used by large corporations, management consultants and accounting firms (such as net present value calculations) are usually inappropriate for assessing small businesses. There is usually not enough time or volume of reliable data to use their traditional frameworks. The frameworks are more relevant for mature businesses that have financial and market size data and well-known industry trends to benchmark against. There is usually an inverse relationship between the volume of data available and the attractiveness of the opportunity, as the more that is known about a market and its profitability, the more likely there are competitors.

The following five-step process enables the filtering of new ideas in a disciplined and systematic manner.

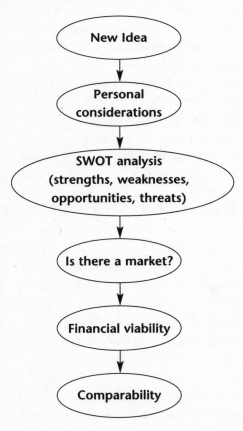

Entrepreneurs should, however, use this initial filter to eliminate only truly dead-end projects, not to reject all ideas by identifying their every short-coming.

How much effort should an entrepreneur devote before rejecting an idea? This will depend on several factors. Business concepts that require significant capital obviously have to be better researched than ventures which are virtually self-financed. Similarly, ventures with more complex operations will require more detailed analysis and planning.

Step 1: Personal considerations

The first step in assessing whether the concept is viable for you is to consider your personal circumstances. Ask yourself these three questions:

- Do you have the skills to launch the business?
- Are you keenly interested in the business?
- Will your family and friends support you?

Skills If you don't have the specialised experience and training to manage a business in your industry you risk making costly mistakes while 'learning on the job' – mistakes that could damage your reputation. Launching any new business requires a number of different skills. You will need to be a generalist with knowledge across a number of areas – finance, sales, marketing, law, tax and operations. Below are three broad categories of skills that are typically required when running a business. While the importance of each skill varies across industries, you will need a basic understanding of each area.

Finance	Marketing	Operations
Budgeting	Choice of location	Stock control
Break even analysis	Market research	Supplier relationships
Financial statements	Distribution	Logistics
Tax returns	Loyalty programs	Staff training
Organising finance	Pricing strategy	Manufacturing
Cash-flow management	Direct marketing	Rosters

The type of industry in which your new business will operate may also require highly specialised technical, regulatory or market knowledge. For example, businesses operating in telecommunications are subject to a complex regulatory regime. Similarly, if you plan to launch an Internet web site retailing surfwear you will need to understand not only the fashion industry but the technology that supports the Internet and how this impacts upon a user's ability to navigate your web site.

It is important to bear in mind, however, that you can acquire new skills through reading journals and textbooks and attending seminars, conferences and short courses of study. As an alternative to study you can always plan to work for a period in the industry to gain the necessary experience and networking opportunities before launching your own venture.

While people with many years of experience in an industry typically generate the most successful ideas, Steve Jobs and Steve Wozniak dropped out of college to start Apple Computer.

Entrepreneurs must also have the capacity to execute their new business concept well. Through their enthusiasm, networks, focus and skill, entrepreneurs must persuade customers, investors, employees and suppliers to support an untested concept. The ability to execute well is particularly important when ideas can easily be replicated. For example, if an innovation cannot be protected by a patent you must launch the business quickly and manage it well so that others don't move in on your business opportunity.

Interest It is not simply enough to think the business will make money. Launching a new business is extremely demanding and can place considerable pressure on your family and friends. Unless you are truly passionate about the business it is unlikely that you will have the discipline required to work the long hours and the ability to cope with the inevitable stresses of tight timetables and near disasters. You need to be intimately involved in every aspect of your business. No employee or consultant will be as committed as you are – they don't have as much to gain (or lose) as you do.

However, projects that appeal to one person may not excite others. You need to determine what you are hoping to personally achieve and assess what sacrifices you are prepared to make. Do you want to make a fortune or will a small profit or enhanced lifestyle suffice? Do you seek public recognition? Do you want to cash out quickly or are you building an empire?

Tip from the trenches

Don't fool yourself into thinking you can launch a successful company while working full-time for someone else. You must be focused on the critical success factors of your business and its core opportunity. Anything that distracts you from giving this 100 per cent focus can lead to failure.

While you might like the industry in which you work, take some time to consider what type of tasks you will have to perform to get the business launched and operating. Will you have to do boring and repetitive work or be required to perform tasks you dislike, such as direct selling of your product by knocking on doors? You can eventually employ staff to do some of this work but you will have to do a bit of everything initially – or maybe longer – so you need to be committed.

Support   Most jobs require reasonably long hours. Launching a new business is particularly time pressured. This is especially true in an era where 'first mover' advantage can mean the difference between success and failure. It is vitally important that you have the support of your spouse, family and friends. Will they put up with you working long hours while you are struggling to launch the new business? It is also important to maintain a balanced lifestyle. There is little point in being successful without any family or friends to enjoy it with.

Step 2: SWOT analysis (strengths, weaknesses, opportunities, threats)

A SWOT analysis is intended to identify the strengths and weaknesses within the business (internal or controllable factors) and highlight opportunities and threats in the external environment (largely uncontrollable factors). This will allow you to utilise your competitive advantages and implement strategies to minimise or overcome your business's weaknesses. Similarly, you will be able to exploit market opportunities to the fullest and protect against threats from the external business environment, such as seasonal downturns. These factors will be different for each business and industry, and they change over time, as markets fluctuate and evolve.

Your SWOT analysis at this stage should be limited to the business's 'key success factors' – strategic influences essential to the business's success.

Strengths/weaknesses   These are factors relating to the internal functions of your business and are largely controllable. They include:
- dedicated and skilled staff
- access to finance
- wide network of contacts
- experienced and focused management.

The extent to which you can control these elements determines whether they are considered a strength or a weakness.

Opportunities and threats   These key factors are external to the business and hard to control. They include:
- economic cycle
- industry reputation
- government/legal prohibitions or regulations
- tax treatment
- technology, scalability and accessibility
- social and demographic trends
- size of target market.

You will need to assess whether these are currently working in your favour or not.

After undertaking a SWOT analysis you will have to make a judgment about whether the weaknesses/threats are insurmountable.

Step 3: Is there a market?

Without a sufficient market for your product or service, your business is doomed before it starts. Chapter three details how to understand your market, but initially you must be able to answer some of the following questions in relation to your selected business idea:

- Who will buy your product or service?
- Why will they buy from you instead of the competition?
- How large is the target market?
- What will your share of the market be?
- What are the basic needs of the target market?
- How does your product or service match or satisfy those needs?

When considering who your customers are it is important to be specific. It is tempting to consider everyone as a prospective buyer. However, products designed to satisfy everyone's needs tend to suffer from 'feature bloat' and cost too much to develop and produce. A specific target market makes the product faster to design and launch. While it may seem counter-intuitive, the smaller the market segment you target, the more you will generally sell.

Customer value   A key principle is that the likely success of a business idea will depend on customer satisfaction. Customers spend money to satisfy a need and it is important to be able to demonstrate that your idea fulfils a need. Entrepreneurs and innovators often focus on the technical details of their product. It is far more important to focus on the customer value. What is your product's 'unique selling proposition' or USP? What is it about your product which sets it apart from other products – what is new and better than currently available products? You must be able to present your idea in a way that makes sense to the consumer. If the consumer cannot understand the advantages of using your product they will not buy it.

Market size It is important to be able to quantify the potential size of the market. You will need to undertake research to calculate the size of the market using verifiable/reliable data from the Australian Bureau of Statistics, trade associations, commerce and trade journals, newspapers and the Internet.

The next step is to do some rough calculations to estimate how much of the market you will be able to capture and whether this will generate enough revenue to justify the costs of establishing the business.

At this stage you are simply doing a 'top-down' analysis to see if the potential market is big enough.

Step 4: Financial viability

You will need to consider the following questions when assessing financial viability:

- Can the business generate enough cash to cover expenses and return a profit?
- Do you have access to sufficient capital to get the business started?
- How long will it be before you can expect the business to break even?

One approach for assessing financial viability is to determine the level of sales necessary to achieve your targeted return. This should cover your salary, cost of capital and a return for the risk taken. You can then assess the likelihood of achieving that level of sales.

Step 5: Comparability

Some entrepreneurs are faced with multiple business opportunities. How do you choose between two new business concepts that seem equally lucrative? Launching one business is demanding enough without the distractions of another venture competing for your time and analytical capacity. Further, unless you have access to an unlimited pool of finance, you can probably only afford to back one concept at a time.

Many large corporations use the discounted cash flow (DCF) they expect from a project as the standard measure of its attractiveness relative to other proposals. However, entrepreneurs often cannot reliably use DCF models to assess multiple opportunities. Cash flows from a new venture are highly unpredictable compared with those from a mature business. Slight changes in (largely unverifiable) assumptions lead to huge differences in projected value.

Issues to consider when choosing between competing opportunities include the following:

Exit probability   Does the business have a high possibility of securing an exit, whether from a trade sale to another business or a public offering of shares onto the stock exchange? Exitable businesses typically have a 'sustainable competitive advantage' from the development of technology, exclusive alliances or distributors, or a deeply embedded brand.

Low capital   Businesses with low capital requirements can be high-growth businesses that can generate funds early and reliably.

Low fixed costs   Businesses with low fixed costs on a month-to-month basis will survive long enough for sales levels to ramp-up to break-even point.

High return   There must be the capacity for high levels of return. Avoid market space with high levels of competition.

Cost of failure   Assess the costs of failure, not only the money you will lose but the damage to your reputation and the time lost in winding the venture up. A business that returns your capital outlay quickly may be preferable to one that will return more in the long term.

CASE STUDY:
George Lewin – Triton

As a 26-year-old TV journalist in 1975, George Lewin invented – almost by accident – the Triton saw bench in his backyard shed.

It all began with George's antique restoring next-door neighbour encouraging him to build a dining table even though George was a novice at woodwork. Having secured a promise of assistance from his neighbour in the event of problems, George bought some expensive wood for the table. His expert neighbour sold up and moved out before he got around to cutting it up, but George decided to continue anyway. After giving up on using a handsaw due to his inability to cut straight and square, George decided to invest in a heavy-duty power saw. To his dismay, this was even less accurate and also scary to use.

Over the next few weeks he used bits of pine, angle-iron and chipboard to design a crude but ingenious saw bench which enabled him to manage the previously uncontrollable power saw. It now became a useful, versatile, accurate and much safer tool. Admittedly the bench looked awful but, in practical terms, it worked!

In this case, George's lack of training in woodwork and his ability to think laterally contributed greatly to his design of the saw bench. Anyone with formal woodwork training would probably not have come up with such an idea. Essentially what he had done was to replicate, very cheaply and simply, the basic functions of a radial-arm saw and a ripsaw bench – two heavy and costly woodworking machines. These tools were widely used, and it was just accepted that they had to be heavy and costly.

George quickly realised that his idea was a winner. He reasoned that there were many handymen and DIY-ers like himself who engaged in weekend hobbies which involved making such things as tables, furniture, toys and boats, as well as repairing things around the house and undertaking extensions and renovations.

His initial limited market research confirmed two things: first, that there was nothing comparable on the market, and second, that a wide range of the population would be interested in a saw bench if the price could be kept to approximately $150–$200.

George applied for a patent, and had a professional steel and aluminium prototype built and presented. His verbal and writing skills enabled him to get a hearing from the highest echelons of the hardware, tool and machinery sector, including retailers, wholesalers and many manufacturers. However, while many distributors could see merit in his invention, none were prepared to take it on.

He almost gave up after sixteen months of effort, expense and frustration, but finally decided to build and sell his benches himself.

Midway through producing his own benches, amidst numerous production problems, he was showcased on the ABC national documentary *The Inventors*. His five minutes of national exposure in 1976 caused an avalanche of responses, with 1000 orders the following day and national distributors begging him for stock. Loads of mail orders followed.

As a totally ill-equipped backyard manufacturer with no formal woodwork training and a huge national demand for his product, he was unable to meet such demand, and the constant design changes were giving him headaches. During the first five years he made almost every mistake in the book and it was only the initial publicity that enabled the business to survive.

The business grew from a backyard operation into a succession of ever-larger factories in Melbourne with an almost 100 per cent Australian infrastructure. The expanded range met with new markets and, over the next twenty-five years, Triton became an iconic Australian brand, with total sales in excess of $300 million, including to hundreds of thousands of overseas customers.

In 1999, George Lewin sold the Triton businesses to Hills Industries Ltd and started the Triton Foundation to help, educate and encourage struggling inventors, like he had once been, and to give them the opportunity to have some exposure via the mass media.

2. THE BUSINESS PLAN

- **Why do a business plan?**
- **Who should draft the business plan?**
- **Features of a good business plan**
- **Overview of the business plan**
- **Common business plan exaggerations**
- **Reviewing the business plan**

WHY DO A BUSINESS PLAN?

A business plan is a written document which identifies your objectives and outlines your strategy for achieving those objectives. It should set out all the key facts about your business – the activities of your business, your financial plan, the industry in general, your competition, your customers, and how you will use your resources to achieve your objectives.

A completed business plan is a summary and evaluation of your business concept. It is a blueprint or road map for your business operations. It will help you to assess whether the business is viable and will allow you to anticipate and plan for potential weaknesses within it. Recent studies show that businesses that develop a written business plan have a greater chance of surviving than those that do not.

A business plan can also be used to help raise finance from lenders or other investors. A well-presented and organised business plan will make a lasting first impression on the lender or investor and demonstrates your standards and business skills (or lack thereof). It allows you to demonstrate that you can handle the diverse aspects of managing the business. Most lenders, investors or venture capitalists will simply not advance funds unless you have a comprehensive plan that shows how you will be able to provide them with a reasonable return on their investment.

The planning process is about making fundamental decisions about what to do and, importantly, what not to do. Small businesses are faced with enormous demands on management time and focus – it is simply not possible to do everything that needs to be done to run your business. Much of the art of strategy is making tough decisions about what you do not have time to do.

It is often said that the process of planning is as important as the plan itself. The activities that members of your team undertake as part of the planning process will ensure they are more effective and more informed as managers and leaders.

The process of planning has a number of other potential organisational benefits:

- It aligns individual visions through vigorous debate about where the business is going and how it is going to get there. Getting the key people to develop a shared view of the business is a powerful lever that ensures everyone is pulling in the same direction.
- Ongoing strategic planning allows you to regularly challenge basic assumptions, identify new risks and changes to critical success factors, and make mid-course corrections to the strategy.
- A good strategic plan that is being actively used to guide the business provides a clarity of purpose that is essential to attract human and financial resources.
- It allows everyone to distinguish between the really important and the simply urgent, allowing resources to be

allocated to the areas of the business that are the most important for long-term success.

When should planning be done?

The frequency of planning depends on the nature of your external environment and the maturity of your company.

Comprehensive and detailed business planning must of course be conducted when starting a new business. If you are in a dynamic and rapidly changing industry then you will need to undertake a comprehensive review of your plan as frequently as every six or twelve months. If your business is well established or in a relatively stable industry then planning can take place less frequently and in less detail. You should also undertake detailed strategic planning when you are considering the launch of a new product or entry into a major alliance. Implementation reviews of your strategic plan are generally undertaken on a quarterly basis.

You should avoid planning when your senior management team are not truly committed to the process – for example, when they are distracted by the departure of another key staff member or if you are in the process of fundraising.

Tip from the trenches
Always balance the extent of your planning. While you need a well-thought-out road map to get started, don't waste too much time over-analysing every detail of your business or your window of opportunity may slip away. At some point you need to stop researching and give it a go.

The actual process of sitting down and writing a comprehensive plan is a good discipline as it will make you think systematically through all the possible risks and assess whether your brilliant concept is really that great after all. It forces you to be realistic about the resources you have and the resources you can obtain.

Where to get help

There is a number of web sites and publications, and a range of computer software, available to assist you in preparing a business plan. You can also get help from industry associations, small business development organisations, chambers of commerce, business advisers or accountants. Listed below are some web sites that may assist you in preparing a sample business plan:

www.avcal.com.au   **www.redherring.com**
www.sbcs.org.au   **www.pwcv2r.com**
www.entepreneur.com

WHO SHOULD DRAFT THE BUSINESS PLAN?

It is important that all the key stakeholders in your business – from fellow owners and investors to key employees and suppliers – are involved in preparing the business plan. People who understand where the business is going are more likely to work towards that goal. They will also feel a greater sense of ownership and belonging if you have taken the time to listen to their views. While you can get help from your accountant or a specialist consultant, it is not advisable to outsource the entire preparation of the plan. Once you lose 'ownership' of your plan you cease to be bound by its discipline.

FEATURES OF A GOOD BUSINESS PLAN

A brilliant plan which resides between the covers of a ring folder and is not referred to is useless if it fails to influence people's day-to-day thinking and behaviour. A practical and useful plan has to combine clear communication with breadth of vision, depth of thinking and appropriate analytical support.

A good business plan will be:

Clear – readers should be able to navigate the plan easily and find topics in which they are particularly interested.

Concise – it is tempting to include all your research and data in the plan and to explore the myriad opportunities available. Focus on the main ingredients and keep it short and focused on the main opportunity.

Logical – ensure the plan has a logical structure and that you group topics together.

Objective – keep your tone objective and allow the reader to weigh up the pros and cons. Over-enthusiastic statements will simply irritate the reader.

Consistent – if several people have had input (for example, the financial officer has written one section and the marketing director another) appoint one person to have overall responsibility for ensuring consistent style, layout and definitions.

Simple – avoid using jargon or getting bogged down in the technical details of your product or service.

Aspirational – the business plan must paint a picture of what the success of the business looks like. It will ideally define a vision of a future that excites people and energises them to make it happen. You need to ask whether your plan offers people the chance to feel involved in something important.

Inclusive – an effective plan includes the input and insights of all the key stakeholders in your business. Participation in strategy formation can be a great motivator for staff, and can help them understand the needs and concerns of all stakeholders, including customers and suppliers.

Manageable – a good plan must bring the business vision down to a practical level. This grounding of the strategy is best achieved through defining the near-term milestones and measurable outcomes. Remember to restrict these to what is manageable – only set five milestones and five outcomes to measure – and make them relevant. Ask yourself the question: Am I just selecting the measures I have, or am I measuring what is relevant?

OVERVIEW OF THE BUSINESS PLAN

Before drafting your plan, gather as much information as possible about the industry, your markets, and your potential products and services. The better you understand your business environment the easier it will be to plan how you are going to operate within it. There are a number of elements that make up the contents of a business plan and they are listed below. Many of these are dealt with in greater detail later in the book. At this point you need to have a clear understanding of what a business plan comprises so you can start collating the information.

A SUMMARY OF THE BUSINESS PLAN

Element	Purpose
1. **Cover page**	Company details should be clearly printed on the cover page.
2. **Table of contents**	This makes it easy for readers to navigate through your plan.

3. Executive summary	Provide a brief one or two page summary that captures the essence of the business plan.
4. Mission/vision	The mission statement captures the purpose, activities and values of your business.
5. Description of industry	Describe the industry you are operating in. How large is it? What are the latest trends?
6. Description of business	Provide a brief description of the proposed or current activities of the business.
7. Products or services	Describe what products and services your business supplies.
8. Identification of market	Discuss and analyse the size and nature of your market.
9. Competitors	Provide an analysis of all your competitors and how you will capture a share of their market.
10. Marketing plan	Describe the strategy you will use to ensure customers know about your business and its products or services.
11. Business goals	Summarise the primary objectives of the business.
12. Directors and management	Provide a brief background of the experience and qualifications of your staff, one of the key assets of your business.
13. Corporate structure	Provide details of the business structure in place, including shares and options on issue.

14. Risk assessment	List the main risks associated with the business.
15. Implementation schedule	Describe the key milestones for the development of your business and when they should be reached.
16. Financial forecasts/statements	Provide historical financial statements and a projected profit and loss statement.
17. Terms of investment	Describe how much you are seeking to raise and the terms attached to the finance.
18. Appendix	Include other documents that support claims made in the business plan.

Preliminary pages

These pages include a cover page and a table of contents. Your cover page should clearly state your company or business name, ACN or ABN, address, email, fax and phone number, as well as contact names and direct phone numbers. The table of contents should make a positive first impression on your reader by indicating that the whole plan is well organised. It should list all the section heads and their corresponding page numbers.

Executive summary

The executive summary describes the highlights of the business plan. In many cases, the quality of the executive summary will determine whether readers will even look at the rest of your plan. The summary should clearly identify the purpose of the plan – is it a proposal seeking equity investment or loan finance, or is it an operating guide? If the business plan is being used to raise finance, the executive summary should specify how much money is required, the purposes for which funding is being sought, and the terms attached to the finance.

The executive summary should also include:

- details of key products, key customers and market area
- the value to the customer
- management expertise
- highlights of the business – your competitive advantages, the barriers to entry and forecast revenues.

Mission statement

sentences

A mission statement is a short (one or two paragraph) statement that captures the essence of your business – its purpose, activity and values.

Purpose   Purpose relates to why the company exists. If this is expressed too broadly it will be meaningless. It is important to focus on outcomes and results, not method. For example, the purpose of a law firm would not be 'to provide legal services' but rather 'to provide innovative solutions for our clients'. *not plain English*

Activity   The main activity or business the company will undertake to achieve its purpose.

Values   The guiding principles or values that guide the stakeholders in the company to achieve its purpose. Examples of values include integrity, innovation, commitment to excellence and creativity.

[handwritten note: Mission / Vision statements pp 36 37 I would disagree with author: Vision statement is how your want your company to be Mission statement is how you're going to do it]

mongst all key

be run past

the direction

e of the hard-

ion statement

at success will

it ponders the

e pursuit of a

ates people to

A useful analogy to consider is that of building a house, for which the strategic plan would be the blueprints and the vision an artist's sketch of the house. Remember that you will never be greater than your own vision of success.

Consider using one or a combination of the following tools and techniques to build your vision.

- Imagine what a day in the life of a customer will be like when you are established.
- Envisage what capabilities your business will have when it is successful.
- Determine your critical success factors, that is, the things that must happen for your business to be successful.

Description of the industry

This section contains:

- the industry outlook and forecast growth potential as well as the latest industry trends and products
- the size of the total market and the latest market trends in relationship to that size

- the social and economic trends that are relevant to your business, such as consumer trends and relevant economic indicators.

Ensure that you quote your sources of information as this will add weight to your research.

Description of business

This briefly describes the business concept:

- a brief history of the business, including development work done, past sales and profits
- what trading name(s) you will use (the name of a product can have an enormous impact on its success)
- what the main activity of the business is – service, retail, manufacture
- what stage the business is at – whether it is a new business, a franchise, a buy-out or an expansion.

You should also include:

- the competitive advantages of your business
- the size and location of the premises
- any equipment required.

Products or services

This section describes in some detail the nature of your products or services, including:

- what the primary (and secondary) uses of your product or service are
- why they are unique or superior to similar products or services already on offer (what is the unique selling proposition?)
- how your product or service will benefit your customers.

If your product or service is merely at a conceptual stage, identify any development work required to get it to market and the time and cost to do so. You should also state whether you have secured any relevant product rights, such as patents, trademarks or franchise rights.

You need to assess the needs of the different customer segments and whether your product or service meets those needs or still requires adaptation. In turn, query whether you should offer a single product or service for all target segments or whether to adjust it for each individual segment.

Identification of market

In this section you need to identify the size and nature of your market. While this is one of the more difficult sections to prepare, it helps substantiate whether your forecasts are viable.

- **Identify your customers' needs** – specify which needs your product or service satisfies.
- **Identify your target market** – clearly specify who your customers are. They should be classified into groups with similar demographics – age, sex, income, residence, education, location (urban, rural), lifestyle (yuppies, active seniors, outdoors) – or buying patterns (brand preference or price consciousness), as well as identifying what their purchasing power is and how much they will spend on your product or service.
- **Determine the size of your market** – specify how large the addressable market is (present the number of customers, unit sales and total dollar sales), whether it is growing or if it is seasonal, such as Christmas decorations. Ensure your estimates are verifiable and based on sound assumptions.
- **Estimate sales** – arguably the heart of your business plan and based on your analysis of the market factors above and your analysis of competitors below.

See chapter three for more discussion of understanding your market.

Competitors

It is important that you understand who your competitors are. You need to identify:

- your top five competitors
- your indirect competitors
- their strengths and weaknesses
- their marketing and pricing strategies
- their share of the market
- how they will react to your market launch
- how they distribute their products
- how sustainable your competitive advantage is
- how you plan to differentiate your business from your competitors to capture a share of the market.

See chapter three for a detailed discussion of competitor analysis.

Marketing plan

Following your assessment of the market, you need to explain your marketing strategy. Your marketing plan should cover the four Ps (place, price, promotion and product).

- **Placement of product** – how you will distribute your products (direct to public, wholesale or retail). Who will sell your products/services – commissioned sales staff or agents?
- **Pricing strategy** – the sale price of your product/service, taking into account your costs, your competitors' pricing, the price sensitivity of your customers, and your break-even point.
- **Product benefits** – the key benefits of your product or services, such as whether you will offer your clients

guarantees or service warranties, and what after sales service you will provide.

- **Promotion plan** – how you will promote the business. Explain how you propose to use different types of promotions such as advertising, sponsorships, trade fairs, competitions and public relations.

See chapter four for a discussion of marketing strategy.

Business goals

This section of the plan should contain a clear and concise statement of the objectives of the business, for example, targets for revenue, profit margins or market share. You should also consider your longer-term goals, such as the sale of the business or a return on equity targets. A business goal should help to minimise disagreements between the shareholders as to what the business is doing, and why.

Directors and management

This section should include a brief background of the directors and key management employees. Many investors consider the people to be as important as (if not more important than) the business opportunity. They will want to know whether the executive team is capable of running the business successfully. A common mistake is to underestimate the importance of this section of the plan. Outline the history of the key executives, their qualifications and skills, and describe how their experience is important to the business.

You should also describe their roles and responsibilities, and disclose their salaries and what equity stake they will have in the business. At this point you should identify key experience/skills which are lacking and how you plan to fill those gaps.

Consider including a structure chart showing who is responsible for each business area.

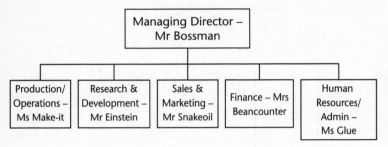

Investors will look for:
- complementary strengths, skills and experience
- whether the team has already worked together
- commitment to the business (not just part-time)
- what distinguishes your management team – what success have they had? What is their standing in the business world?

Tip from the trenches

All successful companies have one thing in common – they attract the best people and retain them by offering attractive packages and a stimulating work environment.

Corporate structure

Here you state the business structure you use or are going to use – sole proprietor, company, trust or partnership (see chapter six). You also need to list:
- details of any shares and options on issue in the company
- a summary of any shareholders' agreements in place
- an organisational chart showing reporting relationships.

You should also name your key advisers – lawyers, accountants, PR or management consultants. This will reassure investors that you have the necessary backup.

Risk assessment

In this section you will need to identify the major risk factors facing the business, for example, new competitors, foreign exchange fluctuations, rising interest rates, staff strikes and changing consumer demand. Describe the measures you will take to counteract these risks.

Implementation schedule

Your implementation schedule should show:

- key milestones for the development of your business and when they must be reached
- which milestones/tasks are interdependent
- how your personnel needs will change as your business grows, and how many staff you will need in each part of the business
- the capital investments that will be required in plant and equipment as your business grows.

Financial forecasts/statements

If your business has already commenced trading, include its current financial statements. You will need to include forecast profit and loss statements based on your market analysis. This section will contain:

- summary balance sheet and profit and loss statements (including the past two to three years if applicable)
- summary projected profit and loss (including the detailed assumptions on which the forecasts are based)
- summary cash flow forecast of all earnings and expenditures

on a monthly basis for the next year of operations (ensuring you have included a reasonable forecast of your personal drawings).

A major cause of failure in small businesses is lack of cash and poor management of working capital. You should consider engaging an accountant to prepare or review your forecasts, budgets and financial statements.

Terms of investment

If your business plan is a financing proposal for an investor or lender, include in this section details of how much funding is sought and how you propose to use the funding. You will also need to include details of the security you are willing to provide. Given that most small businesses fail, investors and lenders must protect themselves against the risk of losing the money they lend you. To do this they may seek security or collateral over your home and any other valuable assets you may have, such as your car, shares or furniture.

Appendix

The following documents, which should be labelled as Appendix A, Appendix B, etc., are likely to be requested by a lender or investor, so you should include them at the back of your plan:

- letters of intent for potential orders, customer commitments and letters of support
- list of product inventory – the type, age and value
- list of leasehold improvements – a description and when made
- list of fixed assets – a description, age and serial numbers
- price lists to support cost estimates
- detailed resumes of the business's founders/executives
- description of insurance coverages

- detailed financial accounts – balance sheets, profit and loss statements and cash flow statements for the last three years
- accounts receivable summary
- copies of legal agreements, such as leases, licences, joint venture agreements and employment contracts.

COMMON BUSINESS PLAN EXAGGERATIONS

Business plans often contain exaggerated claims. Avoid these, as they tend to be transparent to the investor.

COMMON BUSINESS PLAN EXAGGERATIONS

What your business plan says	What it means to an investor
The business has no competition.	Telstra, News Corp and IBM just launched the same business model.
The product is 95 per cent complete.	The balance will cost twice as much as the first 95 per cent and take three times as long to complete.
If we can capture 15 per cent of the market then . . .	There are another twenty companies with the same idea that just got funding.
We conservatively estimate . . .	We plucked a figure out of the air and multiplied it by five.
We estimate investors will make three times the return on their investment.	If absolutely everything goes right you might get your money back in five years.
We have a proven business model.	We have had three customers so far and no-one has complained.

Our executive team have had a great deal of experience in our industry.	They bought the product once before as a consumer and quite liked it.

REVIEWING THE BUSINESS PLAN

A common mistake is for business plans to contain too much detail. Keep your business plan focused. The final document is a *summary* of your planning process. You can always refer to your working papers later to substantiate a particular point.

Ask your key employees and two or three impartial outsiders to critique the finished plan to identify what was overlooked or overemphasised.

Your business plan should be a living and dynamic document which you update and refer back to frequently. After you have launched the business, set aside time each month to update and check the plan. As a minimum you should review your plan every six months. Your ability to get the most value from planning depends on continually checking the progress of the business against your business plan.

3. UNDERSTANDING YOUR MARKET

- **Defining your market**
- **Customer value**
- **Value proposition**
- **Identifying your competitors**

DEFINING YOUR MARKET

It is one thing to have a product or service to sell; it is quite another knowing who to sell it to. You need to target or define your prospective customers so that you'll know who to target with your marketing. You must know your market – *who* they are, *where* they are and *why* they will buy your product/ service. This section considers the following questions: What is a market? What is your total addressable market? What is your addressed market? How is your addressed market segmented?

What is a market?

In simple terms, a market is the potential that exists for the exchange between the producers of goods/services and the buyers or customers of goods/services. In some cases, like commodities such as coal and milk, the market is fairly obvious. In other cases, defining a market is quite complex. It is important to remember that new markets are constantly being created with technological developments and changing customer needs and tastes.

What is your total addressable market? Your total addressable market (sometimes abbreviated to TAM) is the largest possible area of your market which your business could target. In other words, how big is the pie? It is as well defined by who you are targeting as by who you are not targeting. For example, when selling air-travel services over the Internet, your addressable market is 'all travellers likely to travel by air' and excludes all travellers travelling short distances by car, bus or train. Often exclusions are not as obvious as in this example.

What is your addressed market? The next step is to determine your addressed market. In other words, how big is your slice of the pie? This further reduces the number of potential customers through competitors, substitutes and existing behaviours. In the 'online air travel' example, the addressable market is further reduced by the number of air travellers not using the Internet, then by the number of Internet-user air travellers not likely to purchase tickets over the Internet, then by the number of Internet buyers/air travellers purchasing directly from their preferred airlines, and so on.

Too often, a business plan will refer to a market size defined by research written by an industry research firm, which will have used a set of underlying assumptions not at all consistent with the business model defined in the business plan. This leads to a misrepresentation of the addressed market.

How is your addressed market segmented? The next step is to segment or divide your customer base. This should be done in three ways: who they are; how they interact with your business; and why they do business with you.

Who are your customers? Traditional segmentation of an addressed customer base allows you to understand your customers by who they are.

Segmentation	Purpose
Age	Some products are by their very nature aimed at target age groups – holidays for 18–35-year-olds, toys for children, retirement homes for mature adults.
Gender	The issue regarding gender is not simply who is the end-user, for example, of men's clothing, but who actually makes the purchase.
Income bracket	It is important to know the range of income of your typical customer. This impacts on their propensity to buy and capacity to buy.

To discover who your customers are, ask questions like:
- what are their spending habits?
- what are their education levels?
- what are their likes, dislikes, etc.?

How do your customers interact with your business?

Behaviour-based segmentation tries to understand the context in which the customer has an interaction with your business. Of course, behaviour-based segmentation is influenced by who the customers are, such as being a male teenager or a housemaker, but it is not defined by it. The first step in segmenting your market is to understand the context in which your customers are likely to interact with your business. The context should be viewed from the perspective of the customer. In our online air-travel example, the context could be either taking a holiday, travelling for business, or one-off infrequent travel. Another way to look at the context is to identify the customer's intention. Intentions are fundamental needs requiring extensive and integrated planning, decisions and co-ordination.

Why do your customers do business with you? Once you have defined your customer's context, you will need to identify why people choose to deal with your business. What trade-offs do your customers go through when considering interacting with your business. Segmenting in this way is much more powerful than just segmenting by products/ services or demographics/socio-economics because it will let you understand why your customers or prospects interact with your business. In the online air-travel example, the business traveller might value time when placing an order, or the accuracy of the web site and frequency of service of the airline, while the leisure traveller might value scope of travel destinations and value-added services such as insurance and price.

In summary, when segmenting your customer base:
• your segment schemes must support an overall marketing strategy which is simple enough to be executed. For example, can you avoid segments getting confused by multiple messages? Can you maintain a consistent positioning across segments? Can your billing system support multiple price plans? Can customer service answer questions about multiple packages?
• segments should be prioritised by value to your business. Prioritising target segments will allow you to plan your uptake strategy and will ensure you capture the most valuable customers ahead of your competitors.

CUSTOMER VALUE

Make sure you identify the current and potential value of your customers (see chart following) and have an understanding of what they are worth. Such considerations must be made to determine if the market is large enough to justify the investment in pursuing it.

CUSTOMER VALUE MATRIX

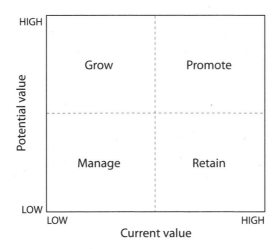

Current value is the customer's value to your business today. Their value is somewhere between low and high, based on their profitability. Some customers are extremely low value because, for instance, they transact with you in a costly way.

This figure provides guidance on how to deal with individual customers, or customer segments.

Manage

If a customer's current and potential value are both low, then you should aim to 'manage' them hard, driving greater efficiencies and seeking to reduce the cost of serving them. You may even decide to put in place strategies to get rid of these customers, as some may be detracting value from your business (by costing you more than you make from them). You certainly don't want to acquire more customers like these.

Retain

If a customer's current value is high and their potential value is low, then you are extracting the most value possible out of these customers and there is no more potential value to extract. You should aim to 'retain' these customers, as they are profitable today. However, in trying to increase their value, beware of over-investing; there is not much more to gain from them.

Grow

If a customer's current value is low and their potential value is high, then they represent a fantastic growth opportunity. This is where you should prioritise and direct your investments. Change the way you serve them in order to create a more profitable relationship, because there is much to gain. Put in place loyalty strategies to ensure you don't lose these customers, and be aware that your competition will try to steal them from you.

Promote

Finally, if a customer's current and potential value are both high, they represent a goldmine customer. These are the ones to 'promote' in your business. The way you're serving them is obviously working; seek to improve your service as much as possible here because they offer a substantial opportunity to grow profits if you can serve them better. Needless to say, you also want to ensure that you are proactively retaining these customers because these are the ones that your competitors have their eyes on.

Enhancing value

However, the good news is that you can influence the potential value of a customer over time to make them more profitable to your business. The marketing, sales, service and loyalty strategies you apply to your customers over the life of the relationship you have with them will impact their behaviours – how they deal with you, talk about you, feel about you and ultimately how they interact with you. If you positively impact their behaviours (for example, by influencing them so that they phone you less for simple requests and instead serve themselves online using your web site, which is a cheaper channel), then you can increase the potential future value of the customer. Further, good customer experiences and service will provide incentives for them to refer you to their family and friends.

VALUE PROPOSITION

You have defined your market size, the part of your market you have addressed, your key customer segments and how valuable they are. The next is to define your value proposition. Without a positive value proposition to all stakeholders in your business, you will find that your entire business is operating inefficiently – you will either need to vastly overspend on marketing to meet your uptake targets, or you will never reach your targets. Defining your value proposition is a simple two-step process: identify where you create value and allocate that value to each stakeholder.

Step 1: Identify where you create value

The first step in defining your value proposition is to understand where your business will create value. The best way to identify where your business creates value is to analyse the value chain relevant to your industry. The easiest way to define the value created by your business is to understand either the inefficiencies you are addressing or the new sources of value you are creating.

The value created by your business needs to meet the following criteria:

- **Measurable** – in our online travel example, one potential value created could be increased quality of service. That statement alone, however, does not properly describe the value created. The increased quality of service comes from a reduction in the number of booking errors and from a reduction in the time to serve. Both of these value statements can be measured.
- **Relevant** – too often, business plans will list up to ten value statements with no indications of where the real value created lies. More than half of these statements are irrelevant. Focus on the key value drivers.
- **Linked to a stakeholder** – sometimes, value to the business is confused with value to the stakeholders. Unless your stakeholders are also shareholders of your business, you cannot state that your image and brand in the market are benefits to your customers.

Step 2: Allocate value to each stakeholder

The second step in defining your value proposition is to allocate the value created to each stakeholder. This step is self-evident, but the following simple rules will help you understand the value as perceived by your stakeholders.

- Identify all stakeholders. Your customers are often not the only stakeholders in your business. It is essential that you create a positive value proposition for your customers, your suppliers and your added-value service providers.
- Ensure you account for the negative value propositions.

CASE STUDY:
Katrina Allen – De Jour

Katrina Allen runs De Jour Tampons, which competes in Australia's $80 million tampon market. When she started the business, she managed to take on multinationals like Johnson & Johnson and Proctor & Gamble. She snatched an 8 per cent market share in the major supermarkets such as Coles, Bi-Lo and Woolworths. In 1999, while still working full-time as Senior Art Director with multinational advertising agency M & C Saatchi, Katrina started the business from scratch. Her simple but compelling business logic has been the foundation for her success.

She first came up with a good idea – an idea that was different and that made her product stand out from the competition. From her observation and extensive market research interviewing 600 women, Katrina identified two changes which could be made to tampons already on the market. First, women her age tended to carry black designer handbags, which did not match the gaudy packaging of most tampons. So, she started packaging tampons in blacks and greys. Second, existing tampon packaging was flimsy and would often come apart in handbags. So she introduced resealable zip-lock plastic bags to hold her products.

She identified the strengths of the tampon business as being that they were fashion-proof, not seasonal, recession-proof, had no use-by date and it was easy to foster consumer loyalty with such a product. Importantly, once established, the products were simple to maintain and had an ongoing demand.

Katrina placed high value on extensive market research so that she would know absolutely everything about her competitors and the market. She gathered information for pricing and sales strategies and conducted a SWOT (strengths, weaknesses, opportunities, threats) analysis. This enabled her to be prepared for whatever came her way and gave her the ability to devise back-up plans as anticipated challenges arose.

It also allowed her to accurately match her product to the target market. Katrina identified her market as young women like herself and had to devise marketing strategies to get their attention. For example, she would try to get coverage in *New Woman* magazine as opposed to the *Financial Review*.

Katrina financed De Jour using a bank loan and her own savings. She controlled the risk by conducting thorough research and consulting extensively with her financial and legal advisers. In this way she knew what to expect and when there would be a return on investment. She found it cost-effective to keep her day job while setting up the business and testing her ideas. She did this by employing a designer to work on her projects.

Katrina learned a valuable lesson from her advertising career – that no matter how good an idea, it will not be given a chance unless it is presented professionally. Her presentation to the supermarkets included packaging, brochures and a document containing the research from 300 women. De Jour was extremely well received and the supermarkets immediately agreed to take on her products.

With her products on the supermarket shelves, Katrina went into overdrive, telling Australian women about the new product. She left samples in the bathrooms of Fashion Week shows and in Portsea pubs during her summer vacation – places where her target market were likely to be. Her hard work proved fruitful as she took a 7 per cent market share over the next eighteen months. She was rewarded with a position in the Australian Businesswomen's Hall of Fame.

Like many successful businesspeople, Katrina avoids trying to do everything herself; she employs the best people to do each job. She selects the best consultants such as accountants and bookkeepers who work together to handle GST, and brokers who deal with supermarkets on her behalf, so that she has time to concentrate on those things she does best.

IDENTIFYING YOUR COMPETITORS

Every business has direct or indirect competitors. Competitive analysis is a critical, although often ignored, element of business plan formulation. It should include identifying the elements of your business model that translate into competitive advantage. In order to analyse your competitors you need to know who they are, understand them, and define your competitive position against them.

Who are your competitors?

The Porter Forces Model (see page 58) provides a framework in which you can analyse your competitors. From it you should be able to define three sets of competitors.

- **Current competitors** – exist today and are the easiest to identify. In our online travel example, travel.com.au would be a current and known competitor. A good source of detailed information about current competitors is their financial statements and reports. Where current competitors are publicly traded, you are likely to find good information in stock brokers' analysis of the market, in research firm reports, in magazine articles, in competitors' advertising, at trade fairs and by doing primary research by talking to a representative of the company.

- **Substitutes** – provide products and services for the same underlying need. In our online travel example, online

PORTER FORCES MODEL

Distribution channel power

- Channels are the forms by which products are distributed from the competitors to the buyers.
- Power is high if:
  - there are few available channels
  - channel members offer buyers unique value-added services, e.g. inventory management
  - there is strong buyer preference for a specific channel or channel type.

Threat of new entrants

- New entrants are companies from a different industry offering products within the same class as competitors.
- Threat is high if there is/are:
  - low barriers to entry
  - high industry profitability and/or growth
  - low buyer switching costs.

Intensity of competition

- Competitors offer products in the same 'product class'.
- Competition is high if there is/are:
  - numerous, balanced competitors
  - mature market growth
  - high exit barriers.

Power of buyers

- Buyers are the purchasers of industry product class.
- Power is high if there is/are:
  - a relatively small number of informed buyers or buyer groups purchasing high volume
  - little or no perceived product differentiation
  - low switching costs.

Threat of substitutes

- Substitutes are products of a different class that offer a similar value proposition to the industry product class. These may emerge from competitors within or outside the industry.
- Threat is high if there is:
  - low substitute cost-to-benefit trade-off
  - rapidly changing technology
  - high buyer willingness to substitute.

Legal/regulation impact

- Regulatory/legal issues emerge from government policies and activities; these issues affect all competitors equally.
- Impact is high if there is/are:
  - a wide span of enforced government authority
  - many unresolved, highly publicised issues impacting the industry.

Power of suppliers

- Suppliers provide the inputs – labour, material, equipment, infrastructure, etc. – to the competitors.
- Power is high if there is/are:
  - few suppliers with no available substitute inputs
  - high supplier switching costs for industry competitors
  - other markets for suppliers' products.

real-estate agents covering holiday accommodations are potential substitute competitors. These are harder to identify, but if their value proposition is more attractive, you are likely to lose a substantial share of your market to these competitors.

- **New entrants** – likely to come rapidly into your market. For example, if an entrepreneur uses a single manufacturer and builds a business retailing a popular product, such as a game console, the manufacturer may develop its own direct channel for getting that product out into the market. As soon as the manufacturer builds its own direct channel it is likely to stop servicing the entrepreneur and to market its own channel rather than the entrepreneur's, thereby killing the entrepreneur's retailing business.

Understand your competitors

It is not enough to identify your competitors, you must also understand the threat they pose to your business. To be most effective, you need to compare your competitors with your business. To do this you need to look at the following:

- **Strategic intent** – usually encompasses strategic partnerships, explicit and implied strategies, and value propositions. Competitors with an established brand and physical presence may suddenly become formidable competitors or, based on their strategic intent, could also be potential partners.
- **Competitive strengths and weaknesses** – what are your competitors' core competencies, weaknesses and sustainable competitive advantages?
- **Performance and capabilities** – your competitors' sales, profits, return on equities/assets, market share, operational efficiencies and financial capacities.

- **What they offer** – must cover markets served, product mix, geographic or channel coverage and the R&D/new product pipeline. For example, an online travel retailer not only competes with Yahoo on the Internet, but also with Yahoo's wireless plays, and offline partnerships. In this case, Yahoo's offering expands far beyond the Internet alone.
- **Business systems** – your competitors' internal mechanisms. These include their organisational structure, their major processes, their high-level cost structures, and their marketing and distribution systems. Often this analysis will allow you to identify short-term opportunities.

First mover versus fast follower

First-mover advantage is often cited as a competitive advantage. However, for first-mover advantage to be a sustainable competitive advantage, the following also need to be true:

- First movers need to quickly erect barriers to entry. Barriers to entry are strong brand equity, key distribution and supplier partnerships locked-in, a control over industry standards or high customer switching costs.
- First movers need to have a sustainable pool of resources to maintain their advantage. Over time, most barriers to entry will be vulnerable to well-funded fast followers.

'Whoever is first in the field and awaits the coming of the enemy will be fresh for the fight; whoever is second in the field and has to hasten to battle will arrive exhausted.'

Sun Tzu, *The Art of War*

Simply put, the first mover as a competitive advantage is valuable but is not sufficient. You need to be sure that your business can leverage its first-mover status into a sustainable competitive advantage.

4. DEVELOPING YOUR MARKETING STRATEGY

- Product and service issues
- Promotion and advertising plan
- Place and distribution strategy
- Price strategy
- Market research

As mentioned in chapter two, your marketing strategy can be divided into four basic components known as the four Ps – product, promotion, place and price. These four components are often referred to as the 'marketing mix'. This chapter also considers the importance of market research.

PRODUCT AND SERVICE ISSUES

Make sure your product is up to scratch before you launch your campaign. There is no point embarking on an expensive and well-targeted campaign only for people to be disappointed that your product or service doesn't match the quality or features you promised.

There are three key product issues:

- features–benefits analysis
- type and level of customer service
- product strategy.

Features–benefits analysis

The first step in preparing your marketing plan is to analyse what benefits your services or product offer and what needs of your customers they fulfil. If you are not absolutely certain of what benefits you provide or their importance to customers, your marketing plan will lack focus.

You will need to prepare a detailed list of the various features of your products and services. For each feature you will then need to identify the various benefits that it will produce for the customer. The next step is to assess which needs of the market segment those benefits satisfy. This of course raises the issue of whether you manufacture one product for all market segments or whether you adjust the product to meet the needs of individual segments.

A feature of your product may have multiple benefits to your customers. It is important to identify as many as possible – as different people will value some benefits more highly than others. A 'features–benefits' analysis is important because:

- the more benefits a product provides to a customer the greater their perception of 'value for money'
- for your advertisements to be successful you must isolate the features that will encourage your customer to buy your products.

Type and level of customer service

A customer's decision to buy will often depend on the level of customer service offered. Attracting new customers is expensive and time-consuming – so it is important to encourage repeat clientele. In order to decide what is the most appropriate type and level of service, you need to consider the cost of providing the service, what your competitors offer, and what the customers expect.

There is a large range of customer service and after-sales care that can be offered, including:

- free samples
- credit sales
- demonstrations
- information brochures
- free quotes/estimates
- trade-in options
- return of goods
- discounts for early payment
- product warranties
- after-sales service
- call centre service
- customer complaints service.

A good customer service strategy will have numerous benefits, including increased customer retention and reduced marketing costs. Superior service therefore becomes a competitive advantage. Some keys to customer service are:

- First impressions count, so ensure staff are always courteous and helpful.
- Listen to what your customers want.
- Avoid jargon by always explaining your product/service in simple plain language, to minimise the risk of confusion.
- Offer a wide range of payment options, such as credit cards and EFTPOS.
- Ensure complaints are handled quickly and politely by always listening carefully to the complaint and not becoming defensive.
- Build loyalty by rewarding repeat customers with discount programs.

Product strategy

The following are the basic components which inter-relate to create product strategy. The needs of your target market should be your key determinant.

- **Product line** – a group of products that have a similar use or features. For example a mobile phone shop might offer a number of different product lines such as mobile phones, batteries and car kits.
- **Product breadth** – the number of product lines offered. The more lines offered, the wider the product breadth. A mobile phone shop which only offered one product line, such as digital phones, would have a narrow product breadth. A shop which offered a large range of product lines, such as hands-free kits, leather cases, car kits etc., would have a wider product breadth.
- **Product depth** – the range of products within a product line. The greater the range of models, colours and brands offered the greater the depth.
- **Product mix** – the product lines you offer.

PROMOTION AND ADVERTISING PLAN

When planning your promotion strategy you need to consider marketing objectives, image, business and product name, competitive advantage, buying motives and where to promote.

Marketing objectives

Many businesses fail to specify their marketing objective. They may have identified a sales or revenue objective and wrongfully assumed that this is also their marketing objective. A marketing objective should not focus solely on sales revenue, but also on changing behaviour and perceptions. It will also change over time as the market, competition and the product all change.

The main objective of your promotion and advertising plan is to convert prospects in your target market into loyal customers. It can also include:

- encouraging existing customers to buy more
- encouraging new customers to try your product or service
- raising awareness of the product and its name
- persuading people of the need for your product
- encouraging existing customers to try other products in the range.

Image Ask yourself what image you want your business to project. Your image should appeal to the people in your target market. This should be based on the package of benefits you are offering your customers. For example, there is no point projecting an image of exclusivity if you are offering bargain-priced goods.

Business and product names An important aspect of image is the name of the product and your company name. The wrong choice can be damaging to the prospects of your business. An imaginative or provocative name can generate public and media attention. Good examples of this are Richard Branson's Virgin label and French Connection UK. Be careful, however, that you do not alienate or repel potential customers.

Your business name should be short and if possible describe your business in some way. However some of the more successful names in recent times have been unique and unrelated to the type of business being operated, such as Amazon.com, Orange, eBay.com.

If you include the name of your local area of operations in your business name, consider what will happen if you expand to other geographical areas. If you are naming the business after yourself, for example Evan Jago Consulting and Co., consider what happens when you want to sell or introduce other partners. A new owner may be uncomfortable about trading under someone else's name, yet not want to lose any goodwill that has been generated.

If you are having trouble coming up with a good name, organise a focus group of four or five people and brainstorm a long list of names that best match the image of the company. Make a short-list of five or so names. Ask your lawyer to check the names are still available. It can be quite challenging to find a name that is still legally available as a company name, business name, trademark and domain name. Before dispatching your product or launching your new business, test the name on a sample from your target market.

Competitive advantage

It is important that your marketing campaign focuses on the features that differentiate you from your competition. What is the unique feature of your business that will make people buy from you rather than the competition? Your competitive advantage could be:

- free installation and training
- extended warranty period
- cheapest prices
- a unique product not offered by others.

Make sure your product or service actually has the features promised and that you have the promised edge over your competitors. Also ensure it is sustainable over time. For example, if you pride yourself on speedy service, make sure as your market share grows the number of customer service staff grows as well. Similarly, there is no point being the cheapest supplier if you are not covering marginal costs.

Buying motives

It is important to consider your customers' basic buying motives and focus your promotion around them. Some of the basic buying motives are a customer's desire:

- to be recognised or gain status
- to protect their family and property from harm
- for long-run savings arising from low maintenance or low operating costs
- to protect and maintain their health
- to derive personal pleasure
- to make life easier by eliminating or reducing time-consuming chores.

Where to promote

Deciding where to promote depends on many factors, such as the nature of the product, the quantity available and how much money is set aside for the promotion campaign.

If you only have a small amount of the product for sale, then mass media, such as television or a national newspaper, may be inappropriate. The damage to your reputation when customers discover the product is sold out could be considerable. The different types of media are discussed in more depth in chapter thirteen.

CASE STUDY:
Anita Roddick – The Body Shop

In 1976, Anita Roddick opened the first store for The Body Shop next to a funeral parlour in Brighton with a $6500 loan. During her widespread travels, Anita had observed that no shops sold bath products in small or sample sizes, and believed there was a demand for such samples. In her first store she sold fifteen natural cosmetic products that she had developed in her garage. She packaged them in small plastic recyclable bottles, keeping costs low.

Business was going well and Anita decided to open a second store in Chichester. Stores were run by family and friends of the Roddicks, who learnt about franchising but did not charge startup or royalty fees. The only requirement was that the franchisees financed the operation in exchange for the use of The Body Shop name. Anita would interview candidates before issuing the rights to a franchise.

The Body Shop was an extraordinary business and differentiated itself from most other cosmetic companies. In her autobiography, *Body and Soul: Profits with Principles – The Amazing Success Story of Anita Roddick & The Body Shop*, Anita writes: 'I hate the beauty business. It is a monster industry selling unattainable dreams. It lies. It cheats. It exploits women.' This mindset was the foundation of The Body Shop's unique philosophy and a critical factor in its success. The Roddicks wanted to create profits with principles, and drive social and environmental reform.

Anita employed unconventional advertising. Rather than pay for advertisements, she allowed quality products to sell themselves. For the first store for The Body Shop, she lined the sidewalk with perfume leading into her store. She also hung potpourri to lure people into the shop. She took advantage of the attention that media can bring by leaking a story to the press that the adjacent funeral parlour was threatened by the success of her business. Soon after, people's curiosity brought them to the shop. Satisfied customers would then recommend the shop to friends. The Roddicks campaigned on social and environmental issues by using their shop windows to display promotions for environmental groups. Their first display was for Greenpeace's lobby against dumping hazardous waste into the North Sea. The Roddicks have also used their trucks and bags to convey social messages. They have supported and promoted the save-the-whales campaign, Amnesty International, rainforest activists and the Friends of the Earth. Anita has campaigned for increased AIDS awareness, for ending animal-testing and for recycling. She focused much of her attention on the empowerment of communities in the Third World. Her campaigns included 'Stop the Burn' (to save the Brazilian rainforests) and 'Trade not Aid'. The Body Shop campaigned against the exploitation of Third World workers by paying them comparable wages to those that are earned by British workers. These crusading efforts for social justice and environmental protection gained much publicity for the Roddicks and their business.

Anita selected employees who shared the same philosophy on environmental and social issues as The Body Shop. Head-office staff were given a day off work each month to work with disadvantaged children. Staff are knowledgeable and respectful of people's space. If you want information, you must ask for it. Information is clearly displayed on containers, which list the ingredients and purpose of the product. The shop provides educational brochures about 'Animal Testing and Cosmetics' and 'What is Natural?'. The Product Information Manual is available to all as a reference for the backgrounds and details of everything sold in The Body Shop. Anita established credibility by educating her customers.

Today, The Body Shop has grown from a single 'hippie' store in England to a multinational company with a presence in many countries.

PLACE AND DISTRIBUTION STRATEGY

This component of the marketing mix deals with how your products and services will be offered for sale. There are a large number of different sales or distribution channels, such as retail/wholesale, direct selling and the Internet.

The basic issue is whether your company will conduct distribution itself, or whether you will outsource to a third party such as a distributor. This decision to 'make-or-buy' will have a considerable impact on your organisational structure and business systems. In turn, the choice of distribution channel will also drive a number of your other marketing decisions.

Many businesses fail to adequately consider their sales channel. It is crucial that you choose a means of distribution that is suitable for your market. You need to keep an open mind about alternative channels. The distribution method you choose is also an important driver of your product – how it will be packaged and priced, your support strategy and advertising strategy.

You should decide *who* will sell your product before you make it or market it. A product sold by mail order will be bundled differently from one sold in a retail store. Don't be afraid to ask potential dealers or distributors whether they would stock your product and how many they think they could sell, to help you decide your best avenues.

Retail/wholesale outlets

If you plan to sell your product via a retail or wholesale outlet you should bear in mind that there are a large range of different options available, ranging from supermarkets and department stores to market stalls and boutique shops. The advantages of outlets include:

- your business can be easily identified
- you can capture passing trade
- you can choose a location close to your target market.

The main disadvantages of outlets are:

- your costs are high, such as lease costs and refurbishment
- you are exposed to external changes – traffic may be re-routed or parking restrictions, which limit the number of customers, may be imposed.

The factors to consider in choosing the location of your premises are set out in chapter nine.

Direct selling

This involves direct selling to customers through television, radio and newspapers. Typically the customer places an order by phone or returns an order form attached to an advertisement. The key attraction of mail order is that it avoids leasing costly retail premises. It also allows you to:

- reach a geographically scattered market
- reach a wide range of market segments by choosing different advertising mediums and strategies
- use different pricing policies depending on market segments
- purchase stock on a 'JIT' (just-in-time) basis – this in turn reduces working capital requirements.

On the other hand:

- advertising/promotion costs will be high
- some products are inherently unsuitable for mail order as it is an impersonal way of selling
- mail order tends to have a poor reputation.

Third-party retailers

Your products could be sold by third-party retailers, who have already established their retail presence and have ongoing access to existing customers. A key issue is to ensure you acquire a good shelf position. The main downside is that third-party retailers will demand a high percentage of the sales price.

Wholesalers

It can be time-consuming to find and make regular contact with a large number of third-party retailers. A wholesaler can take over this activity for you. When choosing a wholesaler make sure they have good relationships with a variety of retailers. Using a wholesaler can be a great way for a new business to achieve rapid and deep market penetration whilst also lowering distribution costs.

Outside agents/distributors

Another option is to engage an external distributor or agent to distribute your product. In essence they assume the job of an in-house salesperson. They only make commission if they sell the product, making them an attractive low-risk channel for new businesses. Be careful of becoming too reliant on one distributor; if they become insolvent it can take many weeks or months to find a new distributor and you also risk losing a large amount of your stock.

Franchising

Franchising has become an extremely popular way of distributing products in Australia. Your business concept is implemented by a franchisee in accordance with your operating manual and guidelines. You are paid an upfront fee plus an ongoing licensing fee by the franchisee. See chapter twenty-one for more details on franchising.

Own sales staff

If your product is complex and requires sales staff to have thorough product knowledge, you should consider using your own mobile sales team. However, as face-to-face visits are expensive, this option is usually only viable when the per-unit margins are high and the number of customers is small.

Internet

A web site with detailed product information is a necessity for many industries. The Internet, however, is not suitable as a distribution channel for some businesses. To assess whether the Internet may generate new sales for your product, consider the following issues:

- Are similar products sold via mail-order catalogues?
- Will customers purchase using credit cards?
- Is it feasible for a free demonstration to be provided on the web site?
- Does the name or picture alone describe the product's purpose?
- Can users install the product themselves?

PRICE STRATEGY

The price at which products and services sell is an important financial consideration. If you set too low a price, you may fail to make an acceptable profit regardless of how many sales you achieve. Too high a price means you may fail to generate a viable level of sales.

In order to decide what price to charge you must consider the interrelation of a number of factors. The overall objective should be to maximise profits by implementing pricing policies that will result in the best combination of sales volume, price and costs, while being consistent with your overall image.

The basis for setting price is the willingness of a customer to pay the price asked, which depends entirely on how they value your product. A common misunderstanding is that price is derived from costs. While costs are important, the cost–price ratio is secondary to the customer value of your product or service.

A common mistake is to underprice your product or service. Price is only one factor that affects a customer's decision to buy – there are numerous other factors that influence the decision, such as quality, convenience and speedy service.

Often different pricing policies can be adopted for different target markets. For example, different telephone tariffs are charged for residential users than for business and commercial users. There is potential for implementing different pricing structures where target markets are sufficiently dissimilar and either sympathetic to such a policy, as in the case of discounts for senior citizens, or unaware of the policy, where target markets are geographically dispersed.

Many new businesses take the prices set by their competitors. The golden rule, however, is not to set your prices too low. You can always reduce prices, but to raise them can be more difficult.

Short-term goals

Price can also be used to achieve a number of short-term goals:

- **Maximising unit profit** – this is where target markets are selected mainly on the basis of their willingness to pay high prices. The level of sales is sacrificed to obtain a high unit profit on each sale.
- **Creating a penetration price** – here, a low price builds up sales volume rapidly. The lower price encourages the customer to try it, and hopefully if the product is good enough, a large percentage of the initial purchasers become repeat customers.
- **Protecting against new competitors** – the business may adopt a short-term pricing policy which makes it difficult for a new company to gain a foothold.

Price elasticity

The relationship between price and sales volume is known as price elasticity. It describes the impact a change in price has on the level of sales. A low price elasticity means changes in price have little effect on sales volume. This is usually the case for specialised businesses with highly differentiated products or well-established top-end brands (for example, prestige cars like Ferrari, fashion labels like Gucci or jewellery from Tiffany's). A high price elasticity means a small change in the price will have a strong impact on the amount purchased. A price increase/decrease will cause sales to drop/rise significantly. This is usually the case for highly competitive businesses with little product differentiation (for example, staple foods like bread, milk and fruit, or home and mobile phone charges).

Pricing by competitors

For your main products or services, you need to consider what prices are currently being charged by your leading competitors. The price difference between competitors may vary from one product to another. Is there a market price that the majority of the competition adopts? Also consider what your competitors have done previously when a new business entered the market.

Pricing policy

The pricing policy you adopt may have long-term ramifications for the success of your business. Outlined below are a number of policies and when they are best used to help you make your decisions.

PRICING POLICIES

Policy	Price	When used
Normal pricing	Charge the market price.	• You do not wish to risk a price war. • Your cost structure will not allow you to charge a lower price. • If you are planning to charge market prices, consider how much they will fall over the next year or two in the normal course of trade.
Premium pricing	Charge a higher price than the competition to generate a higher gross profit on each sale while accepting a lower sales volume.	• Demand for the product outstrips supply. • Price is not a significant factor affecting your customers' decision to buy. • Other factors, such as durability, personalised service and quality drive your customers' decision to buy. • A premium price that is the same as the current market price, but your entry into the market may drive prices below their current levels. • You have limited production capacity, selling capacity or storage space available.

Breakthrough pricing	Charge a lower price than the competition, hoping that increased sales will outweigh a lower gross profit on each sale.	• You are willing to risk a 'price war'. • Unit gross profit is high. • You have low overheads and the competition does not. • It is the only way you can penetrate the market. • The customers' decision to purchase is driven by price. • You have sufficient capital resources to overcome the possible cash problems that can ensue from such action.

Consider the following. If the current market price is $10 for a widget and there is already a reasonably competitive marketplace the different pricing policies would be:

- premium pricing = $10–$11
- normal or market price = $7–$10
- breakthrough pricing = $5–$7.

You will note from this example that the market price may drop materially, simply because of the competitive pressure your own business introduces.

First in category

If your product is a 'first in category', that is, it is the first of its kind on the market, it may be hard to select a suitable price for your product. The best way is to interview your proposed distributors, customers and sales staff. Your distributors will have a good feeling for the price the market will bear. Sales staff may also have a good instinctive feeling for what customers will pay. The best approach, however, is to ask a number of potential customers what they would be prepared to pay, and why.

CASE STUDY:
Cindy Luken – Luken & May

Starting in 1996, entrepreneur Cindy Luken, a former food scientist with Sara Lee, transformed her gourmet biscuit brand Luken & May from a home-based cottage industry to a multimillion-dollar business which has captured the elite biscuit market.

Her list of clients now includes Qantas; David Jones; Myer; Target; Stadium Australia; Sydney Opera House; Starbucks Japan; upmarket UK outlet Selfridges; forty-five chains of four- and five-star hotels; major contract caterers supplying everything from sporting, entertaining and conference venues to schools and offices; and numerous specialty gift shops and gourmet food outlets.

From the outset, Cindy drew from her experience in both small and multinational businesses to establish a fine-tuned combination of close customer consultation, operational and outsourcing systems, quality assurance programs and a technology platform that the major organisations at the time would have been proud of.

She considers herself more entrepreneur than business leader and claims much of the company's success comes from backing her instincts. However, she also emphasises a deep commitment to ensuring attention to detail. Even before the tangible success, Cindy knew she had a winner on her hands. She assessed the worth of the Australian retail biscuit market at about a billion dollars. This was a huge market which had become dull and was in need of stimulation. She identified the opportunity to produce a homemade-looking biscuit that adhered to quality standards. She had the vision to see that such a biscuit would fill this need on both the domestic and international fronts, as there were no premium, exotic, fun or cheeky biscuit products around.

The goal of turning over $5 million within five years was set. Luken & May hit this goal six months into the company's fourth year. However, the success and growth of the business created its own problems, as demand outweighed the capability of the business to supply. Cindy even had to refuse orders from major UK clients because it was not possible to handle the volume and still maintain the strict discipline of paying attention to detail. She strongly believes that if you don't pay attention to detail then things can start falling through the cracks.

Cindy set up a new way to do business. Rather than trying to do everything in-house, she placed the focus on servicing the customer by engaging in close customer consultation and chose to outsource manufacturing and logistics. This was critical in freeing her up to concentrate on creativity, innovation and service. The team at Luken & May have been rewarded for their hard work by industry awards including the Australian Business prize 'Innovate for Success' and the prestigious Jaguar/Gourmet Traveller 'Innovation in Produce' Award for Excellence.

On the product development side, the business has food scientists who are extremely disciplined and systematic; they do not miss a thing. And on the client management side, Cindy has a policy of ensuring that everyone in the office knows what's going on so that if she is not personally available, anyone else could immediately answer customer queries.

The values instilled in the working environment are open communication, integrity and honesty. Cindy's philosophy is simple: 'We must enjoy what we do. We must want to come to work. We must want to work with the people who work here.' There is no doubt that teamwork and pure dedication to quality and service with a passion for creating beautiful products has proved a recipe for Luken & May's success.

In May 2003, Luken & May's brands were sold to Stuart Alexander, a 120-year-old Sydney-based family company whose business is building brands.

MARKET RESEARCH

An important part of developing your marketing strategy is to undertake systematic research into the nature of the market and how it is segmented. This will also let you assess whether your product/service actually appeals to target customers and why. The more detailed your research, the greater the likelihood that you will pinpoint needs in the market which are not being serviced. This procedure, known as market research, can be done internally or you can use an expert consulting company. If you don't do any research you won't know the acceptability of your product until it is too late, that is after you have launched an expensive marketing campaign aimed at the wrong group of prospects or highlighting the wrong features.

While a market research consultant can be costly, using one will ensure you don't miss vital information. They will also make useful conclusions and recommendations based on their experience. They will provide a full range of technical research methods plus the computing power for a comprehensive analysis. They also offer a detailed understanding of the marketing and economic environment.

The key to the success of market research rests with using a systematic approach and completing each step before the next commences. Without market research, marketing decisions can become mere guesswork. To some extent most people do some research, even if it's only to ask the neighbours, family and friends what they think.

The market research process can be broken into the following six steps.

Step 1: Define the objectives

Your market research should answer the following:

- What do prospective customers think of your product?
- Would they buy the product? Why?
- What features do they like or dislike?
- What do they think of the competition?

Step 2: Preliminary investigation

Other studies and published data on the market are analysed in detail. The definition is tested and refined. A good starting point is the Australian Bureau of Statistics (**www.abs.gov.au**). The ABS has a large database of statistics about the Australian market and its demographics.

Step 3: Planning the research

The different techniques and methodology are evaluated and selected. The different methods include questionnaire surveys, sales forecasting, market measurements, motivation research, operations research and factor analysis. The two key issues before conducting any surveys are who you are going to ask and what you want to know about.

When drafting the questionnaire, consider making it anonymous. Think about including some incentive for the person completing the survey, such as a discount or a prize. Keep the survey short and to the point. Consider multiple-choice questions to make it easy to answer.

Step 4: Gathering factual information

The next step is to gather the factual information through telephone interviews, direct mailing of questionnaires, personal interviews, and focus groups.

Step 5: Interpreting the information

The data gathered in the previous step is analysed and segmented according to criteria such as age and income. The data is then tested using computer models, and summarised.

Step 6: Reaching a conclusion

The analysed information is used to form a recommendation for action. The results of the market research should be used to inform and validate the marketing strategy.

5. RAISING FINANCE

- **Finance decision-making**
- **Short-term finance**
- **Long-term finance**
- **Hire purchase and leasing**
- **Equity finance**
- **Types of equity investors**

There are two basic types of finance available – debt and equity. Debt is when you borrow principal that is repaid over time, typically with an interest component. Equity is raised by issuing shares in your business and involves a permanent injection of capital.

Raising finance is one of the more challenging and complex tasks facing entrepreneurs. There are a large number of different types and sources of finance. Make sure you do not spend valuable time pursuing financing options that are inappropriate for your business. You need to match the type/source of funding with your stage of development and business size, and the amount of finance you require.

Tip from the trenches

Don't wait until your current funds are exhausted/inadequate before raising further funds required for the business plan – your negotiating position with funders may be significantly weakened.

Ensure that you raise enough funds – under-capitalising your business may increase the risk of financial failure and/or result in a higher number of time-consuming capital raisings, thereby diverting management attention from running the business.

FINANCE DECISION-MAKING

The main issues to consider before raising finance are:

- What security can you provide?
- How much finance does the business need?
- What will the finance be required for?
- What finance structure is most suitable?
- How much control are you willing to give up? Once you have answered these questions, you will be able to focus your search on the most appropriate sources of finance and enable comparisons of availability, costs and suitability.

Security

A key issue for business owners is the security or collateral required by financiers before lending funds.

In essence, security means that if you fail to make repayments on your loan, the financier may be able to sell certain assets to satisfy the loan moneys owed and any interest in relation to that loan.

Your business may well own assets which can be offered to your financier as security, such as land and buildings, motor vehicles, and plant and equipment. If not, the financier may request that you grant security over your personal assets (or the personal assets of your family) such as your home, investment properties or shares.

In general, if your business has not been profitably trading for more than two years, most financiers will require security before providing loan facilities such as overdrafts, term loans or other finance.

It is also important to bear in mind that when calculating the value of the security you provide, financiers will be very conservative and will also take into account the transaction cost of selling the assets and the risk that the market will soften during the term of your loan. It is not uncommon for valuations of assets put up for security to be some 10–15 per cent less than the going market rate.

It is critical that before you grant security over your home or your parents' home you fully appreciate the seriousness of your decision. If your business collapses not only will your dream of building a business have failed but you could lose your family home.

How much finance does the business need?

The first step is to establish the capital required to fund the business plan. The amount of money needed to start varies tremendously, depending on the scale and nature of the business. Generally, you will have to find capital for two specific purposes: working capital and fixed capital.

Working capital   This is the money needed to operate the business on a day-to-day basis, such as wages, raw materials and stock.

Fixed capital   This is the acquisition of a business or items that will be used in the business for more than one year, such as premises, plant and equipment. Different businesses require different fixed assets to enable the provision of their products or services. For example:

- retail businesses require premises, shop fittings, trolleys, baskets, cash register, delivery van and display stands
- service industries require premises, PC system, printer, desks, shelves, pot plants and lounge suite
- Internet operations require servers, firewalls, PC system and laser printers.

A number of factors will determine what fixed assets you will need to acquire and on what scale. These include the nature of your product/service, the forecast scale of production/sales, the finance you have available (if limited, there will effectively be competition amongst the different types of fixed assets) and any alternative items that will achieve the same or similar results.

What will the finance be required for?

The next step is to itemise what the finance is required for. This will set you on the right path to identifying what kind of finance to secure. In the course of establishing your fixed and working capital requirements you will, by implication, have identified the purposes for which they are required. The table below indicates the different methods of financing for different purposes.

DIFFERENT METHODS OF FINANCING

Purpose	Method
Short-term finance	
Debtors, stock, raw materials,	Overdrafts
and other general working	Creditors
capital requirements	Factoring
Long-term finance	
Business acquisitions, fixed assets,	Loans (medium/long), mortgages
property, motor vehicles	Hire purchase, leases
	Equity/venture capital

The difference between short-term and long-term borrowing is obviously an essential factor in choosing the most suitable type of finance for your business. It is preferable to match the term of a loan with the useful life of the asset that it is financing, and financiers will typically do this. If you used short-term funds to purchase fixed assets, you would most likely be required to repay the loan before the assets had generated adequate cashflows to make the repayments. On the other hand, if you borrowed long-term funds to purchase short-term assets, such as inventory, you would still be paying off the loan after you had used the assets, incurring unnecessary financing costs and unnecessarily utilising available financing facilities.

What financial structure is most appropriate?

Financial structure is the amount of debt versus equity funding you use in your business. Increasing the level of borrowings, known as leverage, has a multiplying effect on your returns, be they profits or losses. The table below shows three different financial structures using an interest rate of 10 per cent.

EFFECT OF LEVERAGING

Assets	$100 000	100 000	100 000
Liabilities – debt	$ 0	60 000	85 000
Equity	$100 000	40 000	15 000
Net profit before interest	$ 30 000	30 000	30 000
Interest expense	$ 0	6 000	8 500
Net profit before tax (NPBT)	$ 30 000	24 000	21 500
Return on assets (ROA)*		30%	24%	21.5%
Return on owner's equity (ROE)**		30%	60%	143%

*NPBT/Assets

**NPBT/Equity

Note the relationship between assets, debts and equity, i.e. as debt increases, the equity contribution required from the owners reduces dollar for dollar. Also, interest expenses increase as the amount of total debt increases, resulting in a reduced net profit before tax (NPBT) when the proportion of debt in the financial structure increases.

However, despite NPBT reducing, ROE *increases* as the proportion of debt increases because of the effects of financial leverage, (i.e. the return (NPBT) per dollar of equity has increased as a result of utilising debt funding). There is an inverse relationship between the amount of leveraging and ROA – the higher the debt the lower the ROA (ROA and ROE are discussed in more depth in chapter eleven). This is because interest expenses increase and reduce profits.

In order to determine the most appropriate financial structure you will need to consider the level of leveraging in other businesses like yours and overall industry profiles. If your sales fall and you are highly leveraged you will fall below break-even point before a business that is not leveraged, i.e. financial risk increases as leverage increases. The maximum amount of leverage achievable will depend on the stage of business development and in most cases will be dictated by the lending bank.

How much control are you willing to give up?

By introducing equity investors, such as corporate partners or business angels, your control over the company will be diluted. Most substantial investors will want to appoint directors to the board. They will expect regular updates on the progress of the business and may want the right to veto certain key decisions (such as entering new alliances or raising capital). Some entrepreneurs don't want to give up some of their equity in the business for fear of losing control. This is a personal decision for the entrepreneur but a dilution in control is a necessary element of raising equity to take advantage of a business opportunity.

SHORT-TERM FINANCE

Short-term finance has the following characteristics:

- it is typically repaid within one year
- it is used to purchase/finance assets that will be quickly turned over in the business, such as trade debtors and inventory
- it is typically self-funding as it is used to purchase/fund assets that will generate the funds necessary to repay the loan when they are sold.

The main sources of short-term borrowing for small businesses are trade credit, inventory financing, overdrafts, trade financing and accounts receivable financing.

Trade credit

Trade credit is simply when your supplier grants you an interest-free period before you have to pay for the goods or services, for example they may give you thirty days from the date of delivery. Trade credit is usually relatively simple to obtain and, unlike bank loans and other forms of finance, does not involve detailed loan applications or negotiations.

You should ensure that your business makes the most of trade credit. If you have been granted thirty-day terms by a supplier you may as well delay payment until the end of that period. An exception to this may be where the supplier has offered a cash discount for early payment, in which case you should weigh up the relevant amount saved by accepting the discount.

Inventory financing

Inventory financing is simply a bank line of credit secured over your inventory. This makes the cash you have tied up in your inventory more available to you. This form of financing is obviously most useful for businesses with physical stocks of inventory and is therefore not useful for service firms. Lending institutions are typically only interested in companies with solid track records. Inventory financing is also not recommended if your stocks are comprised of obsolete or slow-moving inventories.

To maximise your chances of securing inventory financing you will need to demonstrate that you have good systems for maintaining information on your inventory – stock levels, how old the inventory is, and costings. The lender will probably also want to see future orders for merchandise so they can be confident your inventory will move quickly, and may require an additional form of security, such as a personal guarantee.

Overdraft

An overdraft or a short-term line of credit is an arrangement with your bank where you may borrow up to a certain limit on a short-term basis. The lender will set a maximum negative balance, known as the overdraft limit. Borrowings can be made or repaid on a daily basis. You will be required to renew and renegotiate your overdraft annually. Repayments to the overdraft are flexible. It is important to note that an overdraft is repayable on demand although in practice a bank is unlikely to require this unless they are concerned about the business's performance. Overdrafts may be secured (for example, by a charge over the assets of the business) or unsecured.

Overdrafts enable businesses to better manage cash flow. They usually carry a lower interest rate than credit cards but somewhat higher than bank loans for a specific amount and purchase. Interest is calculated daily on the amount outstanding, so you only pay interest on the amount borrowed and only for the period the principal is outstanding.

Overdrafts, like bank loans, are usually only available to profitable, established businesses. They are useful:

- to even out cash flow when fluctuations are predictable, short-term or seasonal
- for purchases that are too large for a credit card but too small for a bank loan (smaller amounts can be rolled into a cheaper form of financing once a sufficiently large amount has accumulated)
- as an insurance policy in case you have a cash shortage
- to finance cost of goods for customer orders already received.

An overdraft is not advisable for purchases of major items of equipment. It is better to get a bank loan which has a lower interest rate and a longer time to repay the amount. It is also not a good form of finance when cash flow shortages may be permanent or for an extensive period, such as more than a year.

To establish an overdraft you will be charged an establishment fee and a monthly administration or commitment fee. All legal fees associated with establishing the facility are also paid by the borrower.

Trade financing

Most banks also provide trade financing to cover the working capital gaps in import and export businesses. The term of such trade finance is for a period up to 180 days. For example, a manufacturer exports a shipment of nuts and bolts to

Europe. His customers in Europe pay on delivery whereas his raw material suppliers in Australia are already owed their invoices. To cover the gap between the receivables on the goods shipped and the raw materials and other costs for producing those goods, a financier can extend a line of credit until the foreign customers have received the goods and paid their invoices.

Accounts receivable financing

There are two methods of accounts receivable financing – factoring and lending.

Factoring   This is when you sell your accounts receivable at a discount to a lender known as a 'factor'. Factoring services are available from most large finance companies and also from specialist factoring companies. The factor assumes responsibility for the collection of your accounts receivable and advances you a percentage of the value of those accounts. In most cases, a small business would only be paid the balance of the accounts receivable, less the factoring fee, when the factor receives payment from your customer. It is important to note, however, that you still bear the risk of bad debts. Not all small or medium-size businesses will be able to obtain factoring finance.

Lending   Most banks and finance companies will also lend your business funds using your accounts receivable as security. They will lend you a cash advance of say 70 per cent of your invoices (debts over sixty days old are typically excluded). The lender will require you to comply with certain debt collection procedures.

LONG-TERM FINANCE

Long-term borrowing is used to finance the purchase of fixed assets, such as equipment, motor vehicles, machinery and property, permanent increases to working capital, the acquisition of an existing business, and/or capital costs when launching a new business. The assets purchased using long-term funding need to generate a level of income adequate to cover not only the principal and interest repayments but also to earn a profit.

This section overviews credit risk assessment by banks, finance submissions, questions you should ask your bank, types of bank debts and the role of the Banking Ombudsman.

Credit risk assessment by banks

While banks use different methods to assess credit risks for applicants, most analysis centres around the three Cs of credit – character, collateral and cash flow.

- **Character** – measures how good your personal credit record is and whether your management team have what it takes to run the business.
- **Collateral** – the level of security you will need to provide to the bank.
- **Cash flow** – you will need to provide a track record of profitability and stability in cash flows. In some cases banks will only lend to a company which has been trading profitably for two years or longer. Some lenders require you to have an annual turnover of at least $250 000.

You will be unlikely to qualify for a bank loan if your business is less than two years old unless you have had successful companies before, you have large personal assets to use as security or you are opening a franchise. Banks are also unlikely to lend to a business which in its recent past has been loss-making, unless the business can demonstrate that current profitability is sustainable.

If you do not qualify for bank finance, you may need to consider seeking equity funding from alternative sources, such as business angels, venture capitalists or private equity investors.

Finance submission

When applying for a loan, the lender will generally require you to submit:

- a detailed business plan
- historical financial statements
- forecasts.

Tip from the trenches

Don't expect to raise money without a thorough business plan. Eighty per cent of businesses seeking bank finance do not have a formal plan and then wonder why they can't raise money.

Your lender will also want to assess:

- whether you have the necessary skills and experience to manage the business
- the amount and purpose of the borrowing
- the source of revenue which will be used to make repayments
- any assets of the company that can be used as security
- the prospects of the business and the industry in general
- your personal credit history
- referees, such as major suppliers/customers.

Most lenders require loans to be protected by some form of security or collateral, such as a personal guarantee, a fixed or floating charge over the assets of the company, or a mortgage over your home. In general it does not matter how strong your forecast cash flows are, the bank will usually require a tangible asset as security. In essence, the bank wants something valuable they can sell to cover the total amount of their loan in case the business fails or repayments cannot be made. For many people the most likely source of such security, in the absence of sufficient business assets, will be the family home.

Lenders usually seek to impose restrictions on you to protect themselves against potential erosion of the value of the business or security through mismanagement during the term of the loan, such as:

- providing the lender with regular financial status reports
- preventing you from borrowing further funds without approval
- minimum levels of working capital
- ensuring you have adequate insurance
- financial covenants, e.g. minimum earnings to debt ratios.

Questions you should ask

Before applying for a loan ensure you ask the bank the following questions (this will assist you in comparing the different banks):

- What is the likely size of the loan they would be prepared to make?
- What are the likely financial covenants they would seek to impose?
- What is the term of the loan?
- Can you repay fortnightly?
- What are the total charges and fees?
- Are there any early repayment penalties?
- Do they lend to companies in your industry and have experience in dealing with small business loans?

Ensure you shop around between the different lenders. Compare the different costs of obtaining a loan – take into account not only the interest rate but also establishment fees, monthly fees, and other charges.

InfoChoice provides an independent information service comparing the terms offered by different financiers. It provides comparative data on interest rates, fees and conditions for a wide range of financial services such as business loans, overdrafts, leases and term deposits. Over the term of a loan the variations in fees and charges between different lenders can produce differences of up to $30 000 on a $500 000 loan.
See **www.infochoice.com.au**

Interest   The rate of interest charged can vary significantly between different lenders, so it is worth comparing rates. Financiers apply a 'margin' to business loans to reflect the risk that they are taking on. The size of the margin typically ranges from 1 to 3 per cent depending on how risky they perceive your business venture over their cost of borrowing those funds. In turn this will be determined by the type and amount of security which is offered, your experience in running a business of that type and the bank's view on the business risk arising from the nature of the industry, your financial trading record, spread of customers, etc.

There are a number of different businesses that will review your account statements to ensure that you are not being overcharged interest or fees by your financier. InterestSavers has designed a software program which checks that you have not been overcharged. They recently conducted a survey and found that of 200 monthly statements over 50 per cent of them had errors and that 90 per cent of those errors were in favour of the lender.
See **www.interestsavers.com.au**

Stamp duty   Bear in mind that if the bank takes security over the assets of the company or your home, you may have to pay stamp duty (ask your solicitor for more information). The rate is payable according to a cost scale that varies in each state.

Services   You should also ensure the lender offers you a full range of services, such as linked cheque and credit card accounts, online or phone banking and leasing services. Some lenders will waive fees on other banking products, such as personal loans, if you take out a business loan.

Term   The term of a bank loan ranges from one to ten years and is usually matched to the useful life of the assets being purchased. The longer the term the greater the amount of interest charged. Note that early repayment penalties may apply if you pay out the loan before the end of the term, particularly with fixed interest loans.

Types of bank debts

Below is an overview of the three main types of bank debts – mortgage, personal loan and term loan.

Mortgages   Mortgage finance is long-term finance for the purchase of land and buildings. Interest rates may be fixed or variable. Repayments are by regular instalments and include principal and interest. Interest-only loans are also available. Mortgages are secured by the property you are purchasing. The term of a mortgage can run fifteen, twenty or thirty years. There are a variety of sources, including mortgage originators, brokers, building societies, banks, finance companies, solicitors' trust funds and insurance companies.

Personal loans   Personal loans are repaid in regular principal and interest instalments. They are typically used for the purchase of motor vehicles, shop fixtures or perhaps the initial stock. They are normally unsecured but sometimes secured against your life insurance policy. The term of a personal loan is usually three or five years. Most banks and finance companies offer personal loans.

Term loans   Repayment of a term loan is typically by regular instalments of interest and principal. Interest rates may be fixed or variable. The loan may be interest-only, requiring regular payments of interest only with the principal repayment either made in a lump sum at the end of the loan term or refinanced with a new loan. These are usually used for the purchase of a business, land, buildings and equipment. Security is generally required. Term loans can run for any period between one and ten years. They are offered by banks, finance companies, building societies, insurance companies and solicitors' trust funds.

The Banking and Financial Services Ombudsman

The Banking and Financial Services Ombudsman considers consumer and small-business complaints about the services provided by banks. It is an independent non-government body. You can complain to the Banking and Financial Services Ombudsman if you are a small business or individual and the loss you are claiming is less than $250 000. The initial consultation will be free, however for further assistance in the claims against your bank, there are fees payable (which are refundable depending on the outcome of your case). See **www.abio.org.au**

HIRE PURCHASE AND LEASING

An alternative method for financing motor vehicles and plant or equipment is through a leasing arrangement. A key advantage of leasing is that it does not require you to make a deposit upfront. The financier, known as the lessor, will buy the asset and then enter a contract called a lease under which you, the lessee, have the right to use the asset for a specified period by making regular lease payments. The main providers of leasing facilities are specialist leasing companies, finance companies, and some equipment or vehicle suppliers.

Hire purchase

Under a hire-purchase agreement, you will be required to fund a deposit yourself and the balance outstanding on the purchase price will be funded by the financier. Repayment is by regular instalments of interest and principal. The financier retains ownership of the assets until all instalments have been paid. A hire-purchase agreement has the following characteristics:

- The term will vary with the type of asset being financed, but is typically three to five years.
- Hire purchase is used to acquire fixed assets such as motor vehicles, shop fittings, plant and equipment.
- The retention of ownership by the lender is effectively a form of security. If you default, the financier may have the right to retain ownership of the asset.

Leasing

The most popular form of leasing is the finance lease. This is similar to hire purchase arrangements in that the ownership of the asset actually remains with the financier or lessor. The term of the contract is usually the asset's useful life. You will be responsible for servicing, insuring and maintaining the asset over the period of the contract. If you want to terminate the lease early you may be liable for a penalty charge.

At the end of the period of the lease, you generally have the option of returning the asset to the financier or offering to purchase the asset for its residual value (this will be a figure nominated in the lease).

It is important to understand, however, that if you return the asset, rather than buying it out, the financier will sell it to the public and you may be liable for any shortfall below the residual value.

There are a number of other types of leases available, as listed below:

- **Sale and leaseback package** – you sell your assets to the financier and then lease them back. The key advantage of this approach is that the lease payments are generally tax-deductible. A common feature of these packages is a repurchase option at the end of the period of the lease.
- **Operating lease** – a short-term hiring arrangement that can be terminated without penalty and with short notice. For example, when you hire a motor vehicle, the rental company is responsible for insurance and maintenance and you simply return it when you are finished.
- **Fleet leasing** – may be a cost-effective option if you need a large number of vehicles. The leasing company will attend to the maintenance and management of the fleet.

Ask your tax adviser to assess the tax effectiveness of each leasing package before you sign any agreements. The table below will give you some helpful pointers on the merits of each lease option.

VEHICLE AND EQUIPMENT FINANCE

Product	No deposit	Tax-deductible repayments	Optional purchase
Hire purchase	✓		✓
Finance lease	✓	✓	✓
Sale and leaseback		✓	
Operating lease		✓	
Fleet leasing		✓	

EQUITY FINANCE

In simple terms equity is when someone owns part of your business. If you have set up a company structure you can introduce new investors to your business by issuing them shares in your company.

The type of investor most suitable for your business depends on how much money you are raising, how much control you are willing to part with and what value they can add to your business, e.g. industry contacts, strategy assistance, etc. Equally important is what stage of the life cycle your business is in.

The search for equity funding is typically an ongoing process. As soon as you have secured one source, start planning and pitching for the next round. Take time to understand alternative forms of finance, such as business angels and venture capital.

Life cycle stages

A common approach to classifying equity funding is to divide businesses into the stage of their life cycle.

Stage 1: Seed   At this stage the business is little more than a concept. The product is usually still in development and the company is concentrating on research and on producing a working model or prototype. Often the founders of the company will fund the business from their personal funds, personal credit cards and from loans from family or friends. At this stage the funding needs of the company are normally between $50 000 and $500 000.

Stage 2: Startup   The startup stage is also known as the 'angel round'. At this stage the concept or products have been developed but the company has no track record and often has not made a profit. This is the riskiest stage for investors as the company needs a large amount of capital but has no reliable indicators of its future success. Many businesses will fail during this phase. The funding needs of the company at this time are typically between $500 000 and $2 million. Depending on the industry, the startup stage can last between six months and several years.

Stage 3: Expansion   This stage is often called the 'second round' and may indeed comprise multiple rounds before the company is ready for stage four. By the expansion stage, the company is fully set up and is building a financial track record. The company now needs funding to expand its existing operational and marketing capacity. At this stage the funding needs of the company are typically between $2 million and $10 million plus. Some companies may be able to meet their financing needs at this time with traditional bank finance, however the bank will usually require personal guarantees from directors and collateral.

Stage 4: Pre-initial public offering (IPO) Pre-IPO funding allows the company to prepare for an IPO. The funds may be used to make a few strategic acquisitions and the pre-IPO investors can provide experience in the IPO process. For example, they may prepare a company for listing by introducing recognised businesspeople to the board. At this stage the funding needs of the company can be anywhere from $10 million to $50 million and upwards.

LIFE CYCLE OF GROWTH BUSINESSES

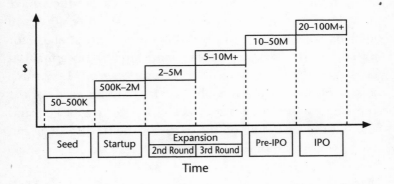

Tip from the trenches

There are no guarantees when raising equity funding. Investors may withdraw for many reasons, even if they have done extensive due diligence or signed a terms sheet (usually non-binding). You may choose to negotiate with multiple investors to mitigate against this, although some investors will want to know they can invest if they conduct extensive due diligence, often at considerable cost.

TYPES OF EQUITY INVESTORS

There are various types of equity investors – family and friends, business angels, venture capital, private equity, private placements, corporate partners or public offerings. They are summarised below.

Family and friends

Raising money from family and friends is a common way of funding a new business concept. In some cases, it may be the only way of obtaining funding on reasonable terms, either because you have no credit history, the business model is completely untested, or you want to maintain secrecy about your plans.

While this source of funding is often relatively easy and quick to obtain, you need to consider the risks before taking money from family or friends.

- If your business fails someone close to you is losing money they may not be able to afford to lose.
- If the business is not the great success you promised, it can become a great source of bitterness and it can taint the personal relationship for years or, worse, forever.
- You need to ask whether you are unintentionally forcing your family or friends into the investment. Make sure their investment is a business decision and not a way of bribing you (or them) in relation to a personal matter.
- Are you comfortable about having to disclose your personal financial situation to them? For example, they will want to know how much money you put in and how much salary you are taking out.
- Will they take up your valuable time asking irrelevant questions or making misguided suggestions?

Raising money from family and friends may not be

preferable if you have another source of finance. Many experts consider family and friends to be finance of last resort. While you may have to give more equity away or pay more interest to a third-party investor by going elsewhere, at least you avoid being dependent on your family/friends. You should also not borrow from family and friends when the amount being invested is a relatively large amount for that person to lend. Only accept their money if you know they would really not be affected if something happened and you could not give them back their money.

To minimise the risks associated with taking funding from family and friends, you need to ensure the following.

- **Disclosure** – ensure you fully disclose all details about your business. Give them a copy of your business plan and ensure they understand all the risks involved with your venture, such as the possibility of new competitors, the reliance on key suppliers, or the untested nature of the products or business.
- **Valuations** – it is always hard to value your business at an early stage, and this is true even for professionals. Your family may typically fall into the category of 'unsophisticated investor' so they may not know how to value your business.
- **Expectations** – make sure you talk openly and frankly about your expectations for the business – when and how you will repay their money, what happens if the business fails, the size of their potential return. Also discuss the ways that you will maintain boundaries between your friendship and the business as there is nothing worse than spending every family meal discussing how your business is going.
- **Legal agreement** – you should ask your lawyer to prepare a short-form agreement that sets out the basis for the

funding between you and the other party. This should include at least the amount being invested, when the money will be repaid, whether the investment accrues interest or dividends and the rate of return, the rights attaching to the investment, what happens when you want to sell the business and a dispute-resolution provision that details how you will deal with a breach of the agreement.

Business angels

An important source of external equity capital for startups is private investors known as business angels. These are typically wealthy individuals who provide finance in the form of share capital. Business angels typically provide seed funding for companies just starting up or emerging from the prototype stage to establish their first operations. The range of funding is anywhere from $50 000 up to $1 000 000.

Some angels provide more than just financing – they will act as your mentor and guide you through the process of setting up your business, introduce you to potential strategic alliances and help find further capital to grow. Angels are often semi-retired senior executives who want to help nurture new businesses. Many have years of business experience and extensive networks of contacts.

Angels will usually invest only in high-growth businesses – you will need to show that they will make a high return within a short period. For example, they will probably not be interested unless they can make four or five times their money within, say, three years.

Funding from angels may not be suitable if:
- you need more money than angels typically invest
- your business is unlikely to grow fast enough to meet the expected returns

• you do not want to give up any control of your business.

Before signing up with an angel ensure that you find out about their background – whether they have experience in your industry sector and what investments they have already made. You should speak to those companies and find out how the angel performed and whether they provided useful contacts. Ask the angel what is expected in return and what their exit horizon is. It will also be useful to know whether they have the capacity to provide further funding if needed. Do not sign anything until you have had your lawyer review the investment documentation between you and your angel.

Locating an angel may be difficult. Your accountant, solicitor and other financial advisers may be able to introduce you to one, or you may find one through the following sources.

• The chamber of commerce in your state may operate a matching service to introduce investors and entrepreneurs.

• Business Angels is an investor network with significant available capital.
See **www.businessangels.com.au**

Venture capital

Venture capitalists are professional investors who provide funding to fast-growing, early to mid-stage ventures, usually in high-growth sectors such as technology, medical devices and life services. They provide large amounts of funding ($500 000 plus) in return for a significant equity holding – typically 35 to 50 per cent – and other rights (for example, the right to appoint a director to the board).

A well-known example of a venture-backed company is LookSmart, which jumped from a valuation in 1996 of $15 million to over US $3 billion when it listed in 1999 on the NASDAQ Board of the New York Stock Exchange, providing the early-stage venture capitalists with a whopping return of over 1000 per cent.

Due to the growing importance of venture capital in funding high-growth ventures in Australia, it has been dealt with separately in depth in chapter nineteen.

Private equity

Private equity investors are similar to venture capitalists except that they tend to invest in mature (i.e. relatively stable revenues, profitable and cashflow positive) businesses. Typical transactions that private equity investors are involved in are management buy-outs (MBOs), management buy-ins (MBIs), leveraged buy-outs (LBOs), public to private transactions, family succession in private businesses and funding mergers, and acquisitions and growth plans of private businesses. Amounts invested are typically $5 million and upwards and a common feature is that a significant amount of leverage (up to 70 per cent) is used in the transactions.

Private placement

A private placement is when a large bundle of shares in your business is sold or issued to a select group of investors. In most cases a placement agent, usually a stockbroking firm or investment bank, will manage the process for a fee. The agent will help you prepare an information memorandum, generate a list of potential investors – often large institutional investors, such as superannuation funds – and assist in pitching to investors. The fees charged can vary considerably, from 3 per cent to as high as 7 per cent (the typical rate charged is 5 per cent) of funds raised.

A private placement is suitable when you need an injection of capital to jump to the next level of growth and you have a proven track record of profitability. A private placement typically takes place in companies who do not want, or are unable, to take venture capital and are too small for a public offering.

A key advantage of a placement is that the company has a considerable degree of control over the terms of the placement – who participates, and the amount and price of equity issued. Also, investors who participate in placements are less likely to want day-to-day control over your operations, unlike venture capitalists or business angels.

Private placements can be quite time-consuming as you will need to prepare a detailed information memorandum that outlines your business, past performance, future plans and viability. The memorandum usually includes detailed accounting information prepared by an independent accounting firm. You will also need to prepare for and attend a number of presentations to investors.

The cost of a placement can be prohibitive as you will need not only a placement agent but also accountants and lawyers who are experienced with the process. Another downside of placements is the level of disclosure required. Your vision and detailed plans for the business become known to investors and competitors alike. This method of fundraising is typically only available for larger businesses.

Corporate partnering

Corporate or strategic partnering is when you form an alliance with another company, often a more mature business, whose goals are similar to your own. The strategic partner provides you with funding, and the day-to-day and strategic operations of both companies become closely aligned.

These alliances are useful when each party brings something different to the table. Your business may have, for example, developed a new technology or product that can be distributed through the other company's existing network. Another example is where you operate within a geographical area and your strategic partner operates in other areas. Together you can service bigger customers.

You should avoid entering into a strategic partnering deal if:

- there is a risk that your partner is merely negotiating/dealing with you to learn as much as possible about your business so they can proceed without you
- the partnership is too one-sided (e.g. you are bringing far more to the table than your partner) such that one party inevitably feels the initial deal struck was unfair
- you are concerned about losing control of your business or dislike a collegiate atmosphere.

For the relationship to be successful, ensure that you:

- negotiate upfront how the parties will divide profits, what assets need to be acquired and who pays for them
- consider upfront how you will divide the ownership of products or intellectual property that you develop jointly (you will also need to consider how you will split any revenue streams from the sale or licensing of those products)
- ask your lawyer to draft a joint venture agreement that includes appropriate confidentiality undertakings and non-compete agreements to protect both partners
- consider working together on a smaller project to ensure the relationship is viable before launching into a full joint venture.

Public offering

An initial public offering (IPO) of shares involves listing your company on a stock exchange, such as the Australian

Stock Exchange (ASX) or NASDAQ in America, and issuing securities to the general public and large financial institutions. An IPO is for mature companies with strong, stable financial performance, preferably offering reasonable growth prospects.

Going public exposes your business to intense scrutiny from regulators and from the financing community, such as brokerage houses. You will also need to make regular reports to your shareholders and the stock exchange, and there are significant ongoing costs associated with maintaining a listing (at least $0.25–$0.5 million per annum).

Potentially, it can be financially fatal for a company to list too early in its life. Not only are there significant ongoing costs but, in reality, many smaller listed companies struggle to raise new funds and attract institutional investors and research coverage despite being listed. Company owners should not therefore take the decision to list before extensively analysing the implications for all stakeholders and seeking professional advice.

To be eligible for listing, the ASX has a number of stringent requirements, e.g. minimum assets test, minimum number of shareholders, etc. (refer to their web site for further details: **www.asx.com.au**).

Summary of equity investors
The table below summarises the main types of equity investors discussed above and the stage at which they would invest in your business.

EQUITY INVESTORS AND THEIR INVESTMENT

Investor	Seed	Startup	Expansion	Mezzanine
	$50 000– $500 000	$500 000– $2m	$2m– $10m	$10m + Pre-float
Family/friends	✓			
Business angels	✓	✓		
Venture capital		✓	✓	
Private equity			✓	✓
Private placement			✓	✓
Corporate partner		✓	✓	
Public offering				✓

6. COMPLYING WITH YOUR LEGAL OBLIGATIONS

- **Registering a business name**
- **Licences and permits**
- **Worker's compensation, minimum wages and superannuation**
- **Australian Business Number**
- **A suitable business structure**
- **Retention of business records**
- **Your company and the law**
- **The role of a lawyer**

This chapter overviews some of your general legal obligations, including registering a business name and obtaining government licences or permits. It also discusses some of the different legal structures that are available – trusts, companies, partnerships and sole traders. You should always seek independent legal advice from a suitably qualified and experienced solicitor when setting up your business to ensure you have complied with all your legal requirements.

REGISTERING A BUSINESS NAME

A business name is the name under which a person or other entity trades. If your trading name is different from your real name, you are required by law to register your business name in each state in which you are trading. For example, if your business trades solely in Victoria, you are only required to register the name in Victoria. If you trade in another state, you will be required to register the name in that state as well.

Choosing the right business or trading name is important from a branding/marketing perspective – see chapter four for further discussion.

You will not be required to register a business name if it is the same as your own name. If you have added extra words, however, to your trading name, then you will have to register the name. For example, if your trading name was simply your given name or initials and family name, such as 'Matthew Carpenter', it would not be required to be registered. However if your trading name was 'Carpenter Strategy Consulting' it would need to be registered.

If you have registered a company with the Australian Securities and Investments Commission (ASIC) and you trade using the name of the company, you will not be required to register a business name. If the company trades using a name other than its registered company name, however, it must also register the trading name as a business name. For example, XYZ Pty Limited is permitted to trade as XYZ without registering a business name in any state, but if the company wants to trade as XYZ Investment Services, it would have to register the name.

Name availability

Once you have chosen a suitable business or company name you or your lawyer will need to check whether it is available for registration. You can do this through the following avenues:

- **Business name searches** – you can search the National Names Index free of charge to check whether your proposed business name already exsists (see **www.asic.gov.au**).

- **Company searches** – you can also do a company name search free of charge on the ASIC web site or contact your state branch (see **www.asic.gov.au**).
- **Trademark searches** – you can do a trademark search free of charge on the IP Australia web site (**www.ipaustralia.gov.au**), apply at the trademarks office (phone 1300 651 010), or ask your solicitor to undertake the searches.
- **Domain name searches** – it is also worth considering whether you will be able to secure an Internet domain name which is similar to your business name. Domain names can be searched on Internet sites such as **www.netregistry.com.au** and **www.melbourneit.com.au**

To register a business name, you will need to lodge an application with your state department of fair trading. The cost of registration is around $130 in each state.

Company names can be reserved for two months by lodging form 410 with the ASIC. ASIC charges a $40 fee to reserve a name. Alternatively, you can register your company name at the same time as you register your company. Simply nominate your company name on your applcation for registration as a company (ASIC form 201).

Registration

The main objective of requiring registration of a business name is to enable the public to find out who is operating the business. Many people make the mistake of thinking that registration gives them ownership of the name. Registration does not necessarily give you exclusive use of the name or any legal protection for use of that name. It does not create any proprietary rights in the name or provide any protection against breach of the intellectual property rights in the name if it is already used by another business. Furthermore it does not stop someone from registering a similar name. The best way to protect a trade name is to register a trademark. Whilst actions under the Trade Practices and Fair Trading legislation, and in passing off, may be used as protective mechanisms, it is often far cheaper (in the long term) and simpler to register a trademark. Logos and pictures can also be protected by registration of a trademark.

Note: Business Name Registrars do not check the trademark registers before registering your business name. It is up to you to ensure your selected business name does not infringe a registered trademark.

Your application for business name registration may be declined if it:

- is the same as or deceptively similar to an existing company name or registered business name
- is an offensive or 'undesirable' name
- improperly includes a reference to royalty, the Olympics or government
- improperly implies you are an educational institution, organisation or charity.

Registration of your business name must be renewed every two or three years, depending on the state you are registered in. If you do not renew in time your registration will lapse and someone else may apply to register the name. A renewal notice will be sent to your principal place of business.

The process and requirements for registration of trademarks are discussed in chapter sixteen.

Displaying your business or company name

Your registered business or company name must be displayed:

- on stationery and correspondence, such as invoices, receipts, letterheads and cheques.
- on external signage at every place you conduct business, not just the principal address.

The name of the company on its documents must be followed by the abbreviation 'Pty Ltd' or 'Pty Limited' for a proprietary company, and 'Ltd or Limited' for a public company, together with the Australian Company Number (ACN) issued by ASIC.

The certificate of registration must be displayed at the location you nominate as your principal place of business.

When displaying the business name, it must be shown exactly as it appears on the registration certificate. For example, 'Global Manufacturing and Import' cannot be shortened to 'Global Imports'.

LICENCES AND PERMITS

The state and federal governments require certain types of businesses to obtain licences or permits to carry out business. As a pre-condition to obtaining a licence you may need to satisfy certain criteria, such as educational requirements, fitness, character or experience, as well as paying a fee. The objective of government licensing is to protect consumers from 'shonky' and untrained service providers.

Tip from the trenches

Engage good legal and accounting advisers early – they will not only help you comply with your legal obligations but can also provide you with useful industry contacts.

The Business Licence Information Service (BLIS) provides a centralised information service in relation to the various licences and permits required to operate a business (see **www.business.gov.au**). The BLIS will also provide you with the necessary application forms. If in doubt as to what licences you need, you should consult your solicitor.

If you are planning to run your business from home you may need to comply with local council regulations.

Industries subject to registration

Special licences, permits, approvals and registrations are required by a variety of different government authorities for a variety of different industries including:

advertising agents

auctioneers

builders/plumbers/
  electricians

conveyancers

dealers/advisers in securities
  and other financial products

employment agencies

importers

medical goods/devices

real-estate agents

restaurants

retail outlets

security guards

tax agents/advisers

travel agents

valuers

Retail outlets and factories are subject to a broad range of additional regulations including:

- health regulations
- safety regulations
- storage of chemicals
- trading hours
- waste disposal
- water/gas/electricity connections.

You will also need a permit to display signs or advertising material outside your premises.

WORKER'S COMPENSATION, MINIMUM WAGES AND SUPERANNUATION

If you are employing staff you are required by law to:
- maintain appropriate worker's compensation to cover employees against accidents
- offer employees minimum wages and conditions
- make contributions to employee superannuation schemes.

See chapter ten for further details.

You may also be required to pay payroll tax once wages reach a certain threshhold. See chapter seven for further details.

AUSTRALIAN BUSINESS NUMBER

The Australian Business Number (ABN) is a single identifier for all business dealings with the Australian Taxation Office (ATO). In the future it will operate for dealings with other government departments and agencies. You need an ABN to register for the goods and services tax (GST) and other elements of the New Tax System. If you do not register you cannot claim GST credits.

All businesses with an annual turnover of $50 000 or more must register for GST and will need an ABN to do this. Organisations with a lower annual turnover may choose to register or not. All non-profit organisations with an annual turnover of $100 000 or more must register for GST and will need an ABN. You can apply for an ABN, GST registration and other elements of the New Tax System on the same ATO form.

The ABN will eventually replace the Australian Company Number (ACN) and the Australian Registered Body Number

(ARBN). If you are trading through a company, your ABN is usually based on your ACN but has two additional leading digits and becomes an eleven-digit number.

Applicants for an ABN need to ensure their activity can be classified as an enterprise. In general, you are not entitled to an ABN where you are not carrying on an enterprise. For example, employees and hobbyists are not entitled to an ABN as they are not carrying on an enterprise. Self-funded retirees also do not need an ABN – they continue to use their tax file number when reporting their annual income to the ATO. However, all companies registered under the *Corporations Act* are entitled to an ABN.

For more information visit the Tax Office's web site (**www.ato.gov.au**).

A SUITABLE BUSINESS STRUCTURE

This section examines the different legal structures that are available to a business and the relative advantages and disadvantages of each. It is important to discuss your options with your tax, accounting and legal advisers before making a decision. For an overview of the tax implications of legal structures see chapter seven.

In summary, the following business structures are available:

- **Company** – the law regards a company, unlike other structures, as a separate entity from its owners. A company can take action in its own right, own property, and be owned.
- **Sole trader** – a sole trader is a person doing business in their own name. The individual who operates the business takes on all rights and liabilities associated with the business. All of the property of the business is owned by the sole trader.
- **Partnership** – a partnership is a legal structure that allows individuals to do business collectively. An action by

one partner is assumed to be taken by all of the partners acting together. All rights, liabilities and property are jointly owned or owed by the partners.

- **Trading trust** – when property is placed in a trust, the nominal owner of the property is legally bound to use that property for certain purposes only (and not for their own enjoyment).
- **Other structures** – there is a range of other structures available including incorporated associations, cooperatives and limited partnerships.

Company

Unlike partnerships and sole traders, a company is a separate legal entity from the shareholders – it can incur debts, sign contracts, and can sue or be sued. A company can own property and must submit its own tax return. The owners of a company (its shareholders) have no direct claim to the assets of the company, unless it is placed into liquidation. In general, creditors of a company have no claim against the company's owners unless the owners have personally guaranteed or provided other security for the company's liabilities. However, there are exceptions to this (see your solicitor for details).

Ownership and control are also separate in a company. The shareholders own the company but the directors exercise most of the control over the business. The directors need not own any shares and a shareholder is not required to have a seat on the board.

You can buy an existing shelf company from an accountant, solicitor or shelf company specialist for around $700. A shelf company is simply a company that has been incorporated but has not traded.

Companies are registered with the Australian Securities

and Investments Commission (ASIC). On 1 July 2006 the cost of registering a company with ASIC was reduced from $800 to $400. Once registered you will be issued with an Australian Company Number or ACN.

Types of companies There are two basic types of companies – proprietary and public. Proprietary or private companies are not permitted to have more than fifty shareholders (this excludes any employee shareholders). There is no limit on the number of shareholders in a public company, although they are subject to more rigorous disclosure requirements.

Shares in a company Ownership of a company is divided into shares. There may be one or more classes of shares. Each share is equivalent to each other share in its class, in terms of the ownership and the voting rights it confers. A share only represents ownership of the company – it does *not* represent any ownership of the company's assets.

Limited liability Under the *Corporations Act*, a shareholder's liability is limited to the amount of capital they contributed, plus any unpaid calls (a 'call' occurs when a company demands that shareholders make a further payment for shares that are only partly paid). Directors of a company, however, *can* be personally liable to the company's creditors if the directors knew that the company was trading while it was insolvent (this is the case whether or not the directors hold shares). It is also common for lenders, landlords and key suppliers to request shareholders of small companies to personally guarantee the company's debts, which negates limited liability for any shareholders who sign. There are also other circumstances where directors, promoters and controllers of companies may be personally liable. You should contact your solicitor for further advice.

Reporting   If a company satisfies any two of the following requirements . . .
- gross operating revenue of more than $10 million
- gross assets of more than $5 million
- more than 50 employees

. . . then it is a 'large proprietary company' and must lodge an audited financial report with ASIC. Public companies must lodge audited financial reports with ASIC regardless of their size. Smaller proprietary companies are not required to prepare a financial report unless 5 per cent of shareholders require it.

Shareholders   The company is a much more flexible structure than a partnership in terms of handling growth. As a partnership gets larger and larger, the structure becomes more and more unwieldy. It also becomes more risky as a greater number of partners can bind the partnership. The company structure, on the other hand, is specifically designed to accommodate growth, as companies are permitted a large number of shareholders.

Directors   Private companies are only required to have one director, while public companies must have three directors. Every company must have at least one director resident in Australia. (Public companies must have two directors resident in Australia.) Directors must be at least eighteen years old and are subject to complex duties under the *Corporations*

Act. Make sure you understand your obligations and be aware that a breach of these duties may result in large fines or imprisonment. For more information contact:

- The Australian Institute of Company Directors: (02) 8248 6600
- The Australian Securities and Investments Commission: **www.asic.gov.au**

Advantages There are a number of advantages to your business being a company:

- As shareholders, you are subject to limited liability.
- Companies can expand easily and can continue to do so regardless of how many people own a stake in the company.
- It is easy to introduce new owners by issuing or transferring shares to them. Similarly, it is relatively easy for existing owners to leave the company by selling or cancelling their shares.
- A company's constitution can be tailored to give a wide array of different possible structures, which can accommodate widely differing interests.
- Because a company is a separate corporate entity, it continues to exist despite the death or departure of its members or managers.
- Shareholders can also be employees, which gives flexibility in structuring payments as superannuation.
- Companies are taxed at a concessional rate (30 per cent) of tax relative to individuals (see chapter seven).

Disadvantages It's also important to consider the disadvantages of your business being a company:

- A company is relatively expensive to establish – it costs

$400 to register, or about $700 to acquire through a shelf company service.

- Companies have high compliance costs which include ongoing costs and administration requirements. Companies must also submit separate taxation returns.
- Minority shareholders may find it difficult to prevent their interests being subjugated by majority shareholder action.

Sole trader

A sole trader is someone who owns and runs the business by themselves. This structure is suitable for people who don't like sharing their profits or diluting their control.

A sole trader business has no legal existence apart from its owner. All of the property of the business, such as leases, stock and office equipment, is owned directly by the owner. It makes no difference if the owner keeps separate accounts for the business.

This results in the following legal consequences, among others:

- The income of the business is the owner's personal income.
- The owner is responsible for any liability of the business and business creditors can satisfy liabilities out of the owner's non-business assets.
- When someone deals with a sole-trader business, it is the owner who is legally obliged to carry out the deal.
- The owner is personally responsible for any wrongdoing of the business, even if it is committed by an employee.

Advantages   Whether it is better to be a sole trader or a company is a matter of circumstances. There are a number of advantages to being a sole trader:

- As all of the rights, obligations and property of the business are in the owner's name, there is no need for any sort of additional legal arrangement. As a result, setting up a business as a sole trader is simpler and easier than any other form of business.

- Maintenance of a sole-trader business is easier. As a sole trader, there are no requirements for some of the administrative tasks required for other business structures, such as annual meetings, lodgement of returns or the passing of resolutions for certain actions.
- There are no costs for establishment, and minimal costs for upkeep. A business name can be registered at a fraction of the cost of a company.
- A sole trader is not required to consult anyone in making decisions that affect the business.
- The minimal legal disclosure regulations attached to a sole trader mean you have the greatest privacy.
- Just as the owner owns the assets of the business, so all of the profits of the business are owned by the owner. There is no need to share profits nor is there any obligation to use the profits for the good of the business.

Disadvantages There are a number of disadvantages to the sole-trader structure, including the following:
- The sole trader is liable for all the obligations of the business. In the event that the business is not able to meet its debts, the owner must cover the shortfall from personal funds.
- A sole trader may not offer shareholdings to other people – as such the only way to raise capital is by borrowing debt.
- As the owner *is* the business, both legally as well as commercially, it can be difficult to sell the business if the owner dies or simply wishes to get out. In order to effectively sell the business, every right and obligation of the business

must be specifically transferred from the old owner to the new owner.

- Companies are presently taxed at a lower rate than individuals. Sole traders have to pay tax at the individual rate.

Going into business as a sole trader is simple, as there are no legal structures that need to be set up. Sole-trader businesses with an annual turnover of more than $50 000 will need to apply for an Australian Business Number (ABN) for tax purposes and register for GST.

If you wish to trade under any name other than your own, you need to register a business name with the department of fair trading in your state.

Partnerships

Partnership is legally defined as 'the relationship that subsists between persons carrying on a business in common with a view to profit'. As with a sole trader, a business run by a partnership has no separate legal existence. The partners arrive at a partnership agreement, which may or may not be written (although it is strongly recommended that you get a solicitor to draft a formal agreement, which will cost around $5000). The partnership agreement sets up the rights and obligations of the partners.

With a partnership, the business is made up of all of the partners acting together. Under this arrangement, every one of the rights, obligations, assets and liabilities of the business is *owned* or *owed* by each of the partners, both separately and as a group. As a result, each of the partners has an interest in all of the property and the profits of the business. For example, this means that each partner owns a portion of the profits from a customer sale that only one partner worked on. Each partner is also liable for debts incurred by the other partners, even if they were incurred without the partner's knowledge.

Partnerships are limited to no more than twenty partners, except in the case of some particular partnerships. For example, medical practitioner and stockbroking partnerships have a limit of fifty members, legal partnerships 400 members and accountancy partnerships 1000 members.

Joint and several liability   Each partner is individually responsible for all of the debts and liabilities of the entire business. As with sole traders, the liability of partners is not limited to the assets of the business – if a debt is greater than the available funds of the business, a creditor can recover from the personal funds of the partners.

A creditor can recover debts from all of the partners. The law refers to this as 'joint and several liability'. Under joint and several liability, each individual is bound to pay the full amount of any debt. A creditor can recover the entire amount of any debt from any partner, even if another partner was responsible for creating the liability. Each partner is also deemed to be fully responsible for any wrongdoing of the business, even if that wrongdoing was actually committed by an employee or another partner. Thus, if an employee's negligence causes damage worth \$500 000, and the business is sued for that amount, every partner is liable for the entire \$500 000.

Control of the business   The basic principle of the partnership – that the business is shared between the partners – extends to control of the business as well. Each partner will have an equal say in controlling the business, unless the partnership agreement specifies otherwise. A partnership cannot exist without an agreement between the partners. The agreement does not necessarily have to be written, it can be verbal. It is recommended, however, that before you commence a partnership you formally document the different rights and obligations of the partners.

The partnership agreement should cover the following issues:

- names and addresses of partners
- contributions to be made by each partner at the commencement of the business
- the extent to which partners can draw on the joint income and assets of the partnership
- details of bank accounts and signatories
- the role of each partner in the business
- each partner's salary and entitlement to bonuses
- how the business is to be governed – voting rights of the partners should be specifically set out
- deadlock and dispute resolution
- whether a partner can sell their interest
- liability to contribute funds to cover losses or purchases on capital account
- each partner's entitlement to profits and losses
- the process of introducing new partners
- how the partnership is to be dissolved, and how the partnership's assets are to be split up on dissolution
- what happens in the event of the death, retirement or bankruptcy of a partner.

Advantages   As with companies and sole traders, partnerships have a number of advantages and disadvantages built into the structure. The advantages include the following:

- A partnership can split the income of the business between the partners. If the partners are members of the same family, the income can be evenly split so as to minimise the amount of a family's income which is in higher tax brackets.
- As the income of the business is really the income of the partners, losses of the business can be offset against other income of the partners. If the partnership agreement allows, it is possible to split income on a different basis to losses.
- If the partners desire, it can be possible to access assets of the business easily. This must be expressed in the partnership agreement.
- Joint and several liability means that creditors will have greater security for any loans advanced to the partnership, meaning that they will be more willing to take the risk. However, a partnership structure restricts equity finance to what is contributed by new and existing partners.

Disadvantages On the negative side of the partnership structure, you need to bear the following points in mind.
- Each partner is personally responsible for each and every debt of the partnership. As every partner is bound by the actions of any one partner, partners can find themselves liable for a debt that was incurred without their knowledge or consent.
- As each partner has an interest in the partnership, making decisions for the business requires considering the interests of all of the partners. As these interests can diverge, and disagreements can arise, a partnership-based business can encounter management difficulties. This can be alleviated with a carefully constructed partnership agreement.
- A partnership is a legal relationship between a set group of

partners. If any one of the partners leaves that set group, the previous partnership no longer exists and a new partnership must be formed. This dissolving of the partnership may constitute a disposal of an interest for capital gains tax purposes. If a partnership wishes to trade under a name other than the names of each partner, it must register a business name.

Trusts

Under a trust structure, a trustee owns the assets on trust for the beneficiaries, which are often family. The trustee may manage the business or another person may manage the business, in which case they are called the manager. The general rule is that a trustee may not benefit from the property of the trust. The trustee is entitled to be reimbursed for expenses, but is not entitled to be paid fees, unless the trust deed provides for this or all the beneficiaries agree to the payment. For example, trustees cannot sell the property and keep the proceeds for their own use.

The specific rights, restrictions and powers of the trustee, manager and beneficiary are set out in a document called a trust deed. This sets out the objectives of the trust, and describes the investment/business guidelines and how the income is distributed.

Types of trust   There are two basic types of trust – unit trusts and discretionary trusts. In a unit trust, the beneficiaries hold 'units' in a trust, similar to how shareholders hold shares in a company. Each unit confers an interest in the trust property and the income of the trust, as determined by the terms of the trust.

The type of trust most commonly used for small business trading trusts is a discretionary trust. In a discretionary trust, the beneficiaries are specified as a class of persons. None of those people has a claim on a fixed proportion of the trust property, unlike a unit trust. The trustee has a discretion to distribute the income of the trust in any way among the beneficiaries.

This means you can apportion income between members of your family (spouse, children, grandchildren) to minimise tax. (Note that if children are under eighteen years old, the maximum they can receive each year, before full marginal tax rates apply, is $416). For example, you could distribute $5000 to your spouse and each of your adult children, and no tax would be payable. However, under the Tax Act, trusts cannot be established for the express purpose of avoiding tax.

In a business context, the trustee is usually a company. The proprietors of the business will be the beneficiaries. Of course, the proprietors may also be the directors of the trustee company or the manager.

Control   Under a trust structure, the principals of the business will still retain full control over the business, as they will control the trustee and any manager, and will be the beneficiaries. However, the trust structure imposes a layer of additional compliance obligations.

Access to assets   The trust structure may also make it harder to access assets quickly. Unless the trust deed provides otherwise, assets cannot be taken out of a trust without the consent of all the beneficiaries – and in the case of some discretionary trusts, it may not be possible to determine who all the beneficiaries are. As a result of the trust law's overwhelming concern for the protection of the beneficiaries, a host of restrictions are introduced that can be inconvenient to a business.

Liability under a trust is similar to liability under a company structure. The entity which is legally conducting the business is the trustee, so all debts and liabilities are incurred by the trustee. However, a trustee is entitled to reimbursement from the property of the trust. The beneficiaries cannot be liable for any debts of the trust, but if the principals of the business are the directors of the trustee as well as the beneficiaries then personal liability for insolvent trading can still attach to them. Creditors will also be likely to look for personal guarantees from the trust principals.

Advantages   Again, there are many advantages and disadvantages to this type of structure. They are summarised below:
- A discretionary trust allows the trustee to split income between the beneficiaries, allowing a family to put as much of a business's income as possible into low tax brackets.
- If the trustee is a company, the trust can take advantage of the corporate structure in terms of limited liability and ease of succession.

Disadvantages   The downside to trusts includes the following:
- The assets of the business are tied up in a complex structure which makes it difficult to access assets easily.
- In order to trade as a trust, a trustee company may need to be set up and a trust deed drafted. The set-up costs for this can be significant. Your solicitor can probably create a simple trust for around $1500, but it can cost considerably more, depending on the complexity of the arrangements and the value of the assets being placed into trust.
- What the trustee can do may be limited by either the trust deed or the law of trusts.

Other structures

There are a number of other business structures available, such as:

- **Incorporated association** – a registered legal entity typically used for charitable, recreational or cultural purposes. Must have at least five members. All profits are applied for the purposes of the association. There is no tax on profits.
- **Cooperative** – a registered legal entity, similar to a company, with at least five members who have equal shareholdings and voting rights. All profits are distributed to members (usually in proportion to their transactions with the cooperative, rather than on the basis of their shareholding) so the cooperative itself is not actually subject to tax. Often used in primary production (such as dairy cooperatives) to pool resources. Contact the Registrar of Cooperatives (the Yellow Pages will list the Registrar in your state) to find out more.
- **Limited partnership** – a blend of companies and partnerships. There are two types of partners – limited partners and general partners. A 'limited partner' is someone whose liability is limited while a 'general partner' is jointly and severally liable for all debts of the partnership.

RETENTION OF BUSINESS RECORDS

One of the more tedious (yet important) aspects of running a business is the maintenance and retention of business records. This section considers the different types of records you will need to keep including tax records, employment records, company registers and financial records. The *Corporations Act* requires financial records to be kept for seven years.

Constituent documents

Some records should be retained during the life of the business such as the constitution of the company, shareholder or partnership agreements, franchise agreements, company registers and minute books, and any title certificates.

Tax records

Every business is required by law to keep sufficient records (in English) to enable the taxable income of the business to be determined. These records must cover income and expenditure and need to be retained for seven years. In addition to income tax records, you must also keep records in relation to other tax areas such as fringe benefits tax, payroll tax and sales tax.

Employment records

If you have an employee who is covered by an award or employment agreement, you must keep, for a period of seven years, records of the employee's name, classification, the applicable award, starting and finishing times, deductions from salary and the reasons for those deductions, leave taken and superannuation contributions made.

Company register

Your company must keep the following registers (known as the 'Company Register'):

- registers of members (shareholders)
- registers of option holders (if you have them)
- minutes of general meetings
- minutes of meetings of directors
- registers of charges created by the company over company property.

Your company must keep the Company Register at its

registered office or principal place of business in Australia. If you have acquired your company through a shelf company service, they will provide you with the Company Register.

The Company Register must be made available for inspection by shareholders. The Register must be updated when changes are made and notification must be given to ASIC upon the occurrence of certain events, such as a change in directors or their details, the principal place of business or registered office of the company, or a transfer or issue of shares. The forms used to notify ASIC of such changes can be obtained from ASIC's web site **www.asic.gov.au**

Financial records

If you are in doubt about the form and content of financial statements or other records which should be prepared or maintained you should seek professional advice from your solicitor or accountant.

A company must keep written financial records that:
- correctly record and explain its transactions and financial position and performance; and
- would enable true and fair financial statements to be prepared and audited.

Financial records include:
- invoices, receipts, orders for the payment of money, bills of exchange, cheques, promissory notes and vouchers
- documents of prime entry
- working papers and other documents needed to explain:
  - the methods by which financial statements are made up
  - adjustments to be made in preparing financial statements.

Financial records may be kept electronically provided that they can be converted, if required, into hard copy. There are numerous software packages available commercially (such as MYOB). Make back-up copies of electronic records regularly, for example weekly or daily.

A company would also normally prepare the following statements regularly (say, monthly) for management purposes, providing to lenders, etc:

- **Statement of financial performance** — shows the company's revenues and expenses, and the profit or loss that results from these items
- **Statement of financial position** — shows the things of value the company owns and the debts the company owes
- **Statement of cash flows** — summarises cash inflows and outflows.

ASIC's list of suggested books and records to be kept

Here are some of the basic financial records that ASIC suggests a company should keep:

Financial statements
Profit and loss accounts (*see Note 1*)
Balance sheets
Depreciation schedules
Taxation returns e.g. income tax, group tax, superannuation, fringe benefits tax, business activity statements and all supporting documents
General ledger
General journal
Asset register
Computer back-up discs
Frequency – suggest at least monthly

Cash records
Cash receipts journal
Bank deposit books
Cash payments journal
Cheque butts
Petty-cash books
Bank account statements, bank reconciliations and bank loan documents
Sales/Debtor records
Sales journal
Debtors ledger
List of debtors
Invoices and statements issued
Delivery dockets
Work in progress records
Job/Customer files
Stock listings
Creditors records
Invoices and statements received and paid
Creditors ledger
Unpaid invoices
All correspondence, annual returns and ASIC forms
Wages records and superannuation records
Registers (*where applicable – see Note 2*)
Members
Options
Debenture holders
Prescribed interests
Charges
Unclaimed property
Minutes of meetings of directors and/or members
Deeds (*where applicable*)

Trust deeds
Debentures
Contracts and agreements e.g. hire purchase and leases.
Inter-company transactions, including guarantees.

Notes
1. Although the *Corporations Act* does not require small proprietary companies to prepare financial statements, unless
   requested by ASIC or shareholders, they are considered a
   valuable tool for managing your company and checking
   its progress and financial position, and may be helpful if
   you are contemplating raising finance.
2. This list is by no means exhaustive and the financial
   records required will vary from company to company.
   Further, the list does not cover the registers you must keep
   if your company holds an Australian Financial Services
   Licence.

Source: Australian Securities and Investments Commission

YOUR COMPANY AND THE LAW

ASIC (the Australian Securities and Investments Commission) is the company law watchdog. The following section is
extracted from a guide prepared by ASIC to let you know
about the most important things the law requires directors
and secretaries of small companies to do. The law imposes a
number of legal obligations on company directors and secretaries. Please note that even if you appoint an agent to look
after the company's affairs, you – not the agent – may still be
held responsible for those legal obligations.

This section covers the following issues:
- What does the *Corporations Act* expect of you personally?
- What work must a director do?

- Can anyone be a director or secretary?
- Can you sell shares to the public?
- What if your company can't pay its debts?
- What do you have to tell ASIC about your company?

What does the *Corporations Act* expect of you personally?

As a director, you must:
- be honest and careful at all times
- know what your company is doing
- take extra care if you are handling other people's money
- make sure that your company can pay its debts
- see that your company keeps proper financial records
- act in the company's best interests, not just in your own interests, even though you may have set up the company just for personal or taxation reasons
- use any information you get through your position properly and in the best interests of the company. It is a crime to use that information to gain, directly or indirectly, an advantage for yourself or for any other person, or to harm the company. This information need not be confidential; if you use it the wrong way and dishonestly, it may still be a crime.

If you have personal interests that might conflict with your duty as a director, you must generally disclose these at a directors' meeting. This rule does not apply if you are the only director of a proprietary company.

What work must a director do?

You and any other directors will control the company's business. Your company's constitution (if any) or rules may set out the directors' powers and functions.

You must be fully up-to-date on what your company is doing.

- Find out for yourself how any proposed action will affect your company's business performance, especially if it involves a lot of the company's money.
- Get outside professional advice when you need more details to make an informed decision.
- Question managers and staff about how the business is going.
- Ensure that the information given to you is adequate and accurate by putting appropriate systems in place.
- Take an active part in directors' meetings.

Only be a company director or a company secretary if you are willing to put in the effort. Avoid any company where someone offers to make you a director or secretary on the promise that 'you won't have to do anything' and 'just sign here'. You could be exposing yourself to many legal liabilities.

Can anyone be a director or secretary?

You must not act as a director or secretary (or manage a company) without court consent if you:

- have been declared bankrupt, or
- have been convicted of various offences such as fraud or offences under company law, such as a breach of your duties as a director or insolvent trading.

If you have been convicted of one of these offences you must not manage a company within five years of your conviction. If imprisoned for one of these offences, you must not manage a company within five years after your release from prison.

If you become bankrupt or are convicted of a relevant offence at a time when you are a director or secretary then you automatically lose that office. In such cases, the company must notify ASIC that you have ceased to act as a director or secretary of the company. ASIC can also ban you from being a company director in certain situations. If you are not allowed to be a company director or secretary, you are not allowed to manage a company. It is a serious offence to set up dummy directors while you really manage the company.

Can you sell shares to the public?

Proprietary companies are generally not allowed to raise money from the public by selling shares. Avoid anything to do with illegal fundraising.

What if your company can't pay its debts?

You must stop your company trading before it is unable to meet its existing debts. You must prevent the company from taking on a new debt if that would mean that it could not meet that debt and its existing debts. If you have reasonable grounds to suspect that the company cannot meet its debts, or won't be able to if you take on more debt, stop and get professional advice.

Your company is 'insolvent' if it can't pay its debts. You would be breaking the law if you let the company trade while insolvent. You could be sued personally by a liquidator or creditors for your own assets, not just the assets of your company, and you could face civil or criminal action.

Common signs of financial trouble are:
- low operating profits or cash flow from the main business
- problems paying trade suppliers and other creditors on time
- trade suppliers refusing to extend further credit to the company

- problems with meeting loan repayments on time or difficulty in keeping within overdraft limits
- legal action taken, or threatened, by trade suppliers or other creditors over money owed to them.

If your company is having difficulties paying its debts, get professional advice quickly. Don't assume that you will be able to trade out of the problem. Delay could be damaging to the company and to you personally.

What do you have to tell ASIC about your company?

Each year you must:

Pay your company's annual review fee   ASIC will send an annual Statement of Company Details to your company or its Registered Agent within two weeks of its annual review date. Your company's review date will usually coincide with the anniversary of its registration. The Statement may be sent electronically, where arrangements have been made with ASIC to do so.

The Statement of Company Details sets out the company's details recorded in ASIC's database, such as the names and addresses of its directors and secretary, registered office, principal place of business, ultimate holding company (if any), shareholders and share details. If these details are correct and no other changes have occurred that require notification to be given to ASIC, then the director(s) need only pass a solvency resolution within two months of the review date and pay the annual review fee invoice that accompanies the Statement. If any details on the Statement are no longer correct, you must update them using Form 484 within 28 days after the Statement of Company Details issue date. ASIC may also require information to be lodged, e.g. where data are missing. To avoid the payment of late fees or other non-compliance action, the annual review fee must be paid within two months of the review date.

Pass a solvency resolution The company's directors must pass a solvency resolution within 2 months after the company's review date, unless the company has lodged a financial report with ASIC within the 12 months before the review date. A **positive** solvency resolution means that the directors are of the opinion that there are reasonable grounds to believe that the company will be able to pay its debts as and when they become due and payable. Notification of a positive solvency resolution does not have to be lodged with ASIC, but you must pay the company's annual review fee. Payment of the fee is taken to be a representation by the directors that the company is solvent. A **negative** solvency resolution means that the directors are of the opinion that there are not reasonable grounds to believe that the company will be able to pay its debts as and when they become due and payable. If the directors pass a negative solvency resolution ASIC must be notified using Form 485 within seven days after the resolution has been passed. If the directors do not pass a solvency resolution within two months of the company's review date, ASIC must be notified using Form 485 within seven days after the end of the two-month period following the review date.

Keep ASIC informed of various changes in your company's details Some of the more common things you must tell ASIC are set out in the following table. The

Corporations Act requires you to tell ASIC about these changes within a certain time period. If you tell ASIC after this time, you may have to pay a late fee.

Type of activity or duty	Form
If you want to keep registers of shares, options or charges at an address other than the company's registered office or principal place of business, you must tell ASIC where they are being kept within 7 days after the change.	**909**
If the officers of the company change, or if any personal details change, such as their residential address, you must tell ASIC within 28 days after the change. You must also lodge the terms of appointment when appointing an alternative director.	**484**
A director or secretary can tell ASIC directly if they retire or resign. A copy of their letter of retirement or resignation from the company must be sent with the form.	**370**
If you change the company's registered office or principal place of business, you must tell ASIC within 28 days after the change.	**484**
If you create a registrable charge on company property, you must tell ASIC within 45 days.	**309 & 350**
If you vary a charge over the company's property, you must tell ASIC within 45 days from the date of the variation.	**311**
You don't have to notify ASIC when a charge is satisfied, but it may be in your interest to do so.	**312**
If the company changes its name, you must tell ASIC within 14 days after the resolution was passed. (New names are subject to availability criteria.)	**205**

If you issue new shares, you must tell ASIC within 28 days from the date of issue.	**484**
Proprietary companies must advise ASIC within 28 days of changes to the top 20 members in each class of share held. Such changes include changes of name and address, increase or decrease in shares held and cessation of membership.	**484**
Proprietary companies must advise ASIC within 28 days of changes to their ultimate holding company.	**484**
If you divide or convert shares into different classes, you must tell ASIC within 14 days from the date of the change.	**211**
You must notify ASIC of a negative solvency resolution within 7 days of the resolution.	**485**
If no solvency resolution is passed within 2 months of the review date you must notify ASIC within 7 days after that period.	**485**
You may apply to change your company's review date if it is considered unsuitable. You must, however, be able to satisfy certain conditions to have the review date varied.	**488**

THE ROLE OF A LAWYER

A critical adviser for any business is its solicitor – they will help you navigate the minefield of legal regulations (from employment law, property, tax and GST to trade practices, and corporate and commercial law). A good legal adviser will not only give you legal advice but will also provide valuable commercial advice and introduce you to potential clients, suppliers and other advisers.

The best way of finding a solicitor is through a personal recommendation from a business colleague or from your other advisers (e.g. accountant or financier). When selecting and appointing a legal adviser:

- Ensure that they have experience in the areas in which you require assistance. There is no point appointing an experienced litigator to help you buy a business.

- Ask them to clearly explain the basis of how fees are charged and what disbursements you will have to reimburse them for.

- If the firm is small or the lawyer is a sole practitioner, ensure that they have access to other specialist skills (such as stamp duty, superannuation or workplace relations) internally or through associated firms. The obvious advantage of using a large firm is that they typically have offices around the country and have access to a broad range of specialists in-house. That said, charge-out rates of national firms tend to be (significantly) higher than sole practitioners/small firms.

- Ensure that you can communicate openly with your adviser. You will probably spend many hours working closely with them and there is little point engaging an adviser who you find it difficult to 'click' with.

- Note that in some states, practitioners can be accredited as a specialist in certain areas (such as small business law).

- If you cannot find a solicitor through personal recommendation, contact the Law Society in your state.

- It is important to 'shop around' and compare a few different law firms for a combination of breadth of skills, experience, price and culture that match with your business.

- Don't be afraid to ask for personal references.

How can a solicitor help your business?

Your solicitor will be able to assist you in many aspects of your business, throughout its life cycle.

When establishing a new business, your solicitor can advise you on:

- the best structure to use (partnership, trust or company)
- registering a business name, domain name and trademark
- settling your property lease
- obtaining permits.

Once you are up and running, your solicitor can assist with:

- preparing contracts with distributors, customers and suppliers
- preparing confidentiality agreements
- preparing service contracts with key staff and contractors
- ensuring compliance with the *Corporations Act*, trade practices provisions and privacy provisions
- procedures for hiring and firing employees
- debt recovery and defending litigation claims
- ensuring compliance with industry-specific requirements such as health regulations or food regulations
- directors' duties.

If you are planning to buy (or sell) a business, your solicitor can:

- prepare and negotiate the sale and purchase agreements
- advise on the stamp duty and tax implications of the transaction
- help negotiate the key terms of the deal including price, earn-outs, restraint periods, etc.

7. TAXATION

- **Tax structure**
- **Income tax**
- **Deductions**
- **Depreciation and amortisation**
- **Dividends**
- **Capital gains tax (CGT)**
- **Foreign considerations and withholding taxes**
- **Grouping/consolidation**
- **Other types of taxes**
- **Tax administration**
- **Where to get help**

This chapter is a general introduction to tax, which is a complex and dynamic area of law. You should obtain independent advice from an appropriately qualified tax adviser, based on your own circumstances. Unless stated otherwise, this chapter assumes that you are trading as a company, which is resident in Australia; the law is different for non-residents and for trusts, partnerships and sole traders. Note the Goods and Services Tax (or GST) is considered in chapter eight.

TAX STRUCTURE
This section compares the different tax implications of structuring your business as a sole trader, partnership, trust or company. Whether you are buying an established business or franchise, or setting up a new business from scratch, the tax and structuring issues for the purchasing entity need to be planned early and with appropriate tax advice. Although the structure

Tip from the trenches

Below are some of the key terms used in this chapter. Other terms can be found in the glossary at the back of the book.

- **ATO** – the Australian Taxation Office, the government authority responsible for collecting and administering tax
- **ABN** – Australian Business Number, an identifier for dealings with the ATO and for future dealings with other government departments and agencies
- **CGT** – Capital gains tax, the tax payable on the sale of an asset where that asset has increased in value from the time that it was purchased (paid at the taxpayers marginal rate)
- **DTAs** – double tax agreements, made between Australia and other countries to ensure that tax is not paid twice on one amount of income
- **GST** – goods and services tax, the tax payable by consumers for any goods or services they purchase (currently a flat rate of 10 per cent)
- **Pay As You Go (PAYG) instalments** – the amounts you pay directly to the ATO to meet your income tax and other liabilities (usually paid each quarter)
- **TFN** – Tax File Number, a unique identifier allocated to each company, which is to be used in all official correspondence with the ATO (including tax returns)
- **Tax rate** or **marginal rate** – the percentage of tax which the taxpayer must pay on their taxable income (30 per cent for companies and up to 46.5 per cent for individuals)
- **Taxable income** – assessable income less allowable deductions. Generally this equates to the income that has been earned by the taxpayer less the costs that were incurred in earning that income.

that is used at this early stage may not have a significant impact on your tax liabilities immediately, it may have a very large impact down the track if the business is successful. Also, there will often be significant taxes incurred in the process of changing structures later (for example capital gains tax, GST and stamp duty may be payable).

Sole trader

An individual operating a business will be taxed at their marginal tax rate. An income in excess of $150 000 will incur the top rate (including the Medicare levy) of 46.5 per cent. Operating losses can be offset against other income earned by an individual, but if you also derive income from different business activities, you need to check the loss quarantining rules that apply to losses from non-commercial business activities.

Partnership

A partnership has to lodge a separate tax return, but each of the partners is still subject to tax. For example, a partnership of individuals will still result in each person being subject to tax at their normal marginal tax rate.

Trust

Discretionary trusts or fixed trusts (e.g. unit trusts) will not normally be taxed. The income is to be distributed to the beneficiaries and subject to tax in their hands.

Company

A company is taxed at a flat rate of 30 per cent. When the net profit is distributed to the shareholders as dividends, further tax can be payable depending on the type of shareholder. A franked dividend means that the profits from which it has been paid have been subject to company tax. A franked dividend paid to an individual will be taxed at that person's marginal tax rate, with a refundable franking credit given for the tax already paid by the company. This protects income from double tax. A corporate shareholder will generally not pay any tax on a franked dividend.

In summary, the relevant factors in choosing an operating vehicle from a tax perspective are outlined in the table below.

	Losses	Rate	Distributions
Trust	Losses remain the trust and cannot be used by trust beneficiaries to reduce their taxable income.	Currently taxed in the beneficiaries' hands.	Flexibility as to distribution of income if discretionary trust; not if unit trust.
Company	Losses remain in company and cannot be used by shareholders to reduce their taxable income.	Taxed at 30 per cent, but full tax to shareholder once dividend distributed.	Distribution to fixed shareholders.
Sole trader	Losses available for offset against other income.	Taxed at marginal tax rate, up to 46.5 per cent top rate on or after 1 July 2006.	No flexibility.

INCOME TAX

In simple terms, your company will be required to pay income tax at the rate of 30 per cent on its profit (called 'taxable income'), which is calculated as 'assessable income' less 'allowable deductions'.

Tax is payable on taxable income

Taxable income = Assessable income – Allowable deductions

Under the tax legislation, the definition of what is 'assessable income' is broad and includes a range of different types of income your company could make, such as:

- consulting fees on any services you provide to clients
- sales of stock or inventory
- dividends received from other investments
- rent received on any premises you rent out to other people
- interest you receive from the bank on any cash in a deposit account
- royalties received for licensing intellectual property or brands, or from franchisees
- the gain you make when you dispose of any equipment.

You can generally claim all the legitimate expenses incurred in running your business – salaries, cost of buying stock or inventory, rent on leased premises, interest on business loans, business travel, etc. – as a tax deduction. However, you cannot claim for personal expenses (driving to work, child care, dry-cleaning, etc.). See the next section, 'Deductions', for more detail.

A simple example demonstrates the key concepts of income tax. Flower Pot Men Pty Ltd provides business planning services to nurseries. It has two employees (Bill and Ben) who are charged out to clients at an hourly rate. The business earned fees of $250 000 over the year. It paid rent on leased premises of $25 000, total salaries to Bill and Ben of $100 000 and had other expenses (such as stationery, electricity and phone calls) of $30 000.

Assessable income		$250 000
Less Deductions:		
Rent	$25 000	
Salaries	$100 000	
Other	$30 000	
Total deductions		$155 000
Equals taxable income		$95 000
Tax rate 30%		
Tax payable		$28 500

DEDUCTIONS
Summary of deductions

Your taxable income can be reduced by claiming allowable deductions. Allowable deductions are certain types of expenses which you have paid during the year and which the ATO recognises as being related to your business. In order to be deductible the expenditure must:
- not be a personal or capital expense, and
- should be spent in order to earn income or have a close relationship with the earning of income.

Sometimes an expense will be both personal and work-related. In this case you should estimate the proportion of use for work purposes and only claim that portion as a deduction. For example, you might use a laptop computer 30 per cent of the time for personal use, in which case you should only claim 70 per cent of the depreciation of that laptop as a deduction.

The following gives a general indication of what expenses are deductible and what are not.

Non-allowable deductions	Allowable deductions
Personal expenses, including:	**Business-related** expenses, including:
• childcare expenses	• motor-vehicle expenses
• driver's licence	• bank charges
• glasses and contact lenses	• equipment such as calculators and computer software
• grooming and haircuts	• home-office expenses
• holidays	• interest and borrowing expenses
• interest on your home loan	• legal expenses
• meals consumed during work hours	• memberships to unions and business associations
• memberships to health funds	• newspapers and journals
• memberships to sporting associations, gymnasiums and health clubs	• occupational clothing, uniforms
• physical injury insurance	• professional indemnity and sickness insurance premiums
• suits	• text books and reference books
• travel from home to work.	• self-education expenses
Capital expenditure: you cannot claim a deduction for capital expenditure (e.g. buying a computer) but you can claim the cost of depreciation of that computer over its effective life. See the next section ('Depreciation and amortisation') for a discussion of these concepts.	• telephone costs
	• tools of trade
	• travel, meals and accommodation expenses on work-related trips
	• superannuation contributions for self-employed people and unsupported members.

Non-allowable deductions	Allowable deductions
Other items which are denied deductibility:	**Other allowable deductions:**
• penalties and fines	• donations
• the first $250 of some self-education expenses	• tax compliances expenses
• excessive payments to shareholders and associates of private companies	• contributions to registered political parties.
• non-compulsory uniforms	**Depreciation of plant and equipment** such mobile phones, computers, desks, etc.
• entertainment expenditure (unless relating to employees).	

Interest and borrowing expenses

You can claim interest paid during the year as a deduction if the money borrowed is used to acquire income-producing assets. For example, if you borrow money to buy shares, or a computer to use for work, you can claim the interest on the loan. You can also deduct interest if the money is borrowed to pay for expenses which are themselves deductible, such as education or travel expenses.

However, if the money borrowed is used for private purposes, such as to buy your home, then the interest is not deductible. The *security* given for a loan is irrelevant to the question of deductibility. For example, if you mortgage an investment property to raise funds for a holiday, the interest on the loan is not deductible.

Borrowing expenses are deductible only if the money borrowed is used solely for income-producing purposes. They include:

- loan application fees
- legal fees
- valuation fees, survey and registration fees
- fees paid in guaranteeing an overdraft.

If the total of borrowing expenses is less than $100, you can deduct the full amount in the year you take out the loan. If the total is greater than $100, you must spread the expenses equally over each year of the loan (or five years, whichever is the shorter period).

Losses

How you treat losses depends on whether they are revenue losses or capital losses.

Revenue losses A revenue loss will arise when your total deductions are greater than your income in a tax year. You are entitled to deduct revenue losses incurred in one year against assessable income earned in later years. Revenue losses can be carried forward indefinitely.

Capital losses A capital loss may occur when you sell an asset for less than its 'cost base' (original purchase price plus any acquisition costs such as stamp duty or legal fees). Capital losses may be offset against your capital gains, so are taken into account when you calculate your net capital gain for the year. If you have a net capital loss, you cannot offset the loss against your non-capital income (i.e. income from employment and business). Instead, the capital loss is carried forward indefinitely until it can be offset against a capital gain (capital gains tax is discussed further, below).

Before a company can recoup tax losses (whether revenue or capital losses) sustained in prior years, it must satisfy a 'continuity of ownership test' that requires that more than 50 per cent of the company's shares be owned by the same persons in the period from the start of the loss year to the end of the year in which loss recoupment is sought. Where there is insufficient continuity of ownership, the 'continuity of business' test applies. This provides that a company must be engaged in the same business in the year of recoupment as that which was carried on immediately before the change in ownership if prior-year losses are to be recouped.

Trading stock/inventory

The general taxation rules relating to trading stock can be summarised as follows:

- Sales of trading stock give rise to assessable income.
- Purchases of trading stock are deductible. Note, however, that a deduction is not available for the purchase of trading stock until the year in which the trading stock first becomes on hand or is sold to another.
- Where closing stock on hand is greater than opening stock, the difference is assessable income.
- Where opening stock is greater than closing stock on hand, the difference is a deduction.
- The value of opening stock must equal the value of last year's closing stock.
- Closing stock on hand can be valued using cost price, market selling price or replacement price. Special rules exist for the valuation of livestock.

DEPRECIATION AND AMORTISATION
Depreciation

When you buy plant and equipment which has a useful or effective life of more than one year, you cannot claim a deduction for money spent to buy that plant and equipment, or the costs associated with buying them. This money is known as 'capital expenditure' and is not deductible. For example, the following items are classified as 'capital expenditure':

- buying a computer, fax machine, photocopier, desk, etc. or the costs of having those items delivered and installed
- buying an investment unit or the conveyancing fees paid when you buy the unit.

Depreciation, also referred to as capital allowances, permits you to claim a portion of the cost of the asset as a deduction over a number of years. Depreciation recognises that some assets wear out or become obsolete over time. For example, a fax machine will be useful for (i.e. have an effective life of) about six years before it becomes so worn out or out-of-date that you have to replace it. If the fax cost $600, you could claim a depreciation deduction of $100 each year for six years.

Depreciation of plant and equipment is based on the effective life of the asset. Taxpayers can self-assess effective life or rely on the 'effective life' tables published by the ATO for many items of plant and equipment. As the ATO's rates are regularly updated, it is important to check for any recent amendments. Ask your accountant or tax adviser for a copy of these tables.

The purchase price of the asset, and the expenses associated with buying and selling it, make up the cost base of the asset. The cost base is then used for calculating the amount of depreciation or capital allowance and the amount of any gain when you sell the asset. Plant acquired partway through the year is depreciable only on a pro rata basis.

You can depreciate assets either on a straight line basis (i.e. same percentage each year over the effective life of the asset) or on a diminishing value basis (i.e. 1.5 times the straight line basis applied each year to the written-down value).

A low-value pool is available for all depreciating assets costing less than $1000. The low-value pool is depreciated over four years using the diminishing value method. Depreciation of 18.75 per cent is available for depreciating assets added to the pool in the year. For the closing balance of undeducted costs in the pool at the end of the previous year, depreciation is calculated at the rate of 37.5 per cent. Disposal proceeds reduce the closing balance of the pool.

There are special rules for small business taxpayers that meet certain requirements. For example, there is an immediate write-off for depreciable assets costing less than $1000 that are fully used for a taxable purpose.

A cost limit applies for depreciation purposes in respect of motor vehicles. That part of the purchase price in excess of the cost limit is not depreciable. Such vehicles are referred to as luxury vehicles. The cost limit for 2005/06 is $57 009.

Capital works deductions

Amortisation of capital expenditure on certain classes of income-producing buildings and structural improvements (collectively referred to as 'capital works'), may be claimed as a tax deduction at the rate of either 2.5 per cent or 4 per cent, depending on the date construction commenced and (in certain circumstances) the use to which the capital works will be put. In contrast to the depreciation regime, there is generally no 'balancing charge' adjustment in respect of the disposal of an item of capital works that is the subject of a capital allowance deduction. However, where the capital works are destroyed or demolished, a balancing deduction is allowable (but only to the extent that the remaining entitlement to a deduction exceeds insurance or salvage recoveries).

Goodwill and intellectual property

There is no tax amortisation of goodwill, but some capital expenditure on industrial and intellectual property (such as patents, registered designs and copyright) may be written off over time.

Black hole expenditure

There are rules that permit tax write-offs for certain 'black hole' expenses. The expenses covered by these rules include expenditure in relation to a business, a business that used to be carried on, a business proposal to be carried on, or to liquidate or deregister a company. These are referred to as 'black hole expenses' because they are neither tax deductible, depreciable nor able to be included in the cost base of an asset for CGT purposes. The rules allow the above categories of black hole expenditure to be amortised over five years, commencing from the year in which they are incurred. New rules relating to black hole expenditure were introduced in 2006 and apply to expenditure after 1 July 2005.

Project costs

There are rules that allow certain capital costs related to 'projects' carried on by taxpayers to be allocated to a project pool and depreciated over the estimated life of the project on a diminishing value basis. The following specific categories of expenses qualify for this treatment:

- mining-related capital expenditure
- transport-related capital expenditure
- certain other specified expenses, such as the costs of creating or upgrading community infrastructure, feasibility study costs, site preparation costs, environmental assessment costs or costs to obtain information or a right to intellectual property associated with the project.

Project pool expenditure will first become deductible in the year in which the project starts to operate. Where a project is abandoned, sold or otherwise disposed of, an immediate deduction is available to the taxpayer for the closing pool value of the previous income year and any further amounts allocated to the pool in that year. Equally, any proceeds from the abandonment, sale or disposal of the project, as well as any other capital amounts derived in connection with the relevant project costs, must be included in the taxpayer's assessable income.

DIVIDENDS

You must declare as income any dividends you receive from a company. Dividends include any distribution made by a company to its shareholders, whether as money or as shares. The amount of tax you pay on the dividend depends on whether the dividend has been franked under the 'dividend imputation system'.

Under the dividend imputation system, dividends paid by Australian companies that have paid a certain amount of tax carry an imputation credit. This credit represents the part of the company's profits that it has paid as company tax. Because the company has already paid tax on those profits, when a share of the profits is distributed to the shareholder as a dividend, the shareholder receives a tax credit toward the tax they need to pay on that dividend.

If the company has paid tax on all of the profits distributed as dividends, the dividend will be 'fully franked' and the shareholder pays no tax on the dividend (unless the shareholder's highest marginal tax rate is greater than the 30 per cent company rate, when the shareholder will have to pay the difference). If the company has not paid tax on the dividend or paid tax on only part of its distributed profits, the dividend is 'unfranked' or 'partially franked' and the shareholder must pay tax on the unfranked proportion of the dividend.

The imputation system is an attempt to eliminate the double taxation of company profits. In the past, both the company and its shareholders have been fully taxed on the same profits.

Australia uses an imputation system of company taxation. Under the imputation system, tax paid by resident companies is imputed to shareholders when they receive franked dividends. The effect of this is that shareholders receive a deduction for their own personal tax returns to ensure that tax is not paid twice on the same earnings.

Generally, the company determines the extent to which a dividend is franked, within the limits of their available franking credits. Accurate records must be kept by the company to verify the amount of the franking credit/rebate that can be passed to shareholders. The franking account balance is not affected by changes in the ownership of the company. Although franking credits/rebates are not available to non-residents, certain dividends received from foreign sources can be paid to non-resident shareholders without withholding tax (discussed below under 'Withholding tax').

CAPITAL GAINS TAX (CGT)

The capital gains tax (CGT) applies, generally speaking, only to disposals of assets acquired (or deemed to be acquired) after 19 September 1985. For assets acquired before 21 September 1999 and held for at least twelve months, gains are calculated after indexing the asset's cost base to the rate of inflation (although indexation is frozen at 30 September 1999). An asset must be held for at least twelve months before indexation applies. Tax on capital gains is levied at the taxpayer's income tax rate. Individuals, trusts and certain superannuation funds may qualify for a discount on the amount of gain included in assessable income, as long as the asset is held for at least 12 months. For individuals and trustees the CGT discount is 50 per cent of the (unindexed) gain. For a superannuation fund the CGT discount is 67 per cent of the (unindexed) gain. CGT applies to events (e.g. disposal) occurring in relation to a CGT asset. CGT asset is defined widely to include most property and rights.

Rollover relief

The CGT legislation provides limited 'rollover relief' (that is, a deferral of CGT) in some situations, for example:

- where an asset is transferred by an individual to a wholly owned company; or
- where a company is interposed into an existing business structure; or
- where certain assets are replaced with similar assets.

Exemptions and concessions

In some situations where a capital gain would otherwise arise, an exception or exemption may be available, to either reduce the capital gain or loss or allow you to disregard it. The most common exceptions and concessions arise in relation to assets acquired before 20 September 1985, the availability of the CGT discount (referred to above) and the disposal by non-residents of assets that are not 'taxable Australian property'. The other common exemptions are gains on disposal of:

- shares in a pooled development fund
- your home (main residence)
- certain compensation or damages for any wrong or injuries suffered by the taxpayer
- winnings from betting, a lottery or other form of gambling, or a game with prizes
- cars, motorcycles and similar vehicles
- collectables acquired for ≤$500
- personal-use assets acquired for ≤$10 000
- assets used to produce exempt income
- inheritance, when received, by beneficiaries of a deceased estate.

There are also various CGT concessions available for small businesses (that is, where the net value of the assets of the tax payer and connected entities is not more than $6 million).

These concessions include:

- an exemption from CGT for assets owned for at least 15 years
- a 50 per cent reduction in CGT for active business assets
- an exemption from CGT if proceeds of sale are used in connection with the tax payer's retirement
- a rollover where the business is sold and another business is acquired.

FOREIGN CONSIDERATIONS AND WITHHOLDING TAXES
Double tax relief

Australia provides relief against international double taxation by granting foreign tax credits in some circumstances and, in others, by exempting the foreign income from Australian tax. The foreign tax credit provisions will apply to taxpayers that derive foreign-source interest, rent, royalties, certain capital gains, pensions and certain business income. Australian companies that receive portfolio dividends and individuals who receive portfolio or non-portfolio dividends are entitled to a foreign tax credit. A portfolio dividend means that you own more than 10 per cent of the voting power of the company paying the dividend.

The amount of the foreign tax credit will be the lesser of foreign tax paid or the Australian tax payable on the foreign-source income.

Australian companies that receive non-portfolio dividends from a foreign company will generally be exempt from Australian tax on those dividends.

In addition to Australia's domestic arrangements that provide relief from international double taxation, Australia has entered into specific Double Tax Agreements with the following countries:

Argentina	Fiji	Indonesia
Austria	Finland	Ireland
Belgium	France	Italy
Canada	Germany	Japan
China	Greece	Kiribati
Czech Republic	Hungary	Korea
Denmark	India	Malaysia

Malta	Romania	Switzerland
Mexico	Russian Federation	Taiwan (Taipei)
Netherlands	Singapore	Thailand
New Zealand	Slovak Republic	United Kingdom
Norway	South Africa	United States of America
Papua New Guinea	Spain	Vietnam
Philippines	Sri Lanka	
Poland	Sweden	

Thin capitalisation

Broadly, Australia's thin capitalisation regime will seek to limit tax deductions (debt deductions) available for financing costs relating to *all debt* funding a taxpayer's Australian operations. The former thin capitalisation regime, which existed prior to 1 July 2001, focused solely on related foreign party debt, but now debt deductions will generally be denied to the extent the relevant prescribed gearing limits are breached.

For most entities, the prescribed debt funding limit is the greater of the following:

- the safe harbour debt amount – broadly, 75 per cent of the average value of the entity's assets, with some adjustments;
- the 'arm's length' debt amount – the amount of debt that the Australian operations could support on an arm's length basis (i.e. from an independent third party) with certain significant factors and assumptions to be taken into account; or
- the worldwide gearing amount – this allows for Australian operations to be geared up to 120 per cent of the Australian entity's worldwide gearing. However, this option is not available if the Australian entity is controlled by foreign entities.

Withholding tax

Withholding taxes generally apply to interest, dividends and royalties paid to non-residents. Withholding taxes are withheld by the company that is to make the payment of interest, dividends or other royalties. They operate as a final tax in that the interest, dividend or royalty that is subject to withholding tax is not also subject to income tax under the ordinary rules.

Interest Interest paid by a resident of Australia to a non-resident is normally subject to a final withholding tax of 10 per cent; this is a final tax and therefore the non-resident is not required to include interest income in an Australian income tax return. If interest income is the only Australian-source income derived by the non-resident, no Australian return is required to be lodged.

While Australia's Double Tax Agreements (DTAs) do not generally reduce the rate of interest withholding tax below 10 per cent, the Protocol to the US–Australia and the UK double tax treaties provide for a withholding tax exemption on interest paid to government bodies and to financial institutions unrelated to and dealing independently with the payer.

Dividends Non-residents are subject to withholding tax on the unfranked portion of dividends they receive from an Australian resident. The dividend withholding tax rate is 30 per cent, subject to Australia's DTAs, which generally limit the rate to 15 per cent. Some treaties contain a graduated rate. For example, the US Protocol provides for a rate of 0 per cent where a US corporate investor, satisfying certain public listing requirements, holds 80 per cent or more of the voting power of an Australian company; a rate of 5 per cent will apply where a US corporate investor holds direct voting interests of at least 10 per cent in an Australian company, otherwise a 15 per cent rate will apply.

Certain partly or fully unfranked dividends that are paid to non-residents may be exempt from dividend withholding tax under the conduit foreign income (CFI) rules. The source to which these dividends may be traced is, in general terms, foreign income that is exempt from Australian tax or relieved of Australian tax by foreign tax credits, for example, the exempt dividends that the Australian company has received from its non-portfolio investments held in foreign companies.

Royalties Australian income-tax law provides that tax is chargeable on all amounts received 'as or by way of royalty'. For purposes of income tax, royalties typically include amounts 'paid or credited' (regardless of whether the payment or credit is periodical) for the use of or right to use copyright, patents, trademarks, industrial equipment, or for the supply of scientific or commercial knowledge or information. The term 'royalty' is broadly defined and can extend to rental payments for the use of certain equipment.

All royalties that are an expense of an Australian business, and are paid or credited to a non-resident, are deemed to have a source in Australia. Therefore, a non-resident will be subject to Australian tax on such royalties, irrespective of where the property giving rise to the royalties is situated, or where the services giving rise to the payment are performed.

Australia has a system of withholding tax to collect tax on royalties paid or credited to non-residents. The royalty withholding tax (at the general rate of 30 per cent) is a final tax.

Where the recipient is a resident of a country with which Australia has concluded a DTA, the terms of the treaty will determine the rate. Most double taxation agreements to which Australia is party provide a rate of 10 per cent royalty withholding tax. The US Protocol and the UK double taxation agreement provide for a general 5 per cent royalty withholding tax rate.

Tax on royalties will be collected by assessment instead of by withholding if:

- the recipient is a resident in a treaty country; and
- carries on business in Australia at or through a permanent establishment; and
- the royalty is effectively connected with that business.

GROUPING/CONSOLIDATION

The Australian Government has progressively introduced legislation to implement a new system of consolidated income taxation (tax consolidation) for entities within a wholly owned group.

Under this regime, if a group decides to consolidate, the Australian resident entities in the group will generally be treated as a single entity for the purposes of income tax.

A 'consolidated group' may be formed if there is a single Australian resident head company and at least one eligible resident wholly owned subsidiary member of the head company. The subsidiary members may be companies, partnerships or trusts.

A consolidated group lodges a single income tax return and keeps consolidated loss, franking and foreign tax credit accounts. All intra-group transactions are ignored. The thin capitalisation rules also apply on a group basis.

Whilst the tax consolidation regime has been substantively

enacted into law, Australian tax authorities have issued many rulings explaining how these provisions operate. It is critical that up-to-date advice be obtained in relation to issues regarding the regime.

OTHER TYPES OF TAXES

This chapter has provided details of only the most common taxes which create the largest liabilities for companies. There are many other taxes which also require consideration, including:

Fringe Benefits Tax (FBT) – imposed at the rate of 46.5 per cent, this is aimed at eliminating any difference in the overall tax burden on cash salary and wages versus fringe benefits. Fringe benefits are generally non-cash parts of an employee's package, such as employer-provided cars, free or low-interest loans, free or subsidised residential accommodation or board, free or discounted goods and services, and expenses paid on behalf of an employee.

Superannuation Guarantee Charge – imposed at the rate of 9 per cent. This is not so much a tax as the minimum contribution that an employer must make to an employee's nominated superannuation fund in addition to the salary paid to that employee.

Stamp duty – imposed on a sliding scale. This is different from state to state (and in some states it is simply called 'duty'). The legislation in each state and territory sets out the party who is liable to pay the stamp duty and the time limits within which it must be paid. Generally, a liability for stamp duty will arise in a particular state or territory if the instrument is executed there, the transaction or instrument relates to property located in the state or territory, or an essential matter or thing is required to be done in that state or territory.

The types of transactions and instruments which are subject to stamp duty include:

- transfers of real property (such as land and buildings) and personal property
- transfers of unlisted marketable securities such as shares (except in Victoria and Tasmania)
- mortgages and charges (except in Victoria and the territories)
- leases of real property (except in Victoria and Tasmania)
- hires of goods (except in Tasmania)
- declarations of trust
- acquisitions of certain interests in land-rich unlisted trusts and companies.

In accordance with the *Intergovernmental Agreement on the Reform of Commonwealth-State Financial Relations*, all revenue raised by the GST is distributed among the states and territories. This agreement also requires the states and territories to progressively phase out stamp duty on various types of transactions.

Payroll taxes – imposed by each state and territory on wages paid by an employer to an employee. Each state and territory has its own legislation with different provisions, rates of tax and thresholds below which no tax is payable. The thresholds below which no payroll tax is payable range from $504 000 to $1 250 000, and the rates of payroll tax range from 4.75 per cent to 6.85 per cent.

TAX ADMINISTRATION
Self-assessment

Australia's tax system works on self-assessment. This means that taxpayers must show all their assessable income and claim only the deductions and offset to which they are entitled on their annual income tax return. The ATO uses the information provided in a taxpayer's annual income tax return to issue them with a tax assessment notice, with a tax refund or tax bill if required.

Therefore, under the Australian self-assessment system, a taxpayer must determine its own taxable income and tax payable each year. On receipt of the return, the ATO will usually issue the assessment without adjustment to the taxpayer's calculations. However, the return may still be subject to further review. The law provides the ATO with a period where it may review a return and increase or decrease the amount payable.

The ATO may amend an assessment up to four years (or two years for certain shorter period of review taxpayers) after the tax became due and payable. Where anti-avoidance provisions apply, the period is four years. Where avoidance is due to fraud or evasion, there is no time limit on amending the assessment. Interest and/or penalties may be due in certain circumstances.

In the case of companies and superannuation funds, which are defined as 'full self-assessment taxpayers', the Tax Commissioner does not issue a formal notice of assessment – the lodged return is deemed to be an assessment. Taxpayers are required to retain records supporting their returns in case of a subsequent tax audit.

There are also formal procedures for objections and appeals.

Annual income tax year

The tax year, or 'year of income', is the year that runs from 1 July to the following 30 June.

If a company wishes to submit tax returns for a different period, it must obtain approval from the Commissioner of Taxation to adopt a substituted accounting period (for example, the year ending 31 December 2005 in lieu of 30 June 2006). If a change in the law applies for 'the year of income commencing 1 July 2005', it will apply to a company with a substituted accounting period ending 31 December in lieu of the following 30 June from 1 January 2005.

The due date for tax returns is published each year in the Commonwealth Government Gazette and should be confirmed. Company returns are generally due starting on the 15th day of the seventh month after the end of the relevant income year, depending on the size of the company or group and certain other criteria.

Companies generally pay their income tax in quarterly instalments, called PAYG (Pay As You Go) instalments, with a final balancing payment generally due on the first day of the sixth month after the end of the year of income. Under these provisions, instalments will generally be due on the 21st day of the month following the end of a quarter. The instalment will generally be based on the company's income in that quarter, so that companies will be required to report certain income details on a quarterly basis. Exceptions generally relate to concessions for small business.

Tax File Number/Australian Business Number

All resident and non-resident taxpayers including companies and individuals, superannuation funds, etc. must show their Tax File Numbers (TFNs) on their income tax returns.

A TFN is obtained from the Commissioner by completing the appropriate form and furnishing the Commissioner with a certified copy of the company's certificate of incorporation or similar document.

Companies and other entities carrying on an enterprise in Australia should also have an Australian Business Number (ABN). Whilst entities will continue to have a TFN, the ABN will be the main reference for dealings with the Federal Government. An ABN will be an essential prerequisite for registration for GST and needs to be quoted to avoid withholding of tax (from payments made to the enterprise, for example by customers) under the PAYG withholding provisions.

Anti-avoidance

The tax legislation has anti-avoidance rules that allow the Commissioner to cancel the effect of any tax benefit that the taxpayer derived or gained from an arrangement if it could be concluded that a person (not necessarily the taxpayer) entered into or carried out the arrangement for the sole or dominant purpose of enabling the taxpayer, or the taxpayer and other persons, to obtain a tax benefit.

An arrangement will be considered to give rise to a tax benefit if it causes an amount to be excluded from the taxpayer's assessable income, an amount to be allowed as a deduction, an amount of a capital loss to be incurred, a foreign tax credit to be allowable or an amount of withholding tax not to be payable.

WHERE TO GET HELP

The Australian Taxation Office has a very useful web site with commentary on a broad range of tax issues: **www.ato.gov.au**

8. THE GOODS AND SERVICES TAX

- **Registration**
- **Accounting**
- **Business Activity Statement (BAS)**
- **Input Tax Credits (ITCs)**
- **Cancellation of registration**
- **Bad debts**
- **Financial supplies**
- **Sale of going concern**
- **The future**

The Goods and Services Tax (GST) was introduced on 1 July 2000. The principal legislation is the *A New Tax System (Goods and Services Tax) Act 1999* ('GST Act'). All legal references are to the GST Act and words in italics are defined in the GST Act.

It is fair to say that most businesses put in some effort to ensure that their systems and procedures were able to cope with the change to a GST and it is also fair to say that many of those businesses have not looked at their GST compliance since that time.

The increase in ATO audit activity means that you need to be more aware of how the GST affects your activities and how your business processes capture the GST payable and receivable to ensure that the right amount of tax is being paid.

Tip from the trenches

Some acronyms you'll need to know when dealing with GST include:

- **BAS** – Business Activity Statement
- **IAS** – Instalment Activity Statement
- **ITCs** – Income Tax Credits
- **FAT** – Financial Acquisitions Threshold
- **FBT** – Fringe Benefits Tax

While a detailed explanation and analysis of the GST law is inappropriate in a book such as this, an appreciation of the basic features of the GST is necessary in order to understand how it affects all aspects of your business.

GST is an indirect tax and is fundamentally different to other direct taxes such as income tax and capital gains tax. GST has been described as a multi-stage, credit offset transaction tax. It has also been described as a tax on consumer spending. Both of these descriptions are correct.

At its simplest, GST is a tax paid on transactions called supplies. *Supply* means all forms of supply and not just sales of goods or services. It also includes the creation, grant and surrender of rights; a grant, assignment or surrender of real property; entering into obligations; agreeing to do something; and agreeing not to do something.

Note that a supply of money is not a supply unless the money is *consideration* for a supply of money. That is, when you pay money for a newspaper there is only one supply, being the supply of the newspaper to you. The money which you give the newsagent is not a supply. However, the interest you pay on a loan is a supply since it is consideration for a supply of money. (See the discussion of financial supplies later in this chapter).

There must be *consideration* for the supply. It need not be in money but must be capable of being expressed in money. *Consideration* includes goods, services and other things given in exchange for a supply, such as in a barter or contra (offsetting or swapping) situation.

The supply must also be made in the course or furtherance of an *enterprise* that the *entity* making the supply *carries on*. *Entity* includes not only sole traders and companies, but also *partnerships* and trusts. It is the *entity* which is *registered* for GST.

An *enterprise* has a wider definition than a business. Taken together, an *entity* making a *supply* for *consideration* in the course or furtherance of an *enterprise* has the widest possible meaning and, in simple language, means that just about anything you do in your business is caught by the GST.

The principal exclusion from the definition of enterprise is the services of employees. The supply made by an employee to an employer is not made in the course or furtherance of an *enterprise carried on* by the employee and therefore there is no GST on salaries and wages.

Tip from the trenches

It is not uncommon for sub-contractors, who are not employees, to be paid through the payroll system. Make sure that these payments are recognised as consideration for supplies made by those sub-contractors and that tax invoices are obtained.

Unlike direct taxes, GST is normally paid by the *recipient* of a *supply* but the responsibility to collect and account for the tax lies with the supplier. In most cases, the *recipient* is not concerned whether or not GST has been properly charged, except to the extent that it affects the *price* payable. In cases where GST has been incorrectly charged, or not charged, it is not the *recipient* but the supplier who will be called upon by the ATO to make good the error.

The single most distinctive feature of GST is that the tax is creditable. *Registered entities* which pay GST on *acquisitions* are entitled, in most cases, to offset that GST against the GST they are liable to pay on the *supplies* they make. The GST actually remitted to the ATO is therefore the difference between the GST payable on *supplies* and the GST *input tax credits* on acquisitions. Assuming for a moment that all *supplies* and all *acquisitions* are taxable, the GST actually remitted will be the GST on the difference between the two; that is, the value added by the business, which is why GST is known in some other countries as Value-Added Tax.

There is no list available of supplies which are subject to GST. The simple rule is that all supplies are likely to be taxable unless a provision in the GST Act provides an exemption from the tax charge. There are two main categories of exemption: *GST-free* and *input taxed*.

Both categories mean GST is not payable on the supply but there is a crucial difference in respect of the *input tax credits* on related costs. Subject to some de minimis rules in respect of *financial supplies*, *input tax credits* are not available for costs which relate to *input taxed supplies* (see below).

The main categories of *GST-free* and *input taxed supplies* are listed below:

GST-free supplies
- food (but there are many foodstuffs that are not GST-free)
- health
- education

- childcare
- exports and other supplies that are for consumption outside Australia
- religious services
- non-commercial activities of charitable institutions, and raffles and bingo conducted by charitable institutions, etc.
- water, sewerage and drainage
- supplies of going concerns
- international transport
- precious metals (in specified circumstances)
- supplies from inward duty-free shops
- grants of land by governments
- farmland
- cars for use by disabled people
- international mail.

Input taxed supplies
- financial supplies
- residential rent
- existing residential premises
- precious metals (in specified circumstances)
- school tuckshops and canteens
- fundraising events conducted by charitable institutions, etc.

REGISTRATION

All entities carrying on an enterprise (or a number of enterprises) must register for GST if their annual turnover exceeds, or is expected to exceed, $50 000 ($100 000 for not-for-profits). Registration involves getting an Australian Business Number (ABN). If an *entity's turnover* is less than the threshold, it need not register for GST but must still obtain an ABN. Failure to quote an ABN to a customer could result in that customer withholding 46.5 per cent of the payment to the supplier under the Pay As You Go (PAYG) withholding rules.

The ABN is the means by which an *entity* interfaces with the ATO. Armed with an ABN, GST-registered businesses must complete a Business Activity Statement (BAS). Entities not *registered* for GST must complete an Instalment Activity Statement (IAS).

The BAS is used to report not only GST but also PAYG instalments, PAYG withholding, Fringe Benefits Tax (FBT) instalments, Wine Equalisation Tax and Luxury Car Tax.

Entities which satisfy certain control and accounting requirements can form a *GST group*. *GST group registration* effectively allows all the group members to be treated as though they were a single entity. The group, through its *representative member* (who must be an Australian resident) files a single BAS; all transactions between group members are treated as though they were not *taxable supplies* (i.e. they are effectively ignored for GST purposes). Further information regarding GST groups is available on the ATO web site. Go to **www.ato.gov.au** and search for 'GST Groups'.

Tip from the trenches

If you have a number of entities which satisfy the grouping requirements and there is a considerable amount of inter-entity trading, consider a group registration. This will reduce the amount of GST flowing through the entities with a consequent improvement in cash flow. If forming such a group might take you over the $20 million threshold for monthly reporting, consider forming two groups.

There are also special *registration* requirements for joint ventures whereby the *joint venture operator* assumes responsibility for some of the GST obligations of the joint venturers.

ACCOUNTING

Entities with an annual turnover below $1 million, and some other entities in limited circumstances, can opt to account for GST on a cash basis. Other *entities* will account for GST on an 'accruals' basis.

Under the cash basis GST is attributable to the *tax period* in which payments are made or received.

Tip from the trenches

If you are eligible to use cash accounting, consider the timing of the cash flows through your business. If you only issue invoices occasionally and you get paid promptly, it may actually be beneficial to use accruals accounting so you can claim your input tax credits (ITCs) before you pay your suppliers. Cash accounting does have an advantage in that you never need to worry about GST on bad debts (see below).

Under the accruals basis GST is attributable to the *tax period* in which an invoice is issued or, if earlier, in which any of the consideration is received. Under the accruals system, the entity needs to pay close attention to control of debtors and creditors. Careful consideration of the timing of the issue of invoices and of major expenditure can minimise the cash-flow effect of the GST.

Tip from the trenches

If you are on the accruals basis, consider whether you are able to time the issue of your invoices and your purchases. Ideally, you should consider issuing your invoices at the beginning of a tax period; this will give you the best chance of being paid before you have to pay the GST to the ATO. Consider timing acquisitions towards the end of a tax period; this will allow you to claim the ITC (provided you have a tax invoice) before you have actually paid the supplier. Even if this idea is inappropriate for the majority of your transactions, it may be worthwhile for large sales or major acquisitions, such as capital assets.

There is one crucial issue in connection with *invoices*. Under the accruals system, GST is payable on *supplies* in the *tax period* when an *invoice* is issued (if, as is usual, it is issued before any payment is received). An *invoice* is any document notifying an obligation to make a payment. However, under both the cash and accruals systems, *input tax credits* are only available if the entity holds a *tax invoice* in respect of the *acquisition*. A *tax invoice* is an invoice that contains specific information: the words 'tax invoice', the name and ABN of the supplier, the name, address or ABN of the recipient, the product or service supplied, and its GST inclusive price.

Special attribution rules apply to security deposits, and progressive supplies or supplies made for a period, such as leases.

BUSINESS ACTIVITY STATEMENT (BAS)

Entities with an annual turnover below $20 million can opt to submit a monthly or a quarterly BAS. Above this threshold, the BAS must be submitted monthly and electronically.

Tax periods are months or calendar quarters. However, the start and end dates of *tax periods* can sometimes be adjusted to fit in with the entity's accounting periods, provided there are no more than twelve periods in a year.

Tip from the trenches

Regardless of turnover, if you will normally expect GST refunds you should consider submitting a monthly BAS in order to max-imise the GST cashflow. This will be relevant to entities which make predominantly GST-free supplies. If you have an entity in a group which gets refunds and the others are net GST payers, consider a GST group only for the payers, ideally on a quarterly BAS, while keeping the refund entity on a monthly BAS.

Your monthly BAS must be submitted, along with any GST payable, by the 21st of the month following the end of the tax period. Quarterly BASs are due on the 28th of the month fol-lowing the end of the tax period, with the exception of the December period which is due by 28 February (to accommo-date Australia's love of a January summer break). Note that if you have a special tax period ending on, say, 4 July, a monthly BAS will be due on 21 July and a quarterly BAS on 28 July.

INPUT TAX CREDITS (ITCs)

ITCs are available for the GST incurred on *creditable acqui-sitions*; that is, on *taxable supplies* received by the *entity*. The *acquisition* must relate to the *enterprise*(s) that the *entity car-ries on*. Creditable acquisitions might include stock for resale, capital expenditure on items such as plant and equipment, property rent, equipment lease charges, overheads such as utilities, stationery and professional fees. Any acquisition which is a genuine business expense, and on which you paid GST, is likely to be a creditable acquisition.

However, there are three main categories of exception to this. ITCs are not available for GST incurred on expenditure which:

- is incurred on certain specified costs which would not be deductible expenses for income tax purposes
- is of a private or domestic nature
- relates to making *supplies* which would be *input taxed*.

The first point applies even to *entities* which do not pay income tax; if the expense would be non-deductible if the entity was a taxpayer, the GST will not be creditable.

The third point is where things begin to get complicated. If an *entity* makes, or expects to make, *input taxed supplies*, it will be required to identify the GST on *acquisitions* which relate to that *input taxed supply* and disallow the ITC. For example, an entity which rents out residential property cannot get an ITC for the GST on repairs to the property.

Where the *input taxed supply* is a *financial supply* there is some leeway, in the form of a de minimis limit called the *Financial Acquisitions Threshold* (FAT). The *entity* is still required to identify the GST incurred on expenditure which relates to the *financial supplies* but, if that input tax is less than the lower of \$50 000 per annum or 10 per cent of total input tax for the year, full ITC can be claimed.

There is further leeway if the financial supply is a borrowing. GST on *acquisitions* which relate to borrowing is creditable if the borrowing relates to *supplies* that are not *input taxed*. For example, if an entity borrowed money to purchase new equipment, an ITC would be available. However, if the entity had borrowed the money to enable it to buy shares or a residential property, it would have to consider the FAT.

Tip from the trenches

Monitor the FAT constantly to ensure that you are aware of how you stand, especially if you only make occasional financial supplies. In this way, if further financial supplies are contemplated, you may be able to time them such that the FAT is not exceeded. Remember, however, that the FAT applies to acquisitions which relate to supplies that would be input taxed so, as soon as an intention is formed to make financial supplies, the FAT has to be considered. If there is one area above all others where it is worth seeking the advice of skilled professional advisers, this is it.

You may incur some expenditure in respect of setting up a company, and registering it for GST, before the company is actually brought into existence. The GST Act contains provisions which allow recovery of the ITC once the company comes into existence.

Tip from the trenches

Be aware that the GST Act does not contain similar provisions relating to recovery of ITCs on expenditure incurred prior to registration for GST. It is therefore important to have your GST registration effective at the earliest possible time to ensure that you can claim ITCs on all relevant expenditure.

CANCELLATION OF REGISTRATION

If you cease to *carry on an enterprise* you must deregister for GST. If your turnover drops below the relevant registration threshold, you are no longer *required to be registered* and can apply to be deregistered. However, you must have been *registered* for at least twelve months.

Before considering a voluntary deregistration, be aware that you may have to refund some input tax credits. The *GST Act* provides that you may have to repay the ITC claimed on assets which are still on hand at the time of deregistration.

BAD DEBTS

The recovery of GST on bad debts is only relevant if you use the accruals basis of accounting for GST. Generally you will be liable to pay GST on a *taxable supply* that you make in the *tax period* in which you issue an *invoice*. If you do not receive full payment for that *taxable supply* you are able to claim a *decreasing adjustment* of 1/11 for the GST portion of the unpaid amount. This *adjustment* is available in two circumstances.

The first is if you have written off as bad the whole or part of the debt. You can adjust for the GST (effectively reclaiming it from the ATO) in the *tax period* in which you write the debt off.

The second is where the debt has been overdue for twelve months or more. If you issue the *invoice* on 15 January and your normal payment terms are 60 days, the twelve months will be up in mid-March of the following year and the adjustment will be made in the March BAS.

Note that if you have not paid a supplier for twelve months after the date payment was due, you will have an *increasing adjustment* for the GST. Interestingly, you must make that *adjustment* even if you had not previously claimed the GST as an ITC (for example, if you did not process the *invoice* because you knew you were going to dispute it with your supplier).

Also, you are supposed to make an *increasing adjustment* if the supplier has written the debt off as bad before the twelve months have elapsed. However, if the supplier does not notify you that the debt has been written off, it is hard to see how you can comply with this requirement.

If you have made either a decreasing or an increasing *adjustment* in respect of a bad debt and you subsequently receive or make a payment for the *supply*, you will have a corresponding increasing or decreasing *adjustment* of 1/11 of the amount received or paid.

Tip from the trenches

Monitor your bad debts regularly. Even if it is your policy never to write off bad debts, remember the twelve-month rule and reclaim the GST. If you only write off bad debts annually, consider a shorter write-off period to enable you to claim the GST.

FINANCIAL SUPPLIES

This is probably the most complicated area of GST, not only for those businesses which make *financial supplies* as their main activity but also for those which only make the occasional *financial supply*.

Put simply (and it is not a simple area) *financial supplies* are principally those involving money, life insurance, superannuation, credit and securities.

The crucial aspect of making *financial supplies* is that your ITCs may be restricted. You are required to monitor the GST which you incur on *acquisitions* which relate to the making of *financial supplies*. This monitoring applies over a twelve-month rolling period, looking backwards and forwards from the current tax period.

It is vital to note that you make a *financial supply* not only if you are the supplier (as with normal supplies) but also if you are the *recipient*. That gives you twice as many reasons to look out for *financial supplies*.

As previously mentioned, there are de minimis provisions, the FAT, which may allow you to claim ITCs on *acquisitions* which relate to making *financial supplies*. There are also *reduced credit acquisitions* which may allow you to claim 75 per cent of the ITC which would otherwise be denied.

One final point to note is that it is your intention to make a *financial supply* which may cause you to restrict your ITC, even if you never actually make the *supply*. For example, you may incur GST on costs investigating the possibility of making an IPO. Even if you eventually decide not to proceed with the IPO, the GST on *acquisitions* which relate to that proposed *financial supply* may have to be restricted.

If you regularly make *financial supplies* you should already have a method in place to monitor your ITC. The following tip is aimed at those businesses which do not, as a rule, make *financial supplies* except on an occasional basis.

Tip from the trenches

As soon as you are aware that you might make a financial supply, or as soon as you contemplate making a financial supply, start to identify the acquisitions which relate, to any extent, to that supply. Remember that receiving a financial supply counts as making a financial supply.

Let's assume that on 1 July you decide you need to raise capital and begin to explore two options. One option is a sale of some assets, the other is to dispose of some shares. The sale of assets will be taxable or possibly GST-free if it's a supply of a going concern (see below). The sale of shares will be input taxed although any shares sold to non-resident purchasers are likely to be GST-free as exports.

As the GST Act restricts an ITC to the extent that it relates to making supplies that would be *input taxed*, there is no single definitive (or 'correct') answer to how ITCs should be claimed. This is one suggested way of approaching the question.

As far as possible you should try to isolate costs which relate to the capital raising project ('project costs'). GST incurred after 1 July might be disallowed (subject to the FAT being exceeded) to the extent that the expenditure relates to the input taxed supply of the share sale. In the absence of any better attribution of costs, it might be reasonable to split the ITCs on the project costs 50/50 as relating to taxable and input taxed supplies.

Assuming that you intend that 20 per cent of the shares will be sold to non-resident investors, 20 per cent of the 50 per cent which relates to the share sale could be claimed.

On 1 September you decide to proceed with the share sale and the shares are sold on 1 November. Apart from possibly some residual invoices for work carried out prior to 1 September, it would be reasonable to conclude that all project costs incurred from then on will relate to the share sale and should be split 80 per cent attributable to input taxed supplies and 20 per cent attributable to GST-free supplies. On this basis, 20 per cent of the ITCs can be claimed.

In calculating the FAT you could use the GST on 50 per cent of the project costs incurred between 1 July and 1 September and the GST on 100 per cent of the project costs incurred after 1 September. If you exceed the FAT, the ITCs attributable to the share issue will not be creditable, unless they are eligible for a reduced input tax credit (RITC).

The 80 per cent incurred after 1 September, plus the 10 per cent incurred between 1 July and 1 September, both relate to input taxed supplies but should be further analysed to see if any of them are eligible for the 75 per cent RITC. Eligible expenditure will include underwriting fees, arranging fees and share registry fees.

The ATO might also insist that you allocate a proportion of your general overheads to the project to reflect the use of heat, lighting, office space, stationery, etc. during the life of the project.

Tip from the trenches

If you are acquiring a going concern, GST-free treatment will reduce your stamp duty cost as the stamp duty is imposed on the GST-inclusive figure. If you are selling a going concern on a GST-free basis, be sure to include a gross-up clause to allow you to charge GST if the supply is subsequently ruled to be taxable.

SALE OF GOING CONCERN

Under normal circumstances the disposal of assets used in a business will be a taxable supply. However, special provisions exist to provide GST-free treatment where the assets are disposed of as a 'going concern'. There are a number of criteria to be satisfied but the principal one is that there must be a written agreement between the parties that the supply is of a going concern. If there is no written agreement the supply cannot be

GST-free under these provisions. (It may, of course, be GST-free under other provisions, such as if the assets are exported). In order to qualify as a going concern, the seller must supply to the buyer all things necessary for the continued operation of the business

THE FUTURE

Of necessity, this book has only highlighted certain areas of the GST, although hopefully those areas which are of most concern or interest to small businesses.

The ATO has already issued over eighty Public Rulings and innumerable Private Rulings in connection with the GST and there is no indication that the rate at which rulings are issued will decrease in the near future. Clearly the GST is more complicated than was envisaged when it was proposed in the run-up to the 1998 federal election. This complexity, plus the ATO's increased focus on areas of perceived risk, means that all businesses need to keep on top of the GST, since it affects all their transactions.

The current rate of 10 per cent can only be amended with the unanimous approval of all states and territories plus both houses of the federal parliament. Many commentators have taken that as a sign that the rate will never rise. However, all the GST revenue, after collection and administration costs are deducted, goes to the states and territories; their cooperation in a rate increase cannot be ruled out.

The fact that the GST applies to the great majority of sale and purchase transactions means that for most businesses, even at a rate of 10 per cent, it represents anywhere between 12 per cent and 17 per cent of cash flow. That is a significant number and clearly indicates the need for the GST to be in the front rank of your tax thinking.

9. SETTING UP YOUR PREMISES

- **Working from home**
- **Leasing premises**
- **Serviced and virtual offices**
- **Selecting a retail location**

WORKING FROM HOME

Working from home can be a good way to start out in business while you assess whether your enterprise is really going to work. The impact on your cash flow of leasing and running an office can be sizeable – there is an upfront bond to pay as well as monthly rent payments and other overheads. Working from home will also save you the considerable time, expense and stress of travelling to and from work. As an added bonus your working hours can be flexible enough to allow more time for your family.

Some businesses are better suited to a home-office environment than others. Professional consultants who can attend meetings at client premises and then complete the paperwork at home often find home offices particularly convenient.

The home-based industry in Australia is large. Twelve per cent of Australian households operate a business from home and the industry sectors with the greatest number of home-based businesses are finance, property and business services, followed by the wholesale and retail trades.

The main issues associated with running a home office are

maintaining a professional image, feeling isolated from your industry, maintaining work discipline and legal issues.

Professional image

It is fairly hard to project a professional image if clients attending your home for a meeting are confronted with an untidy home and screaming children. If you invite clients for a meeting:

- ensure you dress professionally
- consider having a separate entrance for clients
- keep your house clean and tidy
- always answer the phone courteously and identify yourself and your business. You should have a separate line installed as this will ensure clients can get through to you even if the line is engaged by a call for another member of your household.

Isolation

A key advantage of working for a large corporation is being close to other people in the same industry. You can always visit a work associate in the next office or cubicle and ask how they dealt with an issue previously, or if they have a suitable industry contact or information source. The isolation of working from home may mean you lose this valuable source of interaction.

The only way to ensure you keep up-to-date is to join networking groups with a particular focus on your industry. Many industries also have professional associations which offer regular seminars or workshops.

Some good ways of networking include inviting individuals in your network to be your guest at a seminar or exchanging faxes of business articles from newspapers/magazines that you think may be of interest.

Discipline

The difficulty of remaining focused on the task at hand can be another problem for home-based businesses. It takes a lot of discipline to work at home and avoid the numerous distractions, such as television, computer games and friends who drop around.

To avoid this keep the same routine as if you worked in a normal office – don't be tempted to sleep in, ensure that you 'arrive' at your desk at the same time every day and keep normal office hours.

You will have to have fairly open discussions with your family and friends to make sure they respect the sanctity of your home office. You will not be able to focus on the tasks at hand if your flatmate or spouse continually drops in to your home office for a chat or coffee.

Some people find the only way to ensure they actually work at home is to prepare in the morning as if they were going in to the office, that is to shave or put make-up on and dress for work. This routine psychologically prepares them for work and also ensures that if a client drops in unannounced they won't be answering the door in tracksuit pants and slippers.

Legal issues

Before you commence running a business from home there are a number of legal issues you will need to be aware of, including insurance, government regulations and displaying registered office details.

Insurance Many home and contents insurance policies expressly exclude home offices and business assets. For example, your policy may not insure business equipment, such as laser printers or computers. You will need to contact your insurer and ensure you have adequate coverage. It is also important to take out normal business insurances as discussed in chapter seventeen. Also note that your car insurance policy may exclude business usage.

Regulations   Local government regulations restrict businesses conducted from home. You may even be required to obtain a permit. Depending on the local government area in which you live, regulations may:

- regulate the type and size of any signs you display outside the premises
- prohibit you from displaying or selling goods on the premises
- prohibit you from carrying on certain types of business at all, such as manufacturing
- prohibit home businesses that will increase traffic or parking congestion
- limit the amount of floor space used for business purposes
- regulate the emission of noise and other pollution
- regulate the number of employees who can work on the premises.

The nature of these regulations varies greatly between different local governments. Also note that state governments impose restrictions on home businesses as well. For example, occupational health and safety legislation may apply to your home business. It is important that you seek advice from your solicitor and contact your local council for details of permits and restrictions applying to home-based businesses.

Do not be tempted to simply ignore local and state government restrictions. Severe fines can be imposed and in some cases the relevant authority may be empowered to close your business down. Most infringements are reported to authorities by disgruntled neighbours or employees.

Signage   If you have incorporated a company or registered a business name and you have recorded your home address as your registered office then you may be required to display a small sign detailing:
- your business/company name
- your Australian Company Number (ACN) or Australian Business Number (ABN), if applicable
- your office hours.

LEASING PREMISES

A lease is a formal legal contract between you (the tenant or lessee) and the landlord (lessor) and guarantees your right to carry on business in a particular location for a set period of time.

Finding suitable premises involves the following steps:

Step 1: Decide whether to lease or buy
Step 2: Determine desired suburb and location
Step 3: Calculate your space requirements
Step 4: Check zoning and need for permits
Step 5: Negotiate and sign lease.

Lease or buy

Buying a freehold property is a major capital investment. The main disadvantage is that you will have business capital tied up in a non-core asset. The repayments and cost of the purchase will probably prove to be more than outgoings associated with a leasehold purchase. Leasing minimises transaction costs as you avoid having to pay the large stamp duty fees payable on the purchase of real estate – around

5 per cent of the business price. Another advantage of leasing is that it provides greater flexibility in moving to more suitable premises if and when your business grows or shrinks. You may find that there are more constraints attached to the operation of a business from leasehold than freehold premises, such as restrictions on uses and alterations.

On the other hand, if you buy a freehold property, you will own an asset that will appreciate in value. In future years this could provide a sound base for raising future finance for expansion. With the acquisition of a lease, the opposite is true; as the years on the lease are used up, it will depreciate in value.

Location for non-retail premises

The question of where your premises should be located depends on the nature of your business (see the end of this chapter for more information on how to choose a retail location). A premium location carries premium rentals, so if you are operating a non-retail business it may be better to divert funds from lease costs into revenue-producing activities, such as a bigger marketing campaign. Leasing an expensive, prestigious office may actually scare clients away. They might think that if you are paying such high rent then you will be too expensive. You should check the types of properties leased by your competitors.

There are a number of factors that can influence where you locate your business.

- **Proximity to resources** – the nature of your product or service might require your premises to be close to available skilled labour, back-up services, or stock and raw materials suppliers.
- **Finance** – the scale of the finance available to you may preclude city centre or main road locations.

- **Geographical concentrations** – you need to consider whether your customers will come to you or whether you will go to them. If your customers are going to come to you, then obviously you will need to be located as close to them as possible. If you will be going to your customers, then your premises will have to be located for easy access to efficient road, rail and air networks for sale and distribution of your goods/services.
- **Image** – the area in which you locate must be consistent with the overall image of your business.
- **Market decline in a locality** – a number of vacant premises or businesses for sale in the area should raise serious doubts about the potential of the area. What has gone wrong?
- **Future changes to a location** – the ideally located premises that you have found might not be as attractive in the future when the bus route is moved, parking restrictions are imposed in front of your premises or the new road cuts off your passing trade.
- **Facilities** – air-conditioning, security and essential services, such as waste disposal, toilet and kitchen facilities, need to be considered.

Space requirements

Early in the process you should calculate, as accurately as possible, your space requirements for administration, storage and/or manufacture. Once premises have been acquired it is difficult and costly to increase your space. Careful thought should also be given to the future expansion rate.

You should sketch out scale drawings of the optimum way of siting your equipment, including desks and reception areas. You may need storage space for stock and raw materials. If you trade in large volumes of stock, storage space will be directly determined by the stock levels maintained, which is driven by the sales level and the frequency of deliveries.

Zoning and permits

Before signing any lease ask your solicitor to:

- ensure that your intended business will comply with zoning regulations
- find out whether there are any statutory requirements with which you must comply, such as development applications, health or building regulations
- find out whether you should obtain any permits.

The landlord

A key step in evaluating a lease is to evaluate the landlord. Talk to some of the other tenants and ask them if the landlord responds to their needs, such as:

- routine maintenance
- sending service people when needed
- returning phone calls promptly.

The lease

Before signing a lease review it carefully and ensure you understand its terms. Have your solicitor review the lease and explain the key provisions to you.

The terms and conditions of an office lease are generally negotiable. The precise terms of a lease will depend largely on the condition of the rental market and on the relative negotiating strength of the parties concerned. For example, if you are leasing space in a shopping centre, the landlord is unlikely to allow much variation to their standard terms.

There is presently no legislation that prescribes mandatory

terms and conditions for commercial leases although there are statutory provisions regulating termination procedures. These must be detailed extensively in your lease. There is, however, legislation in place which governs the minimum terms and conditions of retail leases, including rent reviews. Although the rules vary from state to state, your lease will generally be classified as a 'retail lease' if:

- the floor area of the premises does not exceed 1000 square metres
- the relevant premises are in a shopping centre
- the tenant supplies retail goods.

All representations and details given to you by the landlord (or its agent) should be detailed in the contract. For retail premises, the landlord will be required to provide you with a statement disclosing your major commercial obligations, such as payment of rent, the amount of any outgoings or promotion contributions, etc. The lease will normally contain the following clauses.

Premises   The address of the premises should be clearly identified, including any parking and storage areas, which may carry different identification numbers from your office, shop or warehouse number.

Period of lease   The date for commencement of the lease and the date of expiry should be clearly stated. The term of the lease requires special consideration. While it is difficult to determine your future needs, it is important to carefully negotiate the term of your lease. If the lease is too short you may be forced to find new premises and incur extra costs such as moving all your office equipment and files. For retail businesses, you will also lose the goodwill you have built in that particular location. If your lease is too long you may be locked into premises that are or become unsuitable. It is important that you have the flexibility to downsize your operations if you hit a rough patch, or move to bigger premises if business is booming.

The best way to deal with this issue is to negotiate an option to renew the lease at the end of its term. For example, you could negotiate a 'one + one' lease, which means the term of the lease is one year with an option to extend the lease for another year. If at the end of the first year you decide that you do not wish to stay at those premises, you merely let the option lapse.

Rental amount   The lease should detail the amount and frequency (weekly, monthly, etc.) of rental payments. In order to ascertain whether you are paying a fair rate, obtain multiple quotes from agents for similar properties in the area. As a rule of thumb, rent and outgoings under the lease (discussed below) should be about 5 to 10 per cent of gross sales.

Tip from the trenches

If it is a 'tenants' market', that is, there is an abundance of office space, you may be able to negotiate a favourable rental structure, such as a rent-free period of say two months, or tiered rental rates, which start at a low rate for an initial period of say six months and thereafter increase to a higher rate.

Rent review   The basis for determining any change or review in rent must be stated in the lease, including an adjudication mechanism should there be a dispute between you and the landlord. It is important that you understand the rent review mechanisms contained in the lease, particularly if you are signing a long-term lease. There are a variety of different mechanisms, including:

- annual percentage increases of, say, 2 or 3 per cent per annum
- reviews tied to inflation
- market reviews.

Avoid leases which contain annual market review clauses – there seems little point in negotiating a cheap rent for the first year only for it to increase back to market in the second.

You should check the lease to see if it contains a 'ratchet' clause which prevents the rent from decreasing on a market review. If this clause is included negotiate to have it removed and ensure you have the ability to instigate the market review. This will allow you to benefit from lower rent on a market review at times of market reductions.

Turnover rent   Rent may sometimes be linked to 'turnover' or sales. There will usually be a fixed minimum rent subject to rent reviews or a rent as a percentage of turnover of the business. The higher of the two is payable. Where the rent is to increase by a fixed percentage of the current rent, it is important to consider the cumulative effect on the business of these increases over a number of years. For example a 6 per cent annual rent increase compounding will result in a 50 per cent increase in rent over six years. In general, if the percentage increase is higher than the Consumer Price Index the increases in rent may erode profitability, and in the long term the business may not be viable.

Security bond   You may be required to pay a security bond, typically three months' rent, which will be held in a bank account by the landlord's solicitor or real-estate agent in trust over the term of the lease. Do not pay the bond directly to the landlord. The landlord may accept a bank guarantee instead of a security bond. This is a letter from your bank saying that they will pay the landlord the amount of the deposit if you default. The bank will usually charge you a fee to give you the security but this will free up funds for working capital.

Repairs   The terms of most leases will require you to keep the premises, fixtures and fittings in good repair. It may also require you to attend to periodic painting or a refurbishment when the lease expires.

Outgoings   Many leases require the tenant to pay for all or a proportion of the costs of council/sewage rates, land tax, insurance, maintenance and so on. Make sure these are clearly stated in the lease and obtain an estimate of your proportion of outgoings, as they are additional to your base rent. The lease may also require you to contribute towards common expenses of a building or development, such as cleaning, security, gardening and maintenance, and replacement of air-conditioning plant. Retail leases may also require a contribution to the marketing and promotion of the centre.

Permitted uses   This clause identifies the types of business activities that you are permitted to carry on within the premises. It's a good idea to ensure the permitted uses are stated broadly enough to allow the activities you currently conduct and any changes that you may make in the future direction of the business. The lease may also contain a number of restrictions that are designed to prevent you from creating any nuisances or disturbances for neighbouring tenants.

Assignment of lease   Ensure that you have the right to transfer or assign the lease to a third party. The main reason for this is to ensure that if and when you sell your business you can transfer the lease to the purchaser. If you do assign a lease, you may be required to guarantee to the landlord the performance of the new tenant.

Goodwill   You may be liable to pay the landlord a percentage of the goodwill of the business if you sell. A clause like this should be avoided because it may limit your sales price. Seek assistance from your solicitor.

Other provisions/issues   Your lease is likely to contain a restriction or regulation on parking and storage facilities. There may also be a requirement that you join a tenants' association. The landlord may also have the right to enter and inspect the premises.

It is also a good idea to do a title search on the premises as there may be a mortgage on the property. If the landlord has a mortgage, check to see if the mortgagee has consented to a lease. If not, the mortgagee will not be bound by the lease and may be able to evict you.

You (the lessee) may have to pay for the landlord's costs in preparing the lease, as well as your own legal costs. You are also responsible for the payment of stamp duty on the lease (in New South Wales, stamp duty on a lease is 35 cents per $100 of rent and outgoings paid for the whole of the term of the lease).

All leases with a term of three years and over, including

the length of any option to renew, must be registered with the Land Titles Office. When the term of the lease has expired, and there are no further options, there is no right to remain in possession or to expect a new lease, although most leases will contain a 'holding over' clause which generally provides that one month's notice must be given by either party to end the lease. If you want to stay on or sign a new lease, commence negotiations in advance of expiry.

The cost of legal advice before you sign a lease is relatively small compared with any potential losses that may arise from onerous clauses or provisions you simply have not understood.

SERVICED AND VIRTUAL OFFICES

A serviced office is ideal for many startup businesses. You can hire, on a short-term basis, a fully furnished office with access to meeting rooms, kitchen facilities and office equipment such as computers, phones, facsimiles and photocopiers. A simple furnished space of around 15 square metres will cost around $150–$350 per week (depending on location). This typically excludes telephone rental.

Most serviced offices have receptionists who will answer telephone calls in the name of your business. You may also be able to access secretarial services, typically charged at a rate of around $30 per hour. Use of meeting rooms may also incur additional hourly charges.

The key advantage of a serviced office is that you only pay for the facilities as and when you need them, avoiding the need to pay for excessive office space, underutilised office equipment and idle staff. They are particularly useful as an interim step for untested business concepts and allow you to avoid locking yourself into a long-term lease.

A more recent type of serviced office is a 'virtual office'. These provide a mailing address and receptionist service only as you do not actually have a desk or office space. Meeting rooms are, however, available for an hourly charge. Virtual offices are suitable for consultants who visit the premises of clients for meetings and do their deskwork at home, but want to have a CBD address for mail.

Incubators can also assist startup companies by providing office space at subsidised rates, access to office facilities and access to a range of business advisers. For details about incubators see chapter seventeen.

SELECTING A RETAIL LOCATION

One of the single most important issues for a retailer is the location of the premises. Do not simply select a location randomly or because it is convenient or cheap to lease. It is important that you investigate the size of the catchment area, population and housing demographics, traffic count, the extent and quality of competition, accessibility, parking etc.

This section considers:
- Shopping centre classifications
- Demographic analysis
- Trade or catchment area
- Strip or shopping centre
- Identifying a suitable shopping centre
- Selecting premises.

Shopping centre classifications

The Property Council of Australia classifies shopping centres in the following order:
- **Regional shopping centres** – comprise one or more department stores, one or more discount department stores,

at least two supermarkets and usually more than 80 specialty shops and are about 35 000 square metres or greater

- **Subregional shopping centres** – comprise a discount department store, one or more supermarkets and usually more than 60 specialty shops and are about 20 000 square metres or greater

- **District centres or community centres** – comprise a discount department store, at least one supermarket and usually 30–60 specialty shops, and are about 5000–20 000 square metres

- **Neighbourhood centres** – comprise a supermarket and between 5 and 30 specialty shops

- **Arcades or malls** – comprise specialty shops only.

Demographic analysis

Demographic analysis provides information about the age, sex, ethnic background and rate of growth in the population. All of these factors help identify spending patterns of potential customers.

You should undertake a customised study, based on the type of retail business you wish to establish and the market segment you aim to attract. The study should answer the following questions:

- How many people are in the trading area and what is the historical population growth rate? The rate of population growth is a benchmark for potential growth in retail sales.

- What is the age of the people in the area? How many children, teenagers, elderly people?

- How many families and how many single households?

- What is the ethnicity of the people in the area? The presence of a strong ethnic heritage in the community will influence demand for certain foods and other products.

- What is the rate of unemployment in the area? Low unemployment suggests higher disposable income.
- What is the average income of the families or individuals?
- Where do they work? How do they travel to work?
- What do they do for a living? Are they tertiary qualified?
- Do the families rent or own their homes? How much rent do they pay?
- How many motor vehicles are parked at occupied dwellings?

For example, a trade area with a large proportion of younger families (with small children) will demonstrate certain income and spending patterns. They generally have:

- lower incomes, as they have not been in the workforce for long enough to have been promoted to higher-paid positions; and
- greater need for particular merchandise such as children's clothes and shoes, children's books, toys, nappies, bottles and other goods related to raising children.

If a large proportion of the population is in an older age bracket, there will generally be higher disposable-income levels.

The Australian Bureau of Statistics (ABS) is the official statistical organisation for the Commonwealth and state governments, and publishes a wealth of socio-demographic information. Copies of statistical publications can be obtained from **www.abs.gov.au** or from the ABS in your capital city. Most public libraries also have copies of ABS publications.

Trade or catchment area

A trade or catchment area for a shopping centre is the geographic area in which its consumer base resides. The boundaries of a trade area are governed by a number of factors, in particular geographic features and transport arteries – bridges, hills, rivers, railway lines, freeways and other main roads act as trade barriers. Anything which increases drive time or reduces accessibility will reduce the size of the catchment area. Also, relative distance to other shopping centres affects how far a trade area will extend. Typically, the radius of a shopping centre's trade area is under ten kilometres; some may even be smaller. In rural and other isolated areas, however, some shopping centres may attract customers from fifty to one hundred kilometres away.

Trade areas can also be defined as follows:

- **Primary trade areas** – close enough to the shopping centre to attract the majority of shoppers within that area; and
- **Secondary trade areas** – fall outside this area, and reflect lower percentages of centre patronage.

The location of competing shopping centres affects the distance a potential shopper will travel. If a well-stocked greengrocer or supermarket is located close to a consumer's home they will generally shop there, rather than travel further for a larger selection. The purpose of the visit will also determine how far a consumer will travel. If the purpose is to enjoy 'the shopping experience', consumers are often willing to travel considerably further.

Strip or shopping centre

Retailers should consider whether to locate their shop in a strip or shopping centre. A 'strip' means a shop located on a main street usually with limited off-street parking and forming part of a small cluster of shops. Such a location usually has lower occupancy costs than a shopping centre but typically has lower numbers of potential customers (i.e. a smaller catchment area).

A shopping centre normally has higher daily customer/ traffic flow, more car parking, air-conditioning and a better tenancy mix (often with major anchor tenants such as Woolworths or David Jones which generate a higher customer count for the centre). On the downside, shopping centres have typically (far) higher occupancy costs including rental, outgoings, management fees and promotion fees (often tenants are required to contribute to the cost of promoting the centre).

Identifying a suitable shopping centre

The following table summarises the key issues associated with selecting a suitable shopping centre for your store.

Visibility	• Is the centre visible from a major thoroughfare and does it have a feature that would attract customers? • Can you reach it travelling from either direction, or is it convenient only from one direction?
Competition	• Who is your direct competition? • How many other stores in the centre handle similar product lines? • What are the strengths and weaknesses of your direct competition? • What are their likely turnover/ stockturn/ expenses/ gross margin? • Are there other centres in your catchment area? How does the centre compare in terms of market share captured? • Will there be any large specialty stores in the area that compete with your products?

Traffic flow	• How many cars pass/visit the centre? Is traffic heavier at some times than others?
	• What does the centre interior look like? Do the various shop fit-outs encourage you to come inside?
	• How many people walk past/through the centre?
	• Do the customers in the centre appear to be in your target demographic?
	• Do shoppers come to the centre from outside the immediate area?
Parking/transport	• What is the parking like (at different times)? Is the centre close to public transport like buses and trains?
Surrounding developments	• What are the surrounding developments (i.e. residential, industrial, commercial, parkland)?
Health of centre	• How busy do other businesses in the centre appear to be? Are there many empty shops?
	• How often do stores in the centre change hands?
	• Are any major changes contemplated in the centre or area?
Tenant mix	• What is the tenant mix in the centre? Are other retailers compatible with your business?
	• What is the mix of national and local tenants?
	• Do other retailers (such as anchor tenants, e.g. big department stores like Myer or David Jones) help attract traffic flow?

Layout of centre	• Is the centre compact or is it sprawling (thus hampering foot traffic)?
	• Is it easy to navigate and is there good directional assistance to find particular tenants in the centre?
Promotion by centre	• Does the centre undertake regular promotional campaigns?
Condition	• Is the centre in good condition? How long since it was refurbished? Is there plenty of natural light? Is it well maintained and tidy? Does the centre provide a good shopping experience?

A short down time between tenants is a good sign the centre has a large catchment area. The presence of national retailers is also important.

Shoppers in regional shopping centres demand a favourable 'shopping experience'. Though not as relevant in smaller and/or food-based centres, the search for 'the shopping experience' is becoming very important in larger retail facilities. Quantifying this phenomena is difficult, but low customer traffic and high tenant turnover statistics in centres that are perceived as unpleasant venues in which to shop is a good verifier.

Real-estate agents and business brokers may be able to assist in gathering this information. Statistics on traffic information are available from the road traffic authorities and local councils (which also provide other information). Assistance can also be obtained from chambers of commerce, trade associations, small business agencies and, if applicable, your franchisor.

Selecting premises

Once you have selected the location of the centre, you need
to consider the following issues in relation to the placement
of the shop within the centre:

Signage	Are there any restrictions on signage outside the shop?
Size	Is the size/shape suitable for the type and range of merchandise you wish to stock?
Level	Is it located on the ground or first floor? The ground floor is usually preferable as it has better traffic flow.
Lease terms	What is the length of lease? Is there an option to renew? Can it be assigned or sublet?
Rent	What is the rental (ensure you get a rate per square metre to assist in comparison to other centres)? How does it compare to other premises? How often is the rent reviewed and on what basis (fixed or market based)?
Costs	What are the other costs? Some centres charge management fees, turnover levies, contributions to centre promotions and centre maintenance.
Quiet enjoyment	Do you have protection against 'loss of quiet enjoyment'? For example, what if a major refurbishment of the centre occurs?
Alterations	What renovations, alterations, fixtures, lighting changes, or floor coverings are required? Who will pay for these alterations and what outlay is required? How long will the renovations take before you can move in?

| **Access** | Where do the people enter and exit the centre? Where is your shop located by reference to these access points? Is rear access available (if needed)? |
| **Facilities** | Are facilities for staff adequate? |

10. EMPLOYING STAFF

- **Recruiting staff**
- **The employment agreement**
- **Employee share ownership plans (ESOPs)**
- **Superannuation**
- **Termination issues**
- **Minimum employment conditions**
- **Other issues for employers**

Employers assume a number of legal obligations when they hire staff, and must comply with several legislative regimes, including legislation on minimum wages and work conditions. This is particularly important in light of the new federal WorkChoices legislation (which has been incorporated into the *Workplace Relations Act 1996*) that came into force in March 2006. It is vital that prospective employers are aware of their obligations, and structure and plan the employment process to be able to meet them.

RECRUITING STAFF

The employment marketplace is a highly competitive one where employers vie for the services and skills of good candidates. An employer's ability to hire and retain skilled and motivated talent can make a significant difference to the success of the business.

Employing someone who is unsuitable can be very costly because of the cost of advertising the position, fees paid to recruitment agencies, time taken to interview and the cost of training. Particularly in service businesses this can amount to more than the employee's annual salary.

The recruiting process can be divided into the following steps:

- aims and objectives
- job definition
- key selection criteria
- sourcing candidates
- short-listing applicants
- job interviews
- reference checking.

Aims and objectives

You should consider the role a prospective employee will play in the context of your business plan and the organisation. You also need to identify clearly how that role will contribute to the outputs and the overall success of the business. Where the role sits in relation to the organisational structure will define to whom the role reports and, at a higher level, what the key objectives of the role will be. This review at a higher level is necessary to ensure that there is no doubling up and that there are no gaps in the processes that the role is expected to deliver.

At this stage take the opportunity to re-examine all other positions within the organisation to ensure the current structure is the most suitable to achieve business objectives. This may also present an opportunity to promote an existing member of staff to a more senior position and recruit from outside at a more junior level.

The next step is to decide whether you want a full-time employee, a part-time employee, a casual employee or an independent contractor. In making this decision, it is important to consider:

- how many hours a week you need someone
- whether the work will be ongoing or short term
- what your business can afford
- underlying minimum benefits prescribed by legislation, awards or enterprise agreements.

Full-time   There is no point in hiring a full-time worker if you can only afford to pay them for six weeks and then need to dismiss them. A full-time employee works for a specified number of hours each week, and has entitlement to benefits, such as annual leave, personal leave, and after a minimum period of employment, parental leave and long-service leave. A full-time employee is not suitable if the work is short-term, seasonal, or fluctuates.

Casual   In very broad terms, a casual employee does not provide services on a regular or systematic basis, and there is no promise to provide ongoing work. Casuals usually have no access to personal leave or annual leave, so their hourly wages are higher to compensate for this fact.

Contract   Independent contractors are not employees at all, but are generally contracted to do a specific task or achieve a specific result. It is important to clarify whether a worker is an employee or an independent contractor at the beginning of the relationship, as employers have different tax and legislative obligations to independent contractors.

Job definition
This is probably the most important step of the entire process. Defining clearly what the job is and what it does will drive the entire hiring process. This becomes the benchmark

against which you can measure potential candidates. A good job description will state clearly:

- the purpose or objective of the role
- to whom the person reports
- the key outputs and duties of the role
- the key performance indicators (what is done, when the job is being done effectively)
- the prerequisites needed to do the job effectively – the knowledge, skills and attributes required to do the job.

The best way to describe a job is to first define the outputs required of the role. For example, if one of the outputs of the role is the production of management accounting reports then several additional requirements (or knowledge, skills and attributes) must also be clarified. For instance, a certain level of accounting knowledge will be necessary as well as the knowledge and ability to use certain accounting software packages, attention to detail and the ability to meet deadlines, etc.

When all key tasks have been targeted, a clear checklist is effectively created against which possible candidates' skills, knowledge, qualifications and attributes can be measured and analysed during and after the interview. In doing so, the guesswork and risk of recruiting candidates can be reduced and a more successful outcome is assured for both the employer and the employee.

Key selection criteria

It is important to remember that you will be seeking someone who can fit readily and comfortably into the existing team and begin to work effectively in the shortest possible time. Selection criteria allow you to assess what kind of skills, educational level, previous experience, training and personal characteristics you require from the ideal candidate.

Sourcing candidates

Potential job candidates can be sourced by a variety of means including from your pool of existing employees, advertisements in newspapers or on the web, various employment agencies and your existing network of contacts.

After briefing, many recruitment agencies will take charge of the process and come back with a short-list of three to four candidates that should meet your job description, saving you the time and money of doing it yourself. Even if you use an agency, you will still have to remain quite involved with the process by defining the job, remuneration and requirements, and by participating in the interview and selection process.

Agencies can also provide useful value-added advice on:
• the most appropriate recruitment strategy for the role
• the availability of certain types of skills in the marketplace, i.e. whether the job as it is defined can actually be filled by one person
• the recruitment process
• discrimination issues
• advertising, if necessary
• reference checking
• negotiation of start dates and remuneration
• a range of other information and services.

Recruitment organisations generally fall into a number of categories based on the type of candidates they are involved in recruiting.

Executive search consultancies These agents identify candidates for directors, CEOs and senior executives. They use a search approach, which means they go looking for a certain type of candidate rather than candidates responding to an advertisement. Whilst very effective, this process tends to be time-consuming and expensive. Fees are generally based on a percentage of the total remuneration of the executive placed (around 30 per cent).

Search and selection consultancies These recruit a broad range of candidates covering senior line-management through to entry-level roles. They use a combination of advertised recruitment strategies combined with the use of their databases to source candidates. Search strategies are used for more senior candidates. Fees are levied on a retainer or contingency basis, which means that they only get paid when they find a suitable candidate. Their fees are generally based on a percentage of the final remuneration package of the placed candidate. The percentage fee is generally 15–20 per cent.

Specialist search and selection consultancies These agents are similar to the search and selection consultancies in terms of fees and the way they operate. They tend to focus on a particular industry, such as information technology, sales and marketing, or specific subsets within a particular industry sector, such as programmers, salespeople etc. Both the contingent and retained fee arrangements are used.

There are also agencies that specialise in secretarial and administrative support positions and others in tradespeople/unskilled labourers.

Web-based consultancies Web-based consultancies are becoming increasingly popular and are an effective way of communicating a vacancy to a wide range of potential candidates. Like newspapers, web-based products contain pages and pages of recruitment advertisements but they allow the potential candidate to carry out detailed searches to narrow down the jobs in which they might be interested. In addition, certain web-based products allow the potential candidate to submit their resume 'online', making the process more time-efficient.

Newspapers

Newspapers are filled with pages of recruitment advertisements – so it is easy for your employment advertisement to get lost amongst the other advertisements. When sourcing candidates, it is important to consider where suitable candidates seeking a career might look in a paper. A good place to start is to have a look at where jobs similar to the one you are looking to fill are being advertised. As a general guide, senior executive roles and management roles are advertised in the front section of the newspaper, known as the early and general news section (EGN), whilst all other advertisements are placed in alphabetical order in the employment section. Advertising in the EGN is more expensive than advertising in the employment section, and the advertisements tend to be large.

Consideration should also be given to industry journals or specialist publications when considering advertising for people in a specialist sector. An example of this might be when you wish to recruit a specialist engineer. Placing the advertisement in a specialist industry publication read by engineers is a more targeted approach to the desired audience.

If you decide to use a newspaper advertisement to source candidates, the next step is to write the advertisement. It is important to start with an attention-grabbing headline that will attract the best-suited candidate. This might be 'top flight sales professional required' followed by a subheading that will further attract suitable candidates to your role, such as 'innovative product line' or 'excellent earning potential'.

The next part of the advertisement might be a description of your company and why people would want to work there, followed by a paragraph setting out the broad responsibilities of the role then a short paragraph on the key requirements that candidates will need in order to be successful in that role. Finally, give contact details and the format in which you want the responses, for example written responses only or contact by phone or email.

Tip from the trenches
Surround yourself with people you can trust and who are leaders in their chosen field. Build a team of executives who have had success in the past. The most critical success factor in any business is people.

Short-list applicants

Once you start receiving applications it is necessary to respond in a timely manner. Make a short-list of people based on their responses and whether they fit your criteria. Be sure to write to other applicants to let them know that you do not wish to interview them. Thank them for the time they have taken to respond to your advertisement, explain that their application was unsuccessful and wish them well. Invite the short-listed applicants to attend an interview.

At this stage it may be advisable to ask each applicant to complete a standard application form with comprehensive details of their competencies, education and work experience. The form should also detail the job and its responsibilities, the remuneration being offered, your employment policy, etc. You should also find out when they would be free to commence work in the event that they are successful. Ask each candidate to sign this form as an indication that they fully understand the terms and conditions under which they might be employed.

Job interviews

Before you commence interviewing be clear on what you are looking for from candidates – the experience, skills, knowledge and attributes that are required. Be clear on exactly what the job is, what outputs candidates will need to achieve, what remuneration package you are prepared to offer and other benefits and conditions of employment.

Preparation – prior to the interview, prepare a list of questions focused on eliciting information around the experience, knowledge, skills and attributes required by the role. This will focus your questioning around gathering facts required to help you make a decision based on rational reasons rather than hunches or gut feeling.

Be prepared to answer questions on your company and what benefits employees gain from being associated with it. Remember, people change jobs for a whole range of reasons, it's not just about money.

Discrimination – it is illegal to discriminate on various grounds, including sex, age, disability, religion, race, marital status, family responsibilities, pregnancy, political opinion, national extraction, social origin or sexual preferences. Make sure you stick to the facts and ask questions that are pertinent to the job. (This is discussed in more detail below.)

Candidate's nerves – it is likely that candidates will be a little nervous during the interview, so holding the interview in a non-threatening place, preferably in a meeting room where you will not be interrupted, is important. Interruptions to an interview are seen as unprofessional and indicate a lack of importance placed on the interviewee. Thank the interviewee for coming and put them at ease.

Ice-breakers – you could start by using an ice-breaker question, such as 'what attracted you to our company?' This allows the candidate to start answering a relatively easy question, hopefully removing some of their nervousness, and should give you some idea as to what they may be looking for in a new job or employer.

Purpose of interview – explain that the purpose of the interview is for you to get an understanding of them and for them to get an understanding of the role and your organisation. Give them an overview of your company. Tell them that you would like to start by asking some questions and that they will have an opportunity to ask some questions as well later on.

Notes – most importantly, take notes during the interview. Do not rely on your memory. These notes will come in handy when you are reviewing the candidates after the interviews have been completed and will also prove useful when discussing them with other people in your team. They may also be important evidence in an unfair dismissal or discrimination claim as they document the requirements of the position and the candidate's suitability for the role. If an unsuccessful candidate claims that they did not get the job on the basis of discrimination, and it cannot clearly be shown why the candidate was found to be unsuitable, then it might be inferred that discrimination has occurred.

Question time – after you have finished asking your questions allow the interviewee an opportunity to ask some questions about the role and the company. Be prepared to answer questions on things such as working hours, benefits, remuneration, what you are looking for in a candidate, etc.

Post-interview – following the interview, complete your notes. Once you have narrowed it down to one to three suitable candidates, get someone else from your company to interview your final short-list. After you have had a second opinion from a colleague, discuss the final candidates and come up with your preferred choice.

Interview ideas to guard against discrimination

As discussed above, potential employers need to guard against any allegations of unlawful discrimination in the interview process. Some tips to bear in mind are:

- Ensure that the questions asked at the interview are directly relevant to the position you seek to fill.
- Be aware of the prohibited grounds of dismissal and ensure that your questions and conduct at the interview comply with legislative requirements.
- Endeavour to have at least two people present at the interview on behalf of the company.
- Treat all applicants and applications in the same manner.
- Avoid questions that could be perceived to be unlawful or not related to the position, such as whether the applicant is married, whether they are planning to have children or whether their partner minds if they have to work late.

Reference checking

It is important to reference check your candidates to verify not only what they have told you but more importantly to get another employer's perspective on the employee's past performance and to verify your own findings. Verbal reference checks will provide more information than any written reference will provide.

If you have found a suitable candidate and need someone to start immediately it can be tempting to forgo reference checks or to make initial contact with the referee and not follow up, especially if the referee is delayed in coming back to you. Resist this temptation – once you have offered a candidate a position and they have accepted it you have a binding contract. If you then receive unsatisfactory references you will have to pay the employee notice to terminate the contract.

Sometimes the most obvious referee may not provide the best information. You may wish to ask for referees other than previous employers, such as some customers when dealing with a salesperson.

Reference checking should never be done without the prior knowledge of the candidate, no matter how great the temptation. By undertaking indiscriminate reference checking, you may jeopardise the candidate's current position with their existing employer.

Start the reference check by telling the referee that their comments will be held in confidence, and keep it that way. Confirm the candidate's previous job, employment dates and reason for leaving. Ask about the role they held, the responsibilities and their performance. Ask about their interaction with other people. You may wish to focus on specific skills and attributes of the candidate, or strengths and weaknesses of their previous work, or about areas for improvement or specific management needs.

As you come to the end of your reference check you might like to describe the role that the candidate has applied for and ask the referee whether they would recommend the candidate for that role. Another good question is whether the referee would re-hire the candidate if they had the opportunity.

Making a formal offer

Having made your decision on your preferred candidate and completed the reference checks, you are now ready to make a formal offer to your preferred candidate. This is best done initially on a verbal basis and, once agreement has been reached, a formal letter of offer should be given to the candidate. Write sympathetic letters to the unsuccessful candidates and advise the person you have chosen that they have been successful and when and where you would like them to commence working for your organisation.

For further information on the process of recruiting staff, consult the following web sites:

- **www.business.gov.au**
- Wagenet
  www.wagenet.gov.au
- Employment and Workplace Relations Service
  www.workplace.gov.au/workplace/organisation/employer

The right to privacy

As a result of amendments to the *Privacy Act 1988* in 2001, the way in which a private organisation collects, keeps, uses and discloses personal information is subject to regulation. Information generated as part of the recruitment process will be subject to the National Privacy Principles contained in the *Privacy Act*.

The National Privacy Principles regulate the way in which organisations are required to deal with personal information that comes into their possession. Such information should only be used for the purpose for which it was collected.

In general terms, the categories and volume of information sought from candidates should be restricted to the minimum necessary to enable proper informed recruitment decisions to be made, the interviewees should be informed who will have access to the information and how it is to be stored and you should not request sensitive information from the individual unless such information is crucial to the recruitment process.

Pursuant to the *Privacy Act*, candidates have the right to access interview records. As a result, you should ensure that the process of selecting candidates for interview and for the position is structured so that it demonstrably produces objective, consistent and fair results. You should not retain the records, including any written notes of the interview, for any longer than is necessary for the recruitment process and in order for you to respond to any challenges to the appointment. When conducting the interview itself, limit the recording of responses to questions that are relevant to, and not excessive to, making the recruitment decision.

The web site of the Office of the Federal Privacy Commissioner of Australia at **www.privacy.gov.au** is a useful source of more information on this subject.

CASE STUDY:
Gerry Harvey – Harvey Norman

Gerry Harvey, a self-made billionaire, is head of retail giant Harvey Norman. He built his fortune from virtually nothing and there seem to be no tricks – just hard work, ethics and a desire for constant improvement and expansion.

At 18, he started selling vacuum cleaners door-to-door, but failed to make a sale in the first six months. Nevertheless, he persisted and watched others who were succeeding until he started to make some sales. In the next six months, he broke all company records, selling up to thirty vacuum cleaners a week.

Gerry then began an auction business with Ian Norman and also started opening shops which sold electrical goods. By the age of 24, the partnership had three shops. Twenty-one years later, Norman Ross had become a household name with forty-two stores nationwide. It was sold to Grace Brothers for $22 million. Within 10 years, Norman Ross went out of business, providing the impetus for Gerry and Ian to create Harvey Norman in 1982. This time, instead of a chain of stores, they implemented the franchise model where each operator owned their business and had the incentive to work harder. In 1987, Harvey Norman listed on the ASX with twelve stores in Australia. Today that has grown to 166 stores throughout Australia, New Zealand, Singapore and Britain. Annual turnover is in excess of $3 billion and the company employs about 10 000 people.

Gerry Harvey's keys to success are very simple. He believes in doing the basics well. In a nutshell, you must work hard, develop good people skills, have an eye for talent, master the art of delegation and, finally, surround yourself with good people.

He believes that the key to managing people is to treat them with respect and to do the right thing by them. While these should be basic principles, he claims that 80 per cent of bosses treat their people badly.

In contrast to the goal-setting obsession which dominates much of today's corporate philosophy, Gerry does not set specific goals; rather, he has just one goal, which is to make Harvey Norman bigger and better each year. In terms of research, Gerry once again works contrary to mainstream business strategy. He prefers the 'gut feel' method of making decisions rather than undertaking months of research. The success of Harvey Norman is built on extensive advertising, good value, exceptional service and special deals such as the well-known 'buy now – pay later' options.

He provides visible leadership for the business by always being on the lookout for new business ventures, and makes the effort to be informed of everything that goes on in the business.

A very basic principle of Gerry's success is that he loves what he does – buying and selling – and has a gift for being able to put a value to something.

WorkChoices

It is important to understand how the Australian employment and industrial framework affects you and your employees.

Historically, legislation and other industrial instruments have been enacted at both a state and federal level. However, the federal WorkChoices legislation, which came into effect on 27 March 2006 and amended the *Workplace Relations Act 1996*, has meant that there is now a unitary system that will apply to most employees in Australia. WorkChoices will not apply to employees employed by entities that are not constitutional corporations, such as partnerships, trusts and sole traders.

The new WorkChoices legislation regulates many aspects of employment, although state laws continue to govern matters such as discrimination, long service leave, rights of entry and occupational health and safety. The WorkChoices legislation deals with:

- an employee's entitlement to notice upon the termination of the employment relationship;
- the procedure to follow when terminating an employee's employment;
- when industrial action is illegal;
- what employment records are required to be kept and for how long;
- entitlements to annual leave, personal leave, parental leave; and

- how employers and employees can create workplace agreements.

The WorkChoices legislation has introduced a set of minimum terms and conditions of employment for all employees of constitutional corporations, known as the Australian Fair Pay and Conditions Standard (AFPCS). The AFPCS applies to all employees, regardless of their remuneration level, and consists of the following:

- minimum wage (being the federal minimum wage or, if different, the rate set under the Australian Fair Pay and Classifications Scale);
- a maximum working week of 38 hours per week, together with reasonable additional hours;
- 20 days' annual leave per year (plus an additional amount for shift workers);
- 52 weeks' unpaid parental leave;
- 10 days' paid personal leave.

THE EMPLOYMENT AGREEMENT

Once you have selected an employee from a field of candidates, it is important to set out in a written agreement the terms and conditions of the employment relationship. A written contract is a safe approach as it provides evidence of the actual terms of agreement in the event of a dispute. Note however that written employment contracts are still subject to the minimum conditions stipulated in a relevant award or legislation including the AFPCS.

The contract should take the form of either a letter of offer, which the employee signs and returns, or a comprehensive agreement. The letter or agreement should be signed by the employee before the employment period begins. The key provisions that should be included are salary and conditions, location, probationary period, incentive/bonus schemes, duties, expenses and transport, intellectual property, non-competition clause, confidentiality, leave entitlements and termination grounds.

You should obtain independent legal advice before you enter into any agreements with staff.

Salary and conditions

It is important to set out the salary and the circumstances under which the salary will be reviewed to avoid disputes about verbal promises. An example would be:

'Your gross starting salary will be $50 000 per annum, including superannuation. Your salary will be reviewed at least once during each twelve-month period of your employment. The Company will not be obliged to increase your salary at any time.'

Probationary period

You should consider inserting a probationary period in all contracts of employment for new employees. An example of such a clause is:

'This offer is subject to the satisfactory completion by you of a probationary period of three months, at the end of which your position may be confirmed. During the probationary period, your employment may be terminated at the sole discretion of the Company by the Company giving you one week's notice or payment of one week's salary in lieu of notice.'

Incentive/bonus schemes

If you have considered having an incentive or bonus scheme to enhance productivity and reward employees, the employment contract is a good place to specify the basic terms. You can then refer the employee to the bonus scheme rules for more detailed provisions. You should specify clearly the objectives to be met in order for the bonus/incentive to be payable. You should specify when it is payable (e.g. 30 June each year) and what happens if the employment terminates before that date, for example whether they get a pro rata entitlement.

Duties

The employment contract should set out the duties of the position so that in the event of any dispute it is clear what the employee is and is not expected to do. To give you flexibility, you can add words to the effect of 'and such other duties as the employer may reasonably require from time to time'. The duties section should specify who the person reports to.

Expenses and transport

If the job involves any travelling, or if work-related expenses are likely to be incurred, include a section on reimbursement of travel, accommodation and meal expenses, including any proof requirement, such as production of receipts.

Intellectual property

This is a particularly important clause for anyone working in a technology or product development field, for example creating computer software. The business owner needs to ensure that they have the intellectual property rights to products that their employees have developed while in their employ. These rights can be very valuable – indeed for some Internet or software companies they are the only material asset – so it is important to protect them.

Non-competition

Your employees have access to confidential information; will be closely acquainted with your clients and business network; and will understand the strengths and weaknesses of your business. A non-competition clause is a sensible precaution to prevent employee conflicts of interest during employment and to protect your business when the employment relationship ends. Clauses should be no wider than is necessary to protect your legitimate business interests. As non-competition clauses are traditionally difficult to enforce, you should consult your legal adviser at the time of drafting to ensure that they are tailored to your situation.

Confidentiality

It is important to ensure employees are bound to not disclose information about your business, its financial affairs, trade secrets or strategies.

Personal leave, annual leave and long-service leave

Although legislative minimum requirements relating to leave are set out in the AFPCS and other legislation, it is often useful to spell out leave entitlements in the employment contract. The employer then has the option of granting more than the minimum entitlements – this might be an important factor in pursuing and keeping the best staff for your business – and some flexibility in stipulating the way in which leave can be taken.

Termination

If the employment relationship is terminated by one of the parties, it is usually such a turbulent period that it is very useful to have a written agreement to clarify the rights and obligations of the employer and employee, the circumstances in which termination is permissible, and whether notice of termination is required. Employers have a number of legal obligations to consider when terminating an employee (discussed below).

EMPLOYEE SHARE OWNERSHIP PLANS

Many companies establish an employee share ownership plan (ESOP) for their employees. An ESOP gives employees an opportunity to become part-owners of the company and a financial interest in its success. There are a number of ways that ESOPs can be structured – an outline of the more common structures follows. There are a number of advantages and disadvantages associated with each structure – these are listed in the following table.

ESOP structures

Free shares   Under current legislation, a company can issue up to $1000 worth of free shares to each employee in the company without any tax needing to be paid on those shares. Employees must be restricted from disposing of the shares for at least three years and the offer must be made on the same terms to at least 75 per cent of employees.

Options   A second structure for the ESOP is for the company to issue options over shares to employees. The options are usually issued for free but have an exercise price that is payable when they are exercised. The exercise price is usually set at the share price on the date the option is issued, or at a slight discount to it. The options are exercisable after a fixed period has elapsed, e.g. three years after the options are

ADVANTAGES/DISADVANTAGES OF ESOP APPROACHES

Type of ESOP	Immediate ownership	Voting and dividend rights	Immediate liquidity	Cost to company	Cost to employee	Individual incentive	Upfront commitment by employee	Minimum employment period restriction possible	Employee exposed to downside	Easy to administer
Free shares	Yes	Yes	No, until expiry of escrow[1] period	Low (subject to sufficient share premium reserve)	Nil	No	No	No	No	Yes
Options	No	No	No	Nil	Exercise price	Yes	Low (if any)	Yes	No	Moderate
Fully paid shares and loan	Yes	Yes	No, until expiry of escrow period/ repayment of loan	Cost of funds	Loan amount (dividends can be used to repay and service)	Yes	Yes	Yes	Yes (unless loan is limited recourse)	No
Partly paid shares	Yes	Pro-rata to amount paid up/ sometimes full	No	Nil	Issue price (dividends can be used to pay up shares)	Yes	Low	Yes	Yes	Moderate
Unit trust	Indirect	Possible, indirectly	No	Nil	Issue price	Yes	Yes	Yes	Yes	No

[1]The escrow period means that the ASX will not permit you to sell all or part of your shareholding

issued. If employees have performed well and the company's share price has increased, the exercise price will be less than the then prevailing share price and, by exercising the option, the employee will achieve a profit equal to the difference between the share price when the option is exercised and the exercise price. Generally options are used for executive, rather than general employee, share plans.

Fully-paid shares and loans   Under this approach, the company provides loans to employees to purchase shares in the company. The shares are then used to secure repayment of the loan from the company. As an incentive, the loan is usually provided at a low or zero interest rate. In addition, the shares may be offered at a discount to the then prevailing market rate. If the loan is not repaid, the company's recourse is generally limited to the value of the shares and interest payments are often timed to coincide with dividends.

Partly-paid shares   Under the partly-paid shares approach, the company issues partly-paid shares to employees. The shares can either be zero-paid or employees can pay a small amount of the issue price of the shares upfront. Employees then pay up the shares over time – usually out of dividends declared on the shares.

Unit trust   A unit trust is set up to hold shares in the company. Employees are issued with units in the trust, rather than the shares themselves. The rights for employees are governed by the unit-trust deed. The unit-trust deed will allow the employee to redeem the units, i.e. require the sale of the underlying shares and the distribution of the sale proceeds to the employee, after a set period has elapsed or on the termination of the employee's employment.

Before implementing an ESOP, you should seek advice from a tax adviser in relation to the special tax rules applying to ESOPs, and also from a lawyer in relation to the prospectus disclosure requirements for ESOPs.

SUPERANNUATION

Under the Commonwealth Superannuation Guarantee Scheme, all employers in Australia must make provisions for their employees' superannuation. The purpose of the Scheme is to make better provisions for Australians in their retirement than is presently provided by the age pension. The principal obligation of employers is to make a financial contribution to their employees' superannuation fund. An employee's contributions do not count towards the employer's contribution.

The Scheme is self-assessing and employers must make their contributions on a quarterly basis. Contributions are generally deductible in relation to the financial year in which they are paid. As an employer, if you fail to make your payment before the relevant due date, you may lose your tax deduction and have to pay a penalty charge. From 1 July 2003, employers are also required to report in writing to the eligible employees setting out the contributions made on their behalf. These reports must be provided within 30 days of each contribution being made. There are also penalties which are not tax-deductible for failure to provide a superannuation guarantee statement.

The amount of the contribution is a percentage of gross salary. Salary is generally a payment that is periodic or recurrent in nature and includes directors' fees, commissions and non-salary benefits. The contribution is presently 9 per cent of the employee's gross salary.

If you make superannuation contributions to your employees under an award, you will have to check with the trustee of the superannuation fund as to whether it is sufficient to meet your new Superannuation Guarantee obligations.

As a general rule you must pay superannuation contributions for all your employees including full-time, part-time and casual staff and even certain types of contractors. You may not have to make provisions for superannuation for certain categories of employees. These are generally:

- employees paid less than $450 per month
- employees under eighteen years of age and working thirty hours or less per week
- part-time domestic workers (who work thirty hours or less per week)
- employees over the age of 70
- employees working outside Australia, where they are not residents of Australia or the employer is not a resident of Australia.

On 1 July 2005 the federal government's choice of fund legislation took effect, giving most employees the right to select the fund into which their superannuation contributions will be paid.

For further information contact the Tax Office Superannuation Helpline on 13 10 20 or go to the ATO's web site: **www.ato.gov.au**

TERMINATION ISSUES

When an employee is dismissed from their job they may be able to bring a claim that they were unlawfully or unfairly dismissed. If an employee commences a legal action for unlawful or unfair dismissal, an employer immediately faces loss of time, legal expenses and potential damage to their reputation. If the employee wins, then an employer might face quite substantial costs, as well as the possibility of being forced to reinstate the very employee they wanted to dismiss.

An important question in all this is who are 'employees' for the purpose of unlawful/unfair dismissals? Some workers, such as independent contractors and those working as directors/shareholders, may in fact be legally considered to be employees despite the express terms of any contract. As such, they would have the ability to bring an unfair dismissal claim on the termination or threatened termination of their engagement. But generally someone is an employee when the hirer exercises a high degree of control over the worker. The provision of labour only, and long-term arrangements with fixed hours and regular payments, are also indicators of an employer/employee relationship.

Unfair dismissal An employer must not dismiss or threaten to dismiss an employee in circumstances that are harsh, unjust or unreasonable. The following factors are taken into account:

- whether there was a valid reason for the dismissal based on the employee's capacity or conduct
- whether the employee was given the opportunity to respond to the allegation that gave rise to the dismissal
- whether there were any warnings of unsatisfactory performance
- whether the employee was given the opportunity to obtain independent advice
- whether the employee was given the prescribed minimum notice of termination, or was paid in lieu of notice.

Unlawful dismissal   Dismissal or threatened dismissal is likely to be unlawful under the federal legislation if termination arose because of:

- temporary absence from work due to sickness or injury
- membership or non-membership of a union or acting as an employee representative
- the employee being absent from work due to parental leave
- the employee's sex, race, age, disability, nationality, religion, pregnancy, sexual preference, marital status, political opinion or family responsibilities
- the employee seeking enforcement of an award or agreement
- the employee refusing to negotiate in connection with making, signing, extending, varying or terminating an Australian Workplace Agreement.

Exclusions   Some classes of employees cannot claim unfair dismissal. These include:

- employees working for an employer who has 100 or fewer employees (the employees of related bodies corporate are included when calculating this figure)
- employees who are not engaged under an award and whose remuneration is above a certain level, currently set at $98 200 (indexed annually)
- employees engaged for a specific term of employment or for a specified task where the term expires or the specified task is completed
- employees engaged for a reasonable period on probation (generally no more than three months unless the circumstances warrant a longer period)
- employees dismissed during the qualifying period of six months

- casual employees engaged for short periods who have not worked regularly and systematically for a period of 12 months prior to dismissal
- employees whose positions have been made redundant as a result of a genuine operational reason
- employees under a traineeship arrangement.

There may be other remedies available to these employees and an employer should still seek advice before termination of employment or unilaterally varying an employment arrangement in relation to such an employee.

If you want to terminate an employee on grounds of misconduct or poor performance, ensure that you do not act unfairly. Tell the employee that there is a problem with their performance. Give them a chance to respond and to improve their performance. If the conduct or poor performance continues, give them a warning, preferably in writing. Talk to the employee and perhaps let them propose alternatives to being dismissed.

If you feel that you have no alternative but to dismiss an employee, tell them why you are doing so and dismiss them in a sensitive way rather than in a fit of rage. Consider whether the conduct justifies termination without notice – dismissal without notice can only be justified in cases of serious or wilful misconduct. The important thing is to document the dismissal, to give the employee the opportunity to respond, and to give the errant employee a 'fair go'.

If it is decided that in all the circumstances the employee has to go, but their conduct does not justify immediate termination, an obligation exists to give the employee notice of termination, or salary in lieu of notice. You should check whether you have an obligation to give notice under an award, the federal legislation or the contract of employment. The higher notice period should be given.

Unfair contracts In addition, in New South Wales under section 106 of the *Industrial Relations Act 1996*, the Industrial Relations Commission of New South Wales used to have the power to void or vary contracts in relation to which services are performed in New South Wales, or arrangements that are collateral to such contracts, on the grounds that they are harsh, unconscionable or unfair. It also has the power to award unlimited compensation in respect of the perceived unfairness.

As a result of WorkChoices, the right of employees to access this jurisdiction has been removed. Readers should note, however, that at the time of writing the WorkChoices legislation is subject to a High Court challenge by the state governments. It should also be noted that this jurisdiction can still be accessed by independent contractors, although this right is likely to be removed when the federal government's independent contractor legislation comes into force.

MINIMUM EMPLOYMENT CONDITIONS
Industrial awards

Until recently, industrial awards have been made at either a state or federal level. State awards have traditionally covered non-managerial employees in specific occupational groups such as the transport, clerical, construction, manufacturing and hospitality industries. Federal awards bind named respondents. Employers can be respondents to a federal award by being named specifically in the award, by being a member of an employer organisation named in the award or by purchasing the business of an employer who is named in the award.

As a result of the WorkChoices legislation, state awards have become known as notional federal agreements preserving state awards (NAPSAs). NAPSAs will gradually be phased out during a transitional period (the length of which varies depending on whether the awards apply to employees of constitutional corporations or not), after which time the minimum terms and conditions of employment of those employees will be governed by the AFPCS.

In addition, all existing federal awards are to be rationalised and simplified and are likely to become common rule awards; that is, they will apply to specific industries, rather than to named employers. Awards (together with the AFPCS) prescribe the legal minimum terms and conditions of employment in an industry.

Employers cannot agree to the modification of any award provision unless it is part of a certified agreement or an individual Australian Workplace Agreement. Such agreements give employers and employees the opportunity to step outside award regulation and build arrangements that best suit the needs of the business and the type of work they do. However, employers and employees cannot agree to opt out of the minimum terms and conditions enshrined in the AFPCS.

Legislation

In addition, the *Workplace Relations Act 1996* and various state acts regulate industrial and employment matters in certain respects. For example, certain acts provide for entitlements such as paid long service leave and notice of termination.

The number of weeks of notice of termination an employee is entitled to under the *Workplace Relations Act* depends on the number of years of service:

- not more than one year of service – at least one week of notice
- more than one year of service but not more than three years – at least two weeks
- more than three years of service but not more than five years – at least three weeks
- more than five years of service – at least four weeks.

In addition, if an employee is 45 or over and has at least two years of continuous service with the employer, the employee will be entitled to an additional week's notice.

The various long-service leave acts throughout Australia require employees with specified minimum length of continuous service to be entitled to take long-service leave. In New South Wales, the *Long Service Leave Act 1955* provides for two months' long-service leave on ordinary pay on completion of ten years of continuous employment. After an employee has reached five years of service they are, in limited circumstances, entitled to a pro rata payment of long-service leave on termination.

Employees will also be entitled to take gazetted public holidays. These may vary from state to state but generally include:

New Year's Day
Australia Day
Labour Day
Good Friday
Easter Monday
Anzac Day
Queen's Birthday

Christmas Day

Boxing Day

Information specifically about federal awards and minimum employment conditions for employees not covered by any award can be obtained from the Department of Employment and Workplace Relations (their web site is **www.dewr.gov.au**). Copies of the relevant documents for federal awards can be obtained from WageNet (their web site is **www.wagenet.gov.au**).

OTHER ISSUES FOR EMPLOYERS

There are a number of other issues employers should consider when dealing with employees, including discrimination, sexual harassment, occupational health and safety and matters relating to unions.

Discrimination

There is both federal and state anti-discrimination legislation which makes discrimination unlawful even if the accused person did not have any intention to discriminate. This has been discussed above in relation to the interview process. However, generally, employers must take all reasonable steps to prevent discrimination and harassment in the workplace if they wish to try to avoid liability. This means they must actively implement precautionary measures to minimise the risk of discrimination and harassment occurring, such as having written policies on workplace discrimination and harassment, ensuring that employees have had an opportunity to read these policies, and providing training for staff in these policies.

Discrimination can be direct or indirect. Direct discrimination is treating one person less favourably than another because of particular attributes, for example race, sex, sexual preference, age or religion. Deciding not to employ someone because they are disabled, for example, is direct discrimination. Indirect discrimination is a result of treating everyone the same in a way that ends up being unfair to a specific group of people. For example, a rule that everyone must start work at 6.30 a.m. might be indirectly discriminatory to a worker who has carer's responsibilites and can't start at that time.

For more information, go to the Human Rights and Equal Opportunities Commission at their web site: **www.hreoc.gov.au**

Sexual harassment

Sexual harassment is an unwelcome sexual advance or an unwelcome request for sexual favours or any other unwelcome conduct of a sexual nature in circumstances where the person responsible would have anticipated that the other person would be offended, humiliated or intimidated.

The vital part of the definition is the emphasis that harassment is unwelcome conduct. Consensual, welcome and reciprocated conduct does not amount to sexual harassment.

Sexual harassment is unlawful for employers and employees, and an organisation has a legal responsibility to prevent harassment, otherwise it can be liable for the behaviour of its employees.

Every workplace should have a clear policy against sexual harassment that is effectively implemented in the workplace, and a program for dealing with it. Employees should be able to approach someone within the workplace to complain of sexual harassment. They should also be able to approach their union, the Human Rights and Equal Opportunity Commission or the relevant state or territory anti-discrimination agency for information and confidential advice.

Occupational health and safety

States and territories are responsible for making laws about occupational health and safety. The most basic requirement under these laws is the exercise of a duty of care. This is a duty to do everything reasonably practicable to protect the health and safety of others in the workplace. The duty is placed on all employers, their employees, and others in the workplace.

The extent of care that must be exercised depends upon the workplace and the nature of the work. Particularly hazardous workplaces necessitate a higher duty of care, and there may be specific legislation setting out occupational health and safety obligations.

For more information, go to the web site of the Australian Safety and Compensation Council: **www.ascc.gov.au**

Unions

Unions provide support services to their members just as employer associations do for their members. Unions represent their members in negotiating for better working conditions and wage increases, making employment agreements and settling disputes.

Employees have a legal right to join a union and equally have the right not to join a union. Employers have no right to stop their employees joining a union. Nor should employees be coerced into joining a union. Any such activity by employers or union officials may be illegal.

For further information contact the Department of Employment, Workplace Relations' web site: **www.dewr.gov.au**

11. FINANCIAL STATEMENTS AND PERFORMANCE ANALYSIS

- **Accounting systems**
- **Business performance analysis and financial ratios**
- **Financial structure analysis**
- **Sensitivity analysis**
- **Financial reporting for companies**

ACCOUNTING SYSTEMS

A well-designed and implemented accounting system will allow you to record, control and interpret your business's financial performance. More specifically, an accounting system will:

- allow you to satisfy the legal requirements of tax legislation
- provide you with information useful in making key business decisions
- allow you to report to financiers, investors, suppliers and regulators in a meaningful way about your operations
- enable you to quickly identify problems and take corrective action before it's too late
- show how your business has performed this year – data which will enable comparison to prior years, forecasts and also comparison to other businesses
- allow corporations to meet the record keeping requirements stipulated by the *Corporations Act*.

You should seek the advice of a qualified accountant before you set up your accounting system. Ask them to advise you on the accounting requirements for your type of business operations, and what records you must keep for tax and statutory reporting purposes.

Your accountant may be able to recommend a prepackaged accounting system for your computer. Simple systems are relatively inexpensive and if your business involves a large number of transactions, a computerised system is likely to be the most beneficial.

The components of a basic accounting system (shown in the diagram on page 254) are:

Purchases journal – this records all the purchases made by the business, such as stock, equipment, supplies and services. Purchases made on credit must also be entered into the accounts payable ledger.

Sales journal – this records all the sales made to your customers. Sales made on credit must also be entered into the accounts receivable ledger.

Accounts payable ledger – this records the goods and services that you have purchased on credit from suppliers.

Accounts receivable ledger – this records the goods and services that you have sold on credit to your customers.

General ledger – this contains a summary of all the transactions contained in the sales and purchases journals and in your cash book.

Cash book – this records cash receipts and payments. The amount of cash received is also recorded in the general ledger and the accounts receivable ledger. The amount of cash paid is also recorded in the general ledger and the accounts payable ledger.

Standing journal – this allows you to prorate charges that are incurred quarterly, semi-annually or annually that should be allocated monthly to facilitate more accurate monthly reporting. **General journal** – this contains all miscellaneous transactions that do not fit in the above categories. It usually consists of one-off items and correction of errors.

In principle, PC-based computerised accounting systems automate many of the different accounting ledgers, as well as providing other functionality such as financial reports and other statements. How they fit together and interrelate can be seen in the following diagram.

The basic principle underlying any accounting system is that the assets of a business are financed by debt (liabilities), or money the owner has contributed or generated by operating the business (equity).

The accounting system produces three main types of

BASIC ACCOUNTING SYSTEM

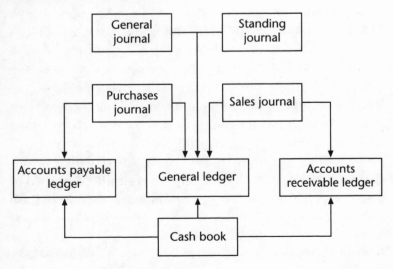

financial statements called the balance sheet, the income statement and the cashflow statement. The balance sheet reflects, at a certain point of time called the balance date, the assets, liabilities and equity of the business. The income statement is a summary of your business's financial operations over a certain period of time. The cashflow statement is a summary of cash receipts and cash payments made by the company over a period of time.

Balance sheets

A balance sheet is frequently called a snapshot of a business, as it relates to one single moment in time. The balance sheet generally represents the historical costs of assets controlled by the business and the value of the liabilities owed by the company at a particular point in time.

The balance sheet on page 254 is based on a fictitious company called Annandale Rocks.

Assets Assets are, in general terms, the items the business controls which will bring future economic benefits as a result of past transactions or events. Assets may be tangible, such as computers or photocopiers, or intangible, such as goodwill or patents. Assets include items which the business owns and items you control, such as certain types of leased assets. Assets are classified as current assets if they can be realised into cash within one year (usually) of the balance date.

Current assets Current assets are typically comprised of cash, receivables, inventory and prepaid expenses. **Cash** consists of funds which are available for immediate use. It represents the money in the business's bank accounts, cash held in cash registers, petty cash and cash equivalents. For

Annandale Rocks Pty Ltd
Balance sheet as at 30 June 2004

	2004 $	2003 $
Current assets		
Cash and cash equivalents	291 240	50 000
Trade and other receivables	450 000	165 000
Inventories	240 000	140 000
Prepayments	10 000	10 000
Total current assets	991 240	365 000
Non-current assets		
Fixed assests	726 667	180 000
Other financial assets	5 000	5 000
Land and buildings	50 000	50 000
Intangible assets	180 000	—
Total non-current assets	961 667	235 000
TOTAL ASSETS	1 952 907	600 000
Current liabilities		
Bank overdraft	—	—
Trade and other payables	150 000	100 000
Provisions	120 000	100 000
Accrued expenses	30 000	12 000
Total current liabilities	300 000	212 000
Non-current liabilities		
Term loan	600 000	—
Total non-current liabilities	600 000	—
TOTAL LIABILITIES	900 000	212 000
Net assets	1 052 907	388 000
Owner's equity		
Issued capital	900 000	300 000
Retained earnings	152 907	88 000
TOTAL EQUITY	1 052 907	388 000

companies complying with Australian Generally Accepted Accounting Principles (GAAP), note that cash held in term deposits longer than thirty days is to be classified as short-term securities.

The main component of **receivables** is usually trade debtors, which are amounts owed by customers to the business. However the entire amount owing from all debtors is unlikely to be received as you (or your accountant) will write off (remove) all debts that are known to be bad debts. An allowance may be made for a percentage of your debts to be uncollectable. This is known as provision for doubtful debts. There are other types of current receivables – essentially non-trade debts due to the business over the next year, such as loans to directors and loans to third parties.

Inventories are the products you have purchased or made for sale to customers. There are three main types of stock or inventory – raw materials, work-in-progress (WIP) and finished goods. WIP is simply those items of inventory that have begun, but not finished, the production process. Inventory should be measured at the lower of cost and net realisable value (NRV). Cost is the aggregate amount of raw materials, labour and an allocation of the overheads, such as rent, relating to the production of that item. NRV is what you can sell the stock for, less selling costs.

Prepaid expenses are expenses that you have paid for in advance and that will expire in the next twelve months. For example, insurance, rent and electricity are often prepaid.

Non-current assets These include investments, property, plant and equipment and intangibles. **Financial assets** are items such as shares, investment property and fixed interest securities. It is common for such financial assets to be a strategic stake in another business. For example, you may own a 5 per cent holding in a key supplier or customer.

There are a number of different types of **property** – freehold land, freehold buildings, leasehold land or leasehold buildings. You should disclose land and buildings separately.

Plant and equipment includes machinery, computer systems and software, telephone systems, motor vehicles, etc. You will need to take into account those items' depreciation. This is a process which recognises that the value of an asset typically reduces over time due to obsolescence and wear and tear. Depreciation is a way of allocating the cash of purchasing an asset over its useful life. Assets that do not decline in value, such as land, are not depreciated.

Intangibles include brand names (also called trade names), broadcasting licences, franchises, patents, mastheads (such as newspaper and magazine titles) and goodwill. Unlike fixed assets, some intangibles, such as brand names, are typically not depreciated by companies as they have an indefinite useful life and therefore may never diminish in value. Intangibles, including goodwill, generated internally by a business cannot be recognised in the balance sheet. It is calculated as the purchase price less the fair value of the net assets acquired. As with fixed assets, intangible assets with indefinite lives and goodwill are subject to an annual assessment of impairment. A recoverable amount is calculated for the asset or for the group of assets. If the recoverable amount calculated is less than its book carrying value, the asset must be written down. Impairment testing is a complex area, and your company should seek advice and assistance from your accountant.

The depreciation of goodwill under Australian GAAP is not permitted. Both the ability to classify intangibles as having an indefinite life and the non-depreciation of goodwill are recent developments. These are part of the recently adopted Australian Equivalents to International Reporting Standards (AIFRS).

Liabilities Liabilities are future sacrifices of economic benefits that the company is presently obliged to make to other companies as a result of past transactions or events. These are typically debts owed by the business to third parties for services or products purchased and financing, such as trade creditors and loans. Liabilities are classified as current liabilities if they are expected to be paid out within twelve months of the balance date. Other liabilities are classified as non-current liabilities.

Current liabilities The main types of current liabilities are trade creditors, borrowings, accrued expenses and provisions. **Trade creditors** are the amounts you owe to suppliers for goods and services received but not paid for by the balance date. **Borrowings** are the amounts owing to lenders at the balance date and due for repayment within one year, such as overdrafts, bank loans, and finance lease liabilities. **Accrued expenses** are obligations that the business has incurred, such as wages, but for which no formal invoice has been received. **Provisions** are a way of recognising a transaction that has occurred but for which the date or exact amount of repayment is uncertain. Common examples are taxes, dividends (if declared) and annual leave for staff. As provisions are usually areas of significant accounting estimates, Australian accounting requirements have become more prescriptive in detailing the nature of items that can or cannot be provided for. General provisions for non-specific events are not allowable under Australian GAAP.

Non-current liabilities   These are liabilities that are not due for repayment for at least twelve months from balance date. Any part of a non-current liability that falls due within one year from the balance sheet date would be listed as part of the current liabilities. The most common forms of non-current liabilities are bank loans, long-term lease liabilities and provisions for employee entitlements.

Equity   Equity is the residual interest in the assets of the company after deducting liabilities. It usually represents the capital contributed by the owners or shareholders plus any earnings or reserves that have been retained in the business.

Income statements

The income statement, also commonly referred to as the profit and loss statement (P&L), is a summary of all the revenues generated by the business and all expenses incurred in obtaining the revenue. The P&L shows the profit or loss over a certain period of time.

Sales and services   This is the amount disclosed as sales revenue for the whole period, whether in cash or by credit, net of discounts, allowances and returned goods.

Cost of sales   To calculate the cost of sales, add the amount of stock purchased at cost during the period to the opening stock, then subtract the closing stock. Closing stock is often determined by doing a physical stocktake at the end of the previous period. If your business provides services, you can include an allocation of those wages directly involved in providing the service.

Annandale Rocks Pty Ltd
Income statement for the year ending 30 June 2006

	2006	2005
	$	$
Sales	1 300 000	1 000 000
Services and advertising	700 000	200 000
Total sales	2 000 000	1 200 000
Cost of sales:		
Opening stock	(250 000)	(150 000)
Purchases	(590 000)	(490 000)
Less closing stock	240 000	140 000
Gross profit	1 400 000	700 000
Operating expenses:		
Salaries and wages	350 000	200 000
Accounting and legal	30 000	20 000
Depreciation	353 333	20 000
Amortisation of brand name	20 000	—
Occupancy	40 000	40 000
General/administration	50 000	40 000
Marketing and advertising	100 000	5 000
Purchase of customer list	200 000	—
IT/software costs	30 000	5 000
Credit card fees	30 000	—
Interest	84 000	—
Net profit before tax	112 667	370 000
Income tax expense	(47 760)	(133 200)
Net profit after tax	64 907	236 800

Gross profit   To calculate gross profit deduct the cost of sales from sales.

Operating expenses   The next step is to calculate your operating expenses. This section should be tailored to fit the needs of your business. You divide your expenses into categories that permit useful analysis of the major cost drivers. Typical operating expenses include:

- salaries and wages – including payments to permanent staff (salary) and casual staff (wages) and on-costs, such as payroll tax, superannuation contributions and long-service leave accruals
- accounting and legal – those fees paid for professional accounting, tax and legal advice
- depreciation – non-cash expenses representing an apportionment of the cost of fixed assets and intangibles over a number of years
- interest expenses – all interest payments to lenders, excluding principal repayments
- general – covering administrative costs, such as postage, telephone and stationery
- marketing and advertising – the cost of purchasing advertising space in magazines, etc. and associated costs, such as commissions and samples
- occupancy – rent, electricity, insurance, rates, repairs and maintenance.

Net profit (loss) before tax   When operating expenses have been deducted from gross profit, the figure obtained is net profit (loss) before tax. If your business earns revenue from non-operating sources, such as rent, dividends or interest, it should be added to net profit before tax.

Income tax expense   This item represents the amount of income tax that is attributable to the net profit before tax.

The income tax expense is affected by whether your business is organised as a trust, partnership or company. The amount of tax to be paid is the provision for income tax that is recognised in the balance sheet as an amount payable to a creditor, being the Australian Taxation Office. The principal difference between your income tax expense and provision is due to the fact that some expenses in the accounting profit or loss account may not be deductible expenses for taxation purposes in the current year, or at all in the future, such as certain types of entertainment expenses.

Net profit after tax   The last item on the profit and loss statement is net profit after tax, which is calculated by deducting income tax expense from net profit before tax.

Cashflow statements

The primary purpose of the cashflow statement is to reconcile the operating profit from your profit and loss account to the movement in cash balances during a period so that the cash performance of the company can be measured.

The cashflow statement will help you determine whether you can pay your employees and suppliers, and meet repayments on the loans which your business may have. Your business may be profitable but due to short-term reasons, such as waiting for payments on sales or having to pay upfront for your stock until you prove your credit worthiness, still require additional finance or short-term credit facilities.

A cashflow statement per Australian GAAP splits the receipts and payments of cash into three principal areas – cash from operating activities, such as sales and purchases; cash flow from investing activities, such as purchases of fixed assets; and cash flow from financing activities, such as the proceeds obtained from drawing down a bank loan.

A cashflow statement for your business can take a variety of forms, however the key aspects are that it:

- reconciles the movement in cash to the operating profit (without this, you will not know whether you have missed any items)
- reconciles the opening cash balance to the closing cash balance for a period so that you can review the movements of cash through your business.

The cashflow statements that meet Australian GAAP requirements are quite complicated. Opposite is an example of a simple cashflow statement.

EBIT   Earnings Before Interest and Tax is the starting point for your cashflow statement – your accounting profit or loss before interest and tax. This will allow you to reconcile your profit or loss to your movement in cash. Even if you made a profit during a period, your company may still have been using a large volume of cash.

Non-cash items   The first major difference between the accounting profit and your actual cash flow will be items such as depreciation and amortisation charges. When your business purchases an asset, there is a cash outflow to buy the asset. For accounting purposes this asset is held in the balance sheet and depreciated through the profit and loss account over the useful life of the asset, i.e. how long you expect it to produce income. Therefore the depreciation charges in the profit and loss are just accounting entries and not actual cash flows. They need to be added back to the profit to reflect the fact that no cash flow occurred.

Annandale Rocks Pty Ltd
Cashflow statement

	2006	2005
	$	$
EBIT	196 667	370 000
Add: Non-cash items		
Depreciation and amortisation		
charge	373 333	20 000
Tax expense	47 760	133 200
Add/less: Movements in working capital		
Movement in debtors	(285 000)	(100 000)
Movement in creditors	88 000	10 000
Movement in inventory/prepayments	(100 000)	(50 000)
Taxes paid	(79 520)	(100 000)
Net cashflow before investing and		
financing activities	241 240	283 200
Less: Investing items		
Capital expenditure	(1 000 000)	(100 000)
Customer list	(200 000)	—
Add/less: Financing		
Net borrowings and repayments	600 000	—
Capital contribution	600 000	—
Net movement in cash	241 240	183 200
Opening cash balance per the balance sheet	50 000	(133 200)
Closing cash balance per the balance sheet	291 240	50 000
Movement per the balance sheet	241 240	183 200

Movements in working capital

Your company's working capital is made up principally of debtors, creditors and inventory. The movement in these items between periods will impact on the actual cashflow and the profit and loss account.

Put simply, a sale of $500 made to a regular customer who pays the account immediately has no effect on the cash flow, as the $500 is shown in the profit and loss account. But if the customer pays sixty days later your cash flow is affected as your business has to wait for its money. Effectively the movement in your working capital reflects the difference between accounting recognition for the transaction in the profit and loss account, and the time when the cash flow actually occurs.

Investing items   Investing items are typically purchases of fixed assets, and investments in shares and other companies, etc. Your cashflow statement should separate out these items so you can see the difference between your operating cash flow, and your cash flow after your investing activities. The reason for this is that operating cash flow will show you whether the business is cashflow generative or not on its day-to-day activities. The investing items should be assessed separately as hopefully they should generate cash flows in the future.

Financing items   Financing activities are typically the sources of capital for the company, being the issue of new shares, bank loans, etc. These items are set out separately to help you assess what the cash from these loans is being used for.

BUSINESS PERFORMANCE ANALYSIS AND FINANCIAL RATIOS

All financial models used to determine business viability and performance comparability revolve around the same theme, being the total return on the investment. That is, how much value is being created in the business through profits, capital growth and any other means.

Business performance can be measured using any array of

performance indicators, financial and non-financial. You will often hear commentary regarding a business's key performance indicators (KPI). A KPI is a measure of business performance against an indicator that the business has set itself as a target. For example, a predetermined return on shareholder equity may be a financial KPI for the company based on its overall result for the period, whereas the percentage of stock requiring rework in a manufacturing process is an example of a non-financial KPI. This KPI would be measuring the quality of the manufacturing process.

The process of analysing your business and setting KPIs for the overall performance is very important, as well as setting KPIs for all sub-processes within the business. The KPIs set, if monitored properly, will help you determine where there are problems in your business and highlight areas that are successful. Close monitoring can also assist in determining at an early stage where things are going off the rails and provide you with time to remedy the situation.

Return on equity

To most business owners and investors, the key overriding factor at the end of the day is the return on equity. That is, for each dollar invested in the business, how many you are getting in return. This is important because if your business is doing very poorly it may be better to put your money in the bank where there is very little risk in obtaining the return. For most investors, the higher the risk the higher the expected return. The providers of capital or finance will want returns commensurate with the risk of the investment, which may be significant given the number of businesses that do not succeed.

The return on equity is derived from two distinct factors, being:

- the ability of the company to earn profits
- capital appreciation in the value of the equity held in the company.

Financial ratio analysis

Financial ratio analysis looks at liquidity measures and management efficiency, and ultimately measures the return on equity from the profits of the business. It does this by measuring the relationship between the various elements contained in the financial statements.

Ratios provide a basis for comparing a business's financial statements, utilising:

- historical ratios, which allow us to assess a trend over time
- benchmarking ratios, by assessing the financial ratios of similar businesses or industry averages
- rule-of-thumb standards, which provide acceptable minimum or maximum ratios to assess the reasonableness of the company's performance – these are based on norms for different industries.

Financial ratios are also used by banks, potential investors and creditors to evaluate your business. These parties may use them to determine whether to lend, invest or sell goods or services to your company. It is not uncommon for banks to stipulate that certain financial ratios be maintained as part of a loan agreement.

There are endless permutations of financial ratios. Some ratios are used specifically in some industries and not in others. Ratios may be used to evaluate the ongoing financial performance of your business or to help derive a value for your business as part of determining the sale price. Ratio analysis is very important in determining the value of a company because the net assets in the balance sheet rarely reflect the actual value of the business; they generally reflect a mixture of historical cost and current market values.

Ratios will give you an overall view of a business's performance and, importantly, the return on equity derived from current period profits.

Sources of data There is a large amount of data available about ratios for different Australian industries, including industry groups and trade associations, chambers of commerce, the Australian Stock Exchange (ASX), the Financial Management Research Centre (which publishes a report *Small Business Profile for Various Industries*), stockbroker reports, and the web sites of individual companies – try looking at companies listed on the ASX operating in a similar industry to yours. Even though these companies may be a hundred times the size of your business you can see how the industry you operate in analyses companies.

Tips for calculating When calculating ratios:
- check that the result appears reasonable – if it is unusually high/low then check you have calculated it correctly
- ensure that the ratio has true relevance for the business you are examining, for example inventory-based ratios are less useful for service businesses
- remember that rules of thumb are not absolute – you must consider all the circumstances and make your own decision based on all the facts.

Background to example When analysing the ratios of a company it is important to understand the business. Our fictional company, Annandale Rocks, is no different. The following are key events that occurred during the accounting period.

In 2005 Annandale Rocks is a retailer of jewellery operating out of a local store. The co-owners are two friends from school, both with keen eyes for jewellery. At the beginning of the 2006 year their online trading and e-business booms and they decide it is time to action their plans to move further into e-commerce. Using their valuation knowledge, they decide to launch an online valuation service. To target their marketing, they purchase a customer list of high-wealth individuals.

For an online valuation, customers can either provide their credit-card details prior to the valuation taking place or pay on account with prior approval. The valuation charges vary on a sliding scale depending on the item being valued. The account customers can also purchase items of jewellery through the web site.

To complete their e-business plans, Annandale Rocks manages to obtain venture capital funding. In exchange for cash of $600 000 and a loan of $600 000 over three years, the investor takes 50 per cent equity in the company.

Three months into the year, the only other online jewellery valuation business on the Internet, eJewel, is forced to liquidate its business. This is a result of the technology stockmarket crash and some poor management decision-making, resulting in the company spending all its cash on brand marketing. Annandale Rocks, sensing a great opportunity to leverage the brand of a first-to-market player, purchases the eJewel brand for $200 000 and rebadges www.arocks.com.au to www.ejewel.com.au. The company uses the remaining funds injected into the business by spending $1 million on developing the web site, related hardware and specialised online valuation software.

The following types of ratios will help to assess Annandale Rocks' performance:
• liquidity ratios

- management efficiency ratios
- overall profitability ratios.

Liquidity ratio

Liquidity ratios test whether the business can meet its current financial commitments as and when they fall due.

Current ratio This shows the current assets available to meet current liabilities.

$$\text{Current ratio} = \frac{\text{Current assets}}{\text{Current liabilities}} = \frac{\$991\,240}{\$300\,000} = \quad 3.3 \quad 1.7$$

	2006	2005

A current ratio of 3.3 to 1 means that current assets equal over three times the current liabilities. The rule of thumb is that the current ratio should be about 1.5 or better. There should be a reasonable excess of current assets to cover current liabilities.

The increase between the years for Annandale Rocks is due to the expansion of the business – debtors have increased substantially, and there has been an increase in stock as well, but the main growth area of the business has been the valuation service, which does not involve the sale of stock.

Acid test ratio This shows the ability of a business's more liquid assets to cover current liabilities.

$$\text{Acid test ratio} = \frac{\text{Current assets} - \text{Inventories}}{\text{Current liabilities}}$$

$$= \frac{\$991\,240 - 240\,000}{\$300\,000} = \quad 2.5 \quad 1.06$$

Inventories are excluded because when sold on credit they become a trade debtor before they become cash. The rule of thumb for the acid test is 1.0 times. It is worth noting that Annandale Rocks' business has changed significantly during the period with a large portion of the business now a valuation e-business. The result is that debtors have increased substantially more than stock, as 35 per cent of sales do not involve stock.

Times interest cover ratio   This shows the ability of the company to service its debt obligations.

$$
\begin{array}{ll}
 & 2006 \quad 2005 \\
\text{Times interest cover} = \dfrac{\text{Profit before interest and tax}}{\text{Interest expense}} & \\
= \dfrac{\$196\,667}{\$84\,000} & = \quad 2.3 \quad \text{N/A}
\end{array}
$$

The ratio is only relevant for the 2006 year as in 2005 the company had no loans. A result of 2.3 indicates that the company can cover 2.3 times its current interest expense and still earn a profit, albeit a diminishing one. This ratio is of particular interest to the financiers of Annandale Rocks' bank loan.

Management efficiency
These ratios measure how well management controls working capital.

Days debtors ratio   This shows how many days it takes to collect cash from debtors.

<table>
<tr><td></td><td></td><td></td><td>2006</td><td>2005</td></tr>
</table>

Debtor days $= \dfrac{\text{Closing trade debtors}}{\text{Sales}} \times (365 \text{ days})$

$= \dfrac{\$450\,000}{\$2\,000\,000} \times 365$ $= \quad 82 \quad 50$

Although Annandale Rocks is turning over a far larger sales volume than last year, the increase in debtors is greater in proportion and it is taking the company longer to collect its debts. The increase in debtor days is often a sign to have a good look at the balance to see whether all the debtors recognised are actually collectable.

Days inventory ratio   This shows how many days it takes to sell inventory from the time raw materials are purchased.

<table>
<tr><td></td><td></td><td></td><td>2006</td><td>2005</td></tr>
</table>

Days inventory $= \dfrac{\text{Closing inventory}}{\text{Cost of sales}} \times (365 \text{ days})$

$= \dfrac{\$240\,000}{\$600\,000} \times 365$ $= \quad 146 \quad 102$

This ratio highlights the performance of the sales of goods, i.e. the items of jewellery side of Annandale Rocks' business. Although sales are increasing at a total level of 67 per cent, the sale of product has only increased by 30 per cent and inventory has increased by 71 per cent, therefore leading to an increase in inventory days. Once again, when we see an increase in the inventory days it is time to look at the stock on hand to determine if all items are saleable at the current price recorded in the books or whether some stock needs to be written off or down to NRV.

274 The Penguin Small Business Guide

Note that use of this formula will vary between industries, with supermarkets using hours and other industries using months as the relevant numerator in the formula.

Cost to income ratio   This details management's ability to control costs as compared to income earned. This is particularly important for service type organisations.

2006   2005

$$\text{Cost to income} = \frac{\text{Costs before tax excluding interest}}{\text{Sales}}$$

$$= \frac{\$1\,203\,333 \times 100}{\$2\,000\,000} \qquad = \quad 60\% \quad 28\%$$

This ratio highlights that the business is moving to a greater fixed-cost basis in the 2004 year. Some of the major costs in 2004 are depreciation and the customer list acquisition. If these two were excluded the ratio would be 30 per cent, very similar to the prior year. However, if Annandale Rocks can drive its valuation volume up, it will flow through to profits with little incremental cost, increasing profits and improving this ratio.

Profitability ratios
Gross margin   This measures the average profit on sales before the deduction of cost of sales.

2006   2005

$$\text{Gross margin} = \frac{\text{Gross profit}}{\text{Sales}} = \frac{\$1\,400\,000 \times 100}{\$2\,000\,000} = \quad 70\% \quad 58\%$$

Gross margin varies tremendously between industries. Once again we must note here that the change in the business has affected this ratio. The gross margin of Annandale Rocks has increased as the cost of sales in this ratio is principally stock. However, 71 per cent of the increased sales came through valuations income, where there is no associated stock cost. The increased cost for these sales is incurred in the operating expense lines, i.e. salaries, depreciation etc., which are not included in this ratio.

Net margin   This measures the profitability of sales after the operating expenses from gross profit.

2006   2005

$$\text{Net profit margin} = \frac{\text{Net profit before tax}}{\text{Sales}}$$

$$= \frac{\$112\,667 \times 100}{\$2\,000\,000} \qquad = \quad 6\% \quad 31\%$$

The increased salary and depreciation charges in 2004 have impacted this ratio. This ratio highlights the differences in ratios. Annandale Rocks, now being 35 per cent a service company, has a ratio that reflects the change in the business. A service company has a higher proportion of operating expenses than cost of sales and this is reflected in the result of this ratio. The low net margin reflects the increased salary and depreciation charges from the web site development.

Return on assets (ROA)   This measures how profitably the business's assets are being employed. The acceptable ROA varies between different industries.

2006 2005

Return on
assets

$$= \frac{\text{Net profit before tax}}{\text{Total assets}}$$

$$= \frac{\$112\,667 \times 100}{\$1\,952\,907}$$

$= \quad 6\% \quad 62\%$

The large reduction in the return on assets is due to the substantial increase in the assets utilised by the business in the 2004 year. This is principally a result of the web site development and the fact that the asset base of the traditional business in 2003 was very low.

Return on equity   The final ratio analyses the return on equity. This ratio measures the rate of profit earnt on shareholders' equity. ROE can be used to compare the earning capacity of the shareholder's investment in that business with returns in alternative investments.

2006 2005

Return on
equity

$$= \frac{\text{Net profit before tax}}{\text{Shareholders' equity}}$$

$$= \frac{\$112\,667 \times 100}{\$1\,052\,907}$$

$= \quad 11\% \quad 95\%$

The movement in the return on shareholders' equity reflects the discussion in the return on assets section above, as well as the additional equity contributed in the 2005 year. However, the return on equity is higher than the return on assets as the company has leverage from earning income from borrowed funds.

FINANCIAL STRUCTURE ANALYSIS

The decision to finance via debt or to inject capital into a company is key to its financial stability. Excessive debt may overly expose the company to changes in the business environment and ultimately liquidation. Conversely, under-utilisation of debt may starve the company of funds and reduce the potential return on investment through lack of leverage of owner's equity. The leverage ratio measures the ownership of total assets.

$$\text{Leverage ratio} = \frac{\text{Total equity}}{\text{Total assets}} = \frac{\$1\,052\,907}{\$1\,952\,907} = \begin{array}{cc} 2006 & 2005 \\ 54\% & 65\% \end{array}$$

The reduction in the percentage reflects the issue of debt during the period. An important question with no absolute answer in financial management is how much debt a company can take on and continue to have long-term viability. The answer is that the acceptable proportion of debt varies between different types of companies and industries, and monitoring this against peer companies will indicate how potential investors and providers of finance will assess your company's financial structure.

SENSITIVITY ANALYSIS

Analysing your business via incremental changes in each of the variables that contribute to the overall return on assets of your company is known as sensitivity analysis. The basic principle behind sensitivity analysis is that relationships are not usually linear, and that if a key variable is changed by a certain percentage, the related change in the percentage and gross return on equity will usually be different.

The following table illustrates the change in return on total equity that results from changing each key input variable by 10 per cent. Sensitivity analysis puts you in a position to rank the key input variables of your company from the most effective to the least effective in maximising your return on owner's equity.

SENSITIVITY ANALYSIS

Key input variable	Change	Net profit before tax	Net profit margin	ROA	ROE	Change in ROE
Sales price	+10%	$200 000	16%	16%	30%	+19%
Cost of sales	−10%	60 000	9%	9%	16%	+5%
Operating costs	−10%	129 000	12%	12%	23%	+12%
Total assets	−10%	35 333	7.4%	8.4%	16%	+5%

An increase in price is far more effective than any other key input variable, whereas reducing assets has very little effect. The sensitivity of return on owner's equity to changes in key input variable can differ significantly between different types of businesses. However, it is worth noting that the increase in price could result in an offsetting decrease in volume.

FINANCIAL REPORTING FOR COMPANIES

Financial reporting requirements for companies vary greatly, depending on the type of company, its size and the users of the information regarding the company. This section does not detail the multitude of tax-related reporting to the Australian Tax Office, such as payroll tax returns, Business Activity

Statement (BAS) returns, annual income tax returns etc., or other non-financial reporting to the Australian Securities and Investments Commission (ASIC). Information on these detailed requirements can be obtained from the ATO (**www.ato.gov.au**) and ASIC (**www.asic.gov.au**).

The level of statutory financial reporting required by the *Corporations Act* is summarised in the following table.

Type of company	Description	Level of reporting
Corporate trustee/ dormant company	No immediate end users of financial information.	Generally not required to prepare a financial report under the *Corporations Act*.
Small proprietary company	To be classified a small proprietary company at least two of the following conditions must be met at the end of the financial year: • consolidated gross operating revenue less than $10 million • consolidated gross asset value less than $5 million • less than fifty employees.	Generally not required to prepare a financial report under the *Corporations Act* except if: • a shareholder with a holding greater than 5 per cent requests it – this report does not require audit or lodgement with ASIC unless specifically requested by the shareholders, and the shareholders can specify which accounting standards it needs to comply with

Type of company	Description	Level of reporting
		• ASIC makes a request • the company is controlled by a foreign entity. The company must however, in all situations, maintain appropriate books and records that can properly explain the transactions and financial position of the company.
Large proprietary company	Any proprietary company that does not satisfy two of the three conditions for a small proprietary company. (It should be noted that at the time of writing these criteria are under review.)	Financial reporting to ASIC complying with Australian Accounting Standards (AASB) and audited.
Listed company	Any company listed on the Australian Stock Exchange.	Same as a large proprietary company and needs to report to ASX at least every half year and year end as well as ASX continuous disclosure requirements.

It is worth noting that in many industries, such as banking and insurance, there are a multitude of government and semi-government organisations that require specific financial-related performance reporting in order for businesses to keep their licences and maintain other regulatory compliance.

There are a number of reliefs that ASIC will give regarding financial reporting if certain criteria are met by the company. There is also a concept known as the reporting entity, which can apply to some of the companies noted above and override the level of financial reporting required. In short, a reporting entity must comply with AASBs.

For financial years ending on or after 1 January 2005, companies are required to comply with the Australian equivalents to International Financial Reporting Standards (AIFRS), including prior year comparatives. Whilst AASBs have been converging with International Financial Reporting Standards (IFRS) over recent years, significant differences remain in areas such as accounting and disclosing financial instruments, business combinations and fixed assets and the impairment of assets, to name a few. By 30 June 2006 the majority of Australian companies will have prepared financial statements in accordance with AIFRS.

In reality, the driver of the level of financial reporting of most businesses of any kind will be the requirements of the providers of capital and finance. Your venture capital partners, banks and private investors will have certain financial reporting requirements to allow them to monitor your business and, most importantly to them, how their investment in your business is performing.

12. PROFIT FORECASTING

- **What is profit forecasting?**
- **Understanding costs**
- **Profit analysis techniques**
- **Applying profit analysis**
- **Establishing a profit forecast**
- **Reviewing a profit forecast**

This chapter aims to assist you to determine your business's future profitability and establish whether the costs involved in operating your business will generate sufficient profit to justify launching or continuing operations.

WHAT IS PROFIT FORECASTING?

There are three key issues that this chapter will help you navigate.

- **Evaluating operations** – once your business is operational, profit forecasts allow you to compare your actual results with the projections. This gives you a standard against which you can evaluate sales performance and cost control and provides early warning signs of any trouble.

- **Identifying resource requirements** – forecasting the expected volume of sales to assist you to manage the amount and timing of stock orders. Understanding your cost structure will help you determine profitability and identify the resources your business needs and when you will need them.

- **Anticipating financing needs** – once you have estimated what resources will be needed you can begin the search for capital as soon as possible. In turn, a realistic profit forecast will inspire the confidence of potential investors.

To forecast your profit you need to forecast key relationships between sales volume, your business's cost structure and pricing policy, and their combined impact on profitability. A simple example will demonstrate the pitfalls that can occur when estimating your profit.

Bob wants to launch a new web site selling mobile phones on the Internet. He estimates that renting a warehouse, buying equipment and building a web site will cost $300 000. He knows the phones can be bought wholesale for $50. He estimates that he will sell 15 000 phones in the first year of trading at a sales price of $100 per phone. His initial calculations based on this information look like this:

Sales revenue (15 000 × $100)	$1 500 000
Less cost of stock (15 000 × $50)	$ 750 000
Less rent and web site costs	$ 300 000
Profit	$ 450 000

Bob, excited by the prospects of making a fortune, quits his high-paying job and asks for seed funding from Uncle Buck. The first question Buck asks is, 'What happens if you only sell half that number?' Bob's instant response is, 'No worries, we'll still make a tidy profit of $225 000 – that's half the profit.' Buck explains, however, that profits will not be exactly halved because not all the expenses have the same characteristics. The cost of stock will logically be reduced by half – only 7500 phones will be purchased for stock. Even if Bob fails to sell a single phone he is still going to have to rent the warehouse, buy equipment, and build the web site. These costs remain the same. So his calculations will now look like this:

Sales revenue (7500 × $100)	$750 000
Less cost of stock (7500 × $50)	$375 000
Less rent and web site	$300 000
Profit	$ 75 000

Bob, undaunted, explains he will simply increase the sales price by 25 per cent, thereby recouping profit lost through reduced sales. The problem, however, in selling phones at $125 is that, given the competitive market, the business will sell even fewer phones. The new calculations would be:

Sales revenue (3000 × $125)	$ 375 000
Less cost of stock (3000 × $50)	$ 150 000
Less rent and web site	$ 300 000
Loss	$ (75 000)

This brief example demonstrates that the three factors that drive profit – sales volume, selling price and costs – are interrelated. Changing one factor may have a major impact on the other factors.

UNDERSTANDING COSTS

In general, there are two types of costs – fixed and variable.

Fixed costs

These are the costs you will have to pay out regardless of the volume of business you are processing. The costs of permanent staff, renting premises and buying extra equipment are all examples of fixed costs. These costs are fixed in the sense that over a short period of time, say twelve months, and for a certain range of sales activity, they are unlikely to change much, if at all. Obviously costs are never truly fixed for a long period of time because, as demand for your products and services grows, so too will your demand for more staff, larger premises, more equipment and so on.

Variable costs

These are costs which vary in direct proportion with changes in sales volume. An example of variable costs are inventories – goods will be manufactured or purchased in direct proportion with sales.

The chart below demonstrates how variable and fixed costs change with sales volume.

INTERACTION BETWEEN FIXED AND VARIABLE COSTS

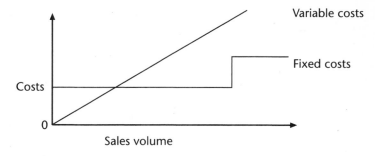

In determining whether a cost is fixed or variable, the fundamental question that needs to be answered is: do the costs change if sales volumes change? You will note from the chart that fixed costs often 'step up' at a certain sales volume, e.g. when additional warehouse space is required to be rented to house more stock. Whilst this point is not dealt with in depth in this chapter, it should be taken into account when reviewing fixed costs. The following table lists some common costs that are typically divided between fixed and variable, however it must be noted that fixed costs for one business may be variable for another. For example, the electricity costs for a company which provides consulting services would generally be fixed, but for a manufacturer operating machinery they would vary with volume of product produced.

EXAMPLES OF FIXED AND VARIABLE COSTS

Fixed	Variable
salaries	inventories
marketing	wages
rent	marketing
insurance	sales commissions
rates	transport costs
depreciation	volume discounts
electricity	royalties
maintenance	
interest	
funding costs	

It is important to understand that items of a capital nature are not a cost, for the purposes of profit forecasting. It is the depreciation of the capital items that needs to be taken into account in profit forecasting and this cost would typically be a fixed cost. The actual purchasing of capital items needs to be taken into account in cash flow forecasts to ensure that funding facilities are available to purchase the assets.

Analysing costs

Throughout the remainder of this chapter we will use the previously mentioned Annandale Rocks business to highlight the concepts being discussed. The following table categorises the costs from the Annandale Rocks profit and loss account (see chapter eleven) into fixed and variable costs.

COSTS OF ANNANDALE ROCKS

	Variable costs ($)	Fixed costs ($)	Total ($)
Sales revenue			2 000 000
Cost of sales	600 000		
Operating expenses:			
Salaries (executives)		200 000	
Wages (casual staff)	150 000		
Accounting and legal		30 000	
Depreciation		353 333	
Amortisation of brand name		20 000	
Occupancy		40 000	
General/administration		50 000	
Marketing and advertising	100 000		
Purchase of customer list		200 000	
IT/software costs		30 000	
Credit-card fees	30 000		
Interest		84 000	
Total costs	880 000	1 007 333	1 887 333
Net profit before tax			112 667

It is worth noting that this allocation process will require some assumptions to be made. For instance, advertising costs are a classic example of a semi-fixed cost. Rightly or wrongly, advertising is often cut by companies when sales volumes are not met. Therefore, it often is more variable than fixed. For the purposes of this example it has been classified as variable, however it is an example of when you need to understand your business and how you run your business to understand its cost structure.

Annandale Rocks has $880 000 in variable costs with sales of $2 000 000. Therefore, the proportion of variable cost is 44 per cent of sales revenue. Using this figure we can estimate the profit or loss for various levels of sales.

ESTIMATES OF PROFIT AND LOSS FOR VARIOUS LEVELS OF SALES

Sales	Variable cost	Fixed cost	Total cost	Profit (loss)
$	$	$	$	$
0	0	1 007 333	1 007 333	(1 007 333)
1 500 000	660 000	1 007 333	1 667 333	(167 333)
2 000 000	880 000	1 007 333	1 887 333	112 667
2 500 000	1 100 000	1 007 333	2 107 333	392 667

As Annandale Rocks has a number of different products and services, it has been assumed that changes in sales volumes affects each of the products and services in proportion to the actual sales mix achieved when $2 000 000 in sales is achieved. This assumption is required as each product and service would have different contribution margins. This concept is discussed later in the chapter.

As you can see, Annandale Rocks needs to turn over between $1.5 million and $2 million to start making a profit.

PROFIT ANALYSIS TECHNIQUES

One of the key questions you need to be able to answer in determining a profit plan is the break-even point, i.e. how much you are required to sell before you start making money. In the previous example we determined that it was somewhere between $1.5 and $2 million, but how much is it exactly? Before calculating this, there is an important concept that should be understood called the contribution margin.

Contribution margin

The contribution margin is a measure of what percentage of your product sales value goes towards offsetting your business's fixed cost. A business with no sales will have a loss equal to its fixed costs and each dollar of sales contributes to a decrease in that loss. The contribution margin is the difference between a dollar of sales and the rate of variable cost per dollar of sales. In the case of Annandale Rocks, sales are $2 000 000 and variable costs are $880 000.

$$\text{Contribution margin} = \frac{\text{Sales} - \text{Variable costs}}{\text{Sales}}$$

$$= \frac{\$2\,000\,000 - \$880\,000}{\$2\,000\,000} = 56\%$$

Once the contribution margin in dollar value has reached the same dollar value of fixed costs, it becomes the rate at which sales contribute to profit. Beyond the break-even point, every dollar of sales will contribute a rate of profit equal to the contribution margin.

The higher the contribution margin, the greater proportion of fixed costs a business has. The reason is that the variable cost for each sale dollar is low. The flip side, however, is that a higher level of sales is required to break even as the quantum of the fixed costs is higher. It is typical of service type companies to have a higher contribution margin than traditional manufacturers.

The key driver in using this profitability measure is understanding your cost structure, as it is a critical component in the contribution margin equation.

Calculating the break-even point

The break-even point is calculated by dividing the fixed costs by the contribution margin.

$$\text{Break-even point} = \frac{\text{Fixed costs}}{\text{Contribution margin}} = \frac{\$1\,007\,333}{56\%} = \$1\,798\,809$$

The profitability tolerance is the difference between the break-even point and the current level of sales. It indicates the extent to which sales volume may decline before the business operates at a loss. Expressed as a percentage of current sales, Annandale Rocks has a profitability tolerance of 10 per cent.

$$\text{Profitability tolerance} = \frac{\text{Current sales} - \text{Break-even point}}{\text{Current sales}}$$

$$= \frac{\$2\,000\,000 - \$1\,798\,809}{\$2\,000\,000} = 10\%$$

The higher the profitability tolerance, the sounder the sales position is. Annandale Rocks could absorb a 10 per cent decline in sales volume before incurring a loss.

APPLYING PROFIT ANALYSIS

There are some key questions that you will face as a business owner in developing a profit forecast. These include:

- What happens to profitability if the selling price increases or decreases?
- What is the increase in the level of sales required to justify additional capital expenditure?
- What additional sales are needed to be generated to justify an increase in a specific running cost?
- What is the contribution margin with respect to individual products sold or services rendered?

Applying the profit analysis methodology discussed above, information can be generated to help answer these questions. It is worth noting that these tools only assist in the decision-making process as there may be strategic or other reasons for making certain decisions.

Changes in selling price

Annandale Rocks wants to cut the average price of all services by 15 per cent in an effort to stimulate sales and increase awareness of its new online business. During the past year sales revenue was $2 000 000, variable cost was $880 000, fixed costs were $1 007 333, and the break-even point was $1 798 809. What level of sales must Annandale Rocks achieve to break even at the lower price? A reduction of 15 per cent in the average price will reduce sales to $1 700 000, assuming at this stage no increase in volume, and lower the contribution margin to 48 per cent.

$$\text{New contribution margin} = \frac{\text{New sales} - \text{Variable cost}}{\text{New sales}}$$

$$= \frac{\$1\,700\,000 - \$880\,000}{\$1\,700\,000} = 48\%$$

With the lower contribution margin of 48 per cent, the new break-even point increases to $2 098 610.

$$\text{New break-even point} = \frac{\text{Fixed costs}}{\text{New contribution margin}}$$

$$= \frac{\$1\,007\,333}{48\%} = \$2\,098\,610$$

A 15 per cent cut in price increases the break-even point from $1 798 809 to $2 098 610. This is a 17 per cent increase in the break-even point. Annandale Rocks will need to assess whether the reduction in prices will stimulate enough extra sales to offset the increase in the break-even point.

New investment

Annandale Rocks is considering the purchase of B2B-capable software for its Internet site. This will add $100 000 in fixed costs per year. Annandale Rocks' contribution margin is currently 56 per cent. How much do sales have to rise to cover the extra fixed costs, assuming the company wants to recoup the costs in one year?

$$\text{Sales increase} = \frac{\text{Increase in fixed costs}}{\text{Contribution margin}} = \frac{\$100\,000}{56\%} = \$178\,571$$

Increasing fixed cost by $100 000 will require extra sales of $178 571, making the total break-even point $1 977 380.

This form of detailed analysis of the company's sales and cost structure will assist a business to obtain external funding, if required, for these sorts of investments. If financiers can see the detailed business case for the investment, then securing funding will be significantly easier.

Cost justification

Annandale Rocks is considering the placement of banner ads on a portal which will cost $2000 per month. Annandale Rocks' contribution margin is 56 per cent. What increase in sales must the banner ads generate every month in order to cover costs?

$$\text{Sales increase} = \frac{\text{Cost of banner ads}}{\text{Contribution margin}} = \frac{\$2000}{56\%} = \$3572$$

Annandale Rocks will need to generate additional sales of $3572 to pay for the banner ads.

ESTABLISHING A PROFIT FORECAST

Earlier we discussed the different types of costs and how they affect the profit or loss given specific changes in the activity of the business. We will now discuss the process of building the profit forecast. Having done so, your forecast can be used to evaluate your operations.

There are many ways you can go about building a forecast and they depend on the stage of your business. An established business has historical data that can be used as a guide for future activities, whereas a startup business with no track record, or a business branching out into new areas, may have to look to industry data or just plain assumptions based on the gut feel of the business owner/manager. While instinct is an important tool in forecasting, applying a little science and discipline is critical in developing a realistic forecast.

The key to profit forecasting is making as many of the underlying assumptions and estimates as realistic as possible. For instance, it is not realistic to increase your sales price by 50 per cent and then forecast a large profit when you know that the market would not bear such an increase. This may seem obvious but in many instances, when a profit estimate doesn't give the result the forecaster is looking for, it is tempting for business owners and managers to just change a couple of variables to ensure the right answer comes out. However, delivering on that answer in reality is a different proposition.

Keep your forecast current so that your profit target remains achievable. Your profit forecast should be revised as often as changing conditions require. The chart opposite illustrates the process of developing the profit forecast for Annandale Rocks in 2007.

Forecasting sales

The first step in building a profit forecast is to prepare a detailed forecast of sales. This is one of the most difficult steps in profit forecasting. A poor sales estimate in either volume or price impacts on your entire forecasting process as many assumptions about costs, such as the number of people you need to employ and equipment required, are affected. If these sales do not materialise and you have forecast to incur fixed costs based on them, then the effect on your forecast can be dramatic.

The best place to start estimating sales is to break down your business into its core products and services. For example, Annandale Rocks has online valuations, retail sales of gems, etc. This allows you to apply differing factors to the anticipated change in sales or, for new products or services, differing take-up factors. For existing products and services, the sales forecast begins by analysing sales for last year.

You will probably find it easier to forecast sales in physical units, such as the number of units sold or the number of clients serviced. The physical units can be calculated into sales dollars when you develop your pricing schedule.

For each sales category you need to consider the factors

PROFIT FORECAST

Annandale Rocks Pty Ltd
Profit forecast
for the year ended 30 June 2007

Sales revenue	$	$
		2 775 000
Cost of sales		
Beginning stock	240 000	
Purchases	588 000	
Less ending stock	(300 000)	528 000
Gross profit (50%)		2 247 000
Operating expenses		
Salaries and wages	850 000	
Accounting and legal	30 000	
Depreciation	453 333	
Amortisation of brand name	20 000	
Occupancy	40 000	
General/administration	60 000	
Marketing and advertising	150 000	
Purchase of customer list	—	
IT/software costs	45 000	
Credit card fees	42 000	
Interest	126 000	1 816 333
Net profit before tax		430 667
Income tax expense		146 427
Net profit after tax		284 240
Proposed dividend		200 000
Addition to retained earnings		84 240

that affect sales. To do this you can develop a business model that maps out:

- the external forces affecting the business, e.g. competition, economic, legal, social, government
- the markets in which your business operates – whether they are expanding, contracting, emerging or mature
- the alliances which your business has – whether they will generate additional sales or save costs
- the customers of your business – whether retail or wholesale, and what is happening to their level of income available to spend on your products and services.

As well as these factors, reviewing the internal forces affecting the company will also help make your sales forecast more accurate. Some of these include reviewing core processes which make/provide your business services, and reviewing your human resources – the availability, experience and competence.

The table opposite represents the 2007 sales forecast for Annandale Rocks. First, actual unit sales for 2006 are divided among product/service lines, being online valuations, retailing precious gems and retailing semi-precious gems. Then total unit sales are multiplied by the 2006 average prices resulting in total revenue of $2 000 000. Next, 2007 unit sales are forecast individually for each product/service line, including a new product for 2007 – online auctioning of precious gems – where Annandale Rocks receives a flat fee of $75 per item.

Annandale Rocks has forecast a 45 per cent increase in unit sales for online valuations, a 10 per cent increase in unit sales for retailing precious gems, and a 50 per cent decrease in unit sales for retailing semi-precious gems. Sales for the new product line have been estimated at 1000, being the conducting of 1000 online auctions in the year.

Annandale Rocks' strategy has been to reposition their

SALES FORECAST

Profit centre	2006		2007	
	Average unit price ($)	Actual units	Unit price ($)	Forecasted units
Online valuations	70	10 000	100	14 500
Retailing precious gems	2 000	500	2 000	550
Retailing semi-precious gems	100	3 000	100	1 500
Online jewellery auctions	75	—	75	1 000
Total units		13 500		17 550
Revenue		$2 000 000		$2 775 000

products and take advantage of their jewellery expertise in the online environment and offer new online services, such as an auction service. Their new product strategy will consist of a narrow product mix with the phasing out of the semi-precious business, which they have determined is not profitable. They expect to be able to increase their unit volume and keep prices constant by mounting a vigorous marketing thrust to build on the eJewel brand and take advantage of the growing use of the Internet for the purchasing of services. This calls for an increase in the advertising and promotion budget. Moreover, Annandale Rocks will need to continue to invest in its IT platform and equipment, including the new auctioning software, and expand its back-up facilities.

Annandale Rocks' objective is to increase unit sales volume by 30 per cent from 13 500 units in 2004 to 17 550 units in 2007. At the same time, they plan to raise the unit price of what they believe will be their largest service – online valuations – by 43 per cent while holding average prices on other product lines. Combined, the increases in unit volume and price are projected to increase sales revenue by 39 per cent from $2 000 000 in 2007 to $2 775 000 in 2008.

Forecasting cost of sales

The next step is to cost all of the product lines that they expect to sell. Annandale Rocks expects the average cost per unit for the retailing business to increase to 10 per cent. With retailing sales of 2050 units, cost of sales will be $528 000. This will produce a gross profit for these product lines of $737 000 and a gross profit margin of 58 per cent. The cost of sales estimate consists of the following items.

- Last year's ending trading stock becomes the next year's beginning trading stock. Annandale Rocks' 2006 balance sheet shows $240 000 in trading stock, which becomes the 2007 beginning stock.
- The total cost of sales, based on an expected retail sales volume of 2050 units, at an average cost of $110 per unit for semi-precious gems and $660 per unit for precious gems, is $588 000.
- The 2007 ending stock is forecast to be $300 000.

The estimate of the amount of the purchases can be worked out by doing the maths backwards.

$$
\begin{aligned}
\text{Cost of sales} &= \text{beginning stock} + \text{purchases} - \text{ending stock} \\
\text{Purchases} &= \text{ending stock} + \text{cost of sales} - \text{beginning stock} \\
&= \$300\,000 + \$528\,000 - \$240\,000 \\
&= \$588\,000
\end{aligned}
$$

It is worth noting that the cost of sales figure has been calculated only for the retailing product lines. The variable costs in the online valuation business and the auctioning business are not considered to be material to the costs of running the business. This is because virtually all costs are of a fixed nature as the IT, staff costs, premises cost, etc. all have to be incurred before one sale is made. Therefore, careful analysis of the operating expenses needs to be undertaken to ensure all expenses have been included.

Forecasting operating expenses

Annandale Rocks' operating expense forecasts are summarised below.

- Salaries and associated costs will increase from $200 000 to $650 000 to employ a brand manager and assistant to help leverage the eJewel brand name, three IT support staff and an auctions manager.
- Wages and associated costs will increase from $150 000 to $200 000 to employ casual staff to handle the increased workload offline of the online business.
- Depreciation will go from $353 333 to $453 333, reflecting the new investment of $300 000 in IT equipment and the auctioning software which will be depreciated over three years.
- Occupancy expense will remain constant at $40 000 as the premises are on a fixed-rate lease.
- General/administration expense will increase from $50 000 to $60 000.
- Marketing expenses will increase from $100 000 to $150 000.
- IT/software costs are expected to increase by 50 per cent to $45 000 as these represent the ongoing maintenance costs and the increase reflects the increase in system usage.
- Credit-card fees are expected to increase at the rate of overall sales to $42 000.

- Interest expense is expected to rise from $84 000 to $126 000, based on $300 000 in new borrowings for the new capital spend.

Total operating expenses are forecast to be $1 816 333 for the year. Net profit before tax is forecast to be $430 667, and net profit after tax will be $284 240. This represents a 338 per cent increase in net profit before tax over 2007. The company intends to pay the shareholders a dividend of $200 000, with $84 240 to be retained in the company.

REVIEWING A PROFIT FORECAST

Once you have completed your profit forecast it is important to rigorously test your assumptions and apply reasonableness tests to ensure it is as accurate as possible.

In the table opposite is a series of actual results and forecast profit and loss statements. All dollar figures have been converted into percentages to permit useful comparison of percentage of sales and expenses from one period to another and to permit comparisons to industry averages. The table contains Annandale Rocks' actual profit and loss statement for the years 2005 and 2006, the forecast for 2007, and the industry averages for the year 2005 (the latest year available). With this information, we can make the comparisons that enable us to evaluate Annandale Rocks' projected profit margins for 2007.

In 2006, Annandale Rocks' gross profit margin was 5.6 per cent of sales. This was a decline of 25.2 per cent over the 2005 gross profit margin of 30.8 per cent. The principal reason was the high costs of setting up the new online business with its higher fixed-cost base. The performance in 2005 was better than the industry average of 26 per cent. It is worth noting, however, that the industry average is for jewellery retailing, a business which in 2007 will only account for

COMMON-SIZE PROFIT AND LOSS STATEMENTS

	2005 actual	2006 actual	2007 forecast	2005 industry average
Sales	100.0	100.0	100.0	100.0
Cost of sales	41.7	30.0	19.0	45.0
Gross profit	58.3	70.0	81.0	55.0
Operating expenses				
Salaries and wages	16.7	17.5	30.6	15.0
Accounting and legal	1.7	1.5	1.0	2.0
Depreciation	1.7	17.7	16.4	2.0
Amortisation of brand name	—	1.0	0.7	—
Occupancy	3.3	2.0	1.4	5.0
General/administration	3.3	2.5	2.1	2.0
Marketing and advertising	0.4	5.0	5.4	2.0
Purchase of customer list	—	10.0	—	—
IT/software costs	0.4	1.5	1.7	1.0
Credit-card fees	—	1.5	1.6	—
Interest	—	4.2	4.5	—
Total	27.5	64.4	65.4	29.0
Net profit	30.8	5.6	15.6	26.0

45 per cent of Annandale Rocks' sales and therefore not be as relevant a benchmark as it was for comparison with 2005. Going forward, the industry used to benchmark the company will have to change to meet the change in the business. The 2007 profit forecast calls for a substantial improvement to 15.6 per cent.

Annandale Rocks' gross profit margin has been improving

significantly each year and exceeds the industry average. How can gross profit margin performance be exceptionally good in the 2006 year and 2007 forecast when the net profit margin performance has not yet reached the levels of 2005? The answer lies in a combination of the business having a higher fixed-cost base and possibly excessive operating expenses. To help determine whether the higher fixed-cost base does not also include excessive operating expenses, that is inefficiency that can be cut out of the business, the cost structure needs to be analysed.

Cost structure

The following table details Annandale Rocks' variable costs and contribution margin.

VARIABLE COST COMPARISON

	2005 actual	2006 actual	2007 forecast
Sales	100.0	100.0	100.0
Variable costs:			
Cost of sales	41.7	30.0	19.0
Wages[1]	8.3	7.5	7.2
Marketing	0.4	5.0	5.4
Other	—	1.5	1.5
Total	50.4	44.0	33.1
Contribution margin	49.6	56.0	66.9

[1] includes variable proportion of salaries and wages only

Annandale Rocks' contribution margin has improved significantly in 2006 and is projected to increase again in 2007. The projected improvement in the contribution margin is principally dependent on the price increases. As such, Annandale

Rocks must be confident that customers will accept the higher prices, otherwise a significant shortfall in profit will occur.

Break-even comparison

To see the effect of the significant increase in fixed costs on the contribution margin, the 2006 actual and 2007 forecast are analysed below.

	2006	2007
Fixed costs	$1 007 333	$1 424 333
divided by		
Contribution margin	56	66.9
equals		
Break-even point	$1 798 809	$2 129 048

The effect of the increase in fixed costs is to increase the break-even point by 18.4 per cent. This increases the risk of variations in sales volume causing the business to make a loss.

A number of profit analysis techniques have been discussed in this chapter. A final point to stress is that all forecasting requires you to make judgment decisions. Once you have completed your analysis you need to stand back from the results and objectively ask yourself, are these projections realistic? It is in this area that your experience and business acumen will have to guide you. If there are some assumptions which you know deep down are a little bullish or overly conservative, challenge them objectively and amend your forecasts if required.

13. MARKETING COMMUNICATIONS

- **Advertising media**
- **Publicity**
- **How to write an advertisement**
- **How much should you spend?**
- **Keeping track of your campaign**
- **The** *Trade Practices Act*

This chapter discusses the main types of advertising media such as mass media (radio, television, newspapers) and more specialised media such as direct mail; it also provides an overview of public relations (such as press releases); how to write an advertisement; and ways of tracking the success of your campaign.

Before embarking on an expensive media campaign, consider:

- **Objective** What do you want this campaign to achieve? Your objective must be more than simply to increase sales – for example, do you want to increase awareness of your brand, attract new customers or persuade existing customers to try new products?
- **Segment** Who are you trying to reach? Carefully consider the target market you are seeking to focus this campaign on (see chapter three for more details).
- **Region** Which geographical area or region are you focusing on? This will be a key driver of the media type which you should use. If you only service a suburb or

regional centre, there is little point undertaking a city- or state-wide television campaign. You are better off using a local newspaper which services your area.

ADVERTISING MEDIA

There are a number of different types of advertising media, including television, radio, newspapers, magazines and journals, public transport, posters and Yellow Pages. The medium that can give your business the most effective result will depend on your advertising budget, your desired image, your target audience and their geographical spread. You can of course use different types of media at the same time.

If your target market covers a broad range of demographics then you should consider using television, radio and newspapers. If your target market is a narrow segment, such as electricians, stockbrokers or lawyers, then the mass media are the most inefficient and expensive means of reaching your market. A niche publication, such as a trade journal, is a cost-effective way to reach your target market whereas a mass media advertisement will reach many people who are not interested in your business. Remember that mass media rates are charged on the basis of deep market reach.

Margaret Gee's Media Guide (**www.mediaguide.com.au**) is updated three times a year and contains a comprehensive listing of radio and television stations, newspapers and magazines in Australia. Other useful features include media contact listings, circulation details, readership profiles and rates.

Television

Television advertising is a powerful medium for reaching a large number of people. It allows you to incorporate visually stimulating images and sounds not possible with newspapers, magazines or radio. Choose the station and broadcast time carefully to match the most likely users and image.

Repeating the same commercial can be boring so consider a range of different commercials either following a theme or with different segments. As with any advertisement, it should clearly identify who you are and how you can be contacted. Ask your friends what their three favourite TV commercials are and then ask them if they can actually name the product in the commercial (in many cases they cannot). A controversial, glamorous or funny ad is not necessarily an effective one. Remember, seek sales not applause.

Television is one of the most expensive media and may be beyond the reach of many small businesses. A prime-time, thirty-second commercial can cost $50 000 or more, while a four-week campaign (including production costs) can cost more than $500 000. You should carefully consider whether a more targeted approach, such as direct mailing, may be more effective. Consider whether this medium matches your image – TV is less than subtle and may not bolster an image based on exclusivity or personal service.

Radio

Radio advertising is another medium for reaching a large number and broad range of people in a local geographical area. According to the Radio Marketing Bureau:

- the majority of people spend some of their media consumption time listening to the radio
- commercial radio reaches almost eight in ten Australians
- commercial radio listeners consistently tune into commercial radio for between eighteen and nineteen hours each week
- listeners are very loyal to their particular radio station – around a third of any given station's audience never listen

to any other radio station – and most people listen to only a small number of stations

- commercial radio has the ability to travel with the consumer as it can be accessed from car, workplace and home.

The loyalty and length of time spent listening creates a strong relationship between the listener and the radio station. Advertisers therefore have an opportunity to leverage that existing relationship for their own brand. But because the listener has the radio on for such long periods, the frequency of message builds very quickly and people can get bored with the same advertising message played over and over again. Change your advertisement to suit the time of day, the day of the week, the lifestyle of the target audience and other factors which come into your marketing and advertising strategies.

You should choose the station and the broadcast times carefully. Different stations have different target markets, often based on listening preferences, age groups, news/information appetite, ethnic background and socio-demographics. A well-crafted radio advertisement can build a personal rapport with listeners. If you want to give a personal feeling you can record your own radio commercials. Most stations will assist you in preparing the commercial and can organise every aspect of the commercial, from script suggestions to selecting the appropriate voice and recording.

Newspapers

Newspapers can be either nationally distributed, such as the *Australian Financial Review*, state-focused, such as the *Sydney Morning Herald* in New South Wales, the *Age* in Victoria or the *Courier Mail* in Queensland, or have a local distribution. Whether you should advertise in a local, state or national paper depends on the area of your target market covered by that paper's circulation. If your business only services your local area, don't waste time and money advertising nationally. Newspapers regularly publish details of their circulation. Remember readership is usually substantially greater as papers are often read by two or three other readers. For example, a newspaper purchased by a café will be read by many customers.

Local newspapers are one of the better media for small retailers. They reach a large number of potential customers and also provide information on future events and other items of interests in a local area that will entice more people to that shopping centre or area.

By pre-booking advertisements early or regularly you can negotiate cheaper rates. If possible, try to negotiate a good position from a layout perspective. The top right-hand corner of the page is usually the most effective.

Magazines

Special-interest magazines, such as golf, sporting, travel, PC, car, etc. are an ideal medium if your product/service appeals to the people who pursue that interest. Special-interest magazines are useful for mail-order business with a narrow product range and a national market. General-interest magazines are quite an expensive advertising medium but they provide an extremely wide coverage, which is really only suitable for businesses with the broadest target markets.

Ambient media

A reasonably new form of media is 'ambient' or non-traditional media. It includes:

- light projections onto walls or footpaths
- placement of products into movies, music videos or TV shows (a well-known example is the use of BMWs in James Bond films)
- poster ads above urinals in bathrooms
- ads painted onto cars and trucks
- trailer ads towed by cars or mopeds.

Ambient media can be a very powerful yet cost-effective way of promoting your business. A well thought out and executed campaign using a novel concept can be memorable and generate mass media coverage.

For example, *Cleo* promoted a recent 'bachelor of the year' competition by launching 10 000 Ken dolls attached to helium balloons over Sydney. The balloons floated to the ground and were collected by curious onlookers who found a small note attached asking them to vote in the competition. The campaign generated news stories on TV and radio. It was conducted by Maverick Communication.

Specialty advertising

Specialty advertising is when you imprint your logo on items that are given to your customers or prospective customers. Your logo can be imprinted on virtually anything, including mugs, pens, baseball caps, T-shirts, calendars and briefcases. Specialty advertising is a cheap and effective means of building name recognition.

Brochures

Brochures are a cost-effective tool for retail- and service-based firms. They can be distributed by mail in response to specific enquiries, left in the foyer or shopfront, or distributed at trade fairs/expos. They can also be distributed via a letterbox drop of a specific area – but remember that people often throw away unsolicited 'junk mail' unread.

Business cards

Your business card says a lot about your company. It not only gives people your contact details but projects your image. A homemade or cheap-looking card implies that you are unprofessional. Use quality card, legible printing and a layout/font consistent with your overall media plan (brochures, letterhead and advertisements).

Yellow Pages

The Yellow Pages can be a cheap means of reaching your target audience. When people are searching through the Yellow Pages – the paper directory or online – it is usually because they are ready to buy the product or service and merely need a provider.

Obviously it helps to have a large advertisement in the Yellow Pages. Studies show that customers are likely to select the largest ad because they assume the company is the biggest supplier.

Contact the Yellow Pages on 13 23 78, or go to their web site: **www.yellowpages.com.au**

Direct marketing

Direct marketing is when you send a personalised letter or email to, or telephone, an existing customer (from your own database) or a potential customer from a targeted mailing list. This type of promotion can be far more effective and targeted than radio, television or newspapers. Most people throw away unsolicited junk mail unread, whereas a personally addressed letter is more likely to be read.

You can purchase a specialised mailing list from a commercial mailing house or broker. On average, a list will cost $200 to $300 for about 1000 names and addresses (20–30 cents a name). When you add postage, printing and designs, a mailing to 1000 people will cost between $1200 and $1600. When buying a list ask the broker to confirm how current it is and the firm who last used it. The broker should also confirm in writing that there are no double-ups of names.

You should also maintain your own personal database of customers and prospective customers. Update this list regularly and use it to send brochures/newsletters or special offers. A telephone directory can also be a useful source of contacts. To save on postage, consider including your advertisement in monthly accounts or packages.

Direct marketing is a more personal way of communicating than mass media. It allows you to convey more information than a short radio commercial or five-line newspaper advertisement. You can, for example, enclose a detailed pricelist or product brochure.

Direct marketing can however backfire and erode customer loyalty as people become annoyed by the invasion of privacy. To minimise this risk, use direct mail sparingly, try novel concepts (enclose a free chocolate bar or other gift) or make sure you have something newsworthy to communicate (new product, new store or a discount sale).

Email

Another method of direct marketing is using email. It is a convenient and inexpensive way of getting information to your clients and potential clients.

Ensure you keep your email newsletters concise – people have a short attention span when it comes to emails. There are a number of commercially available database management software systems such as Microsoft Outlook, Majordomo and Revnet.

A word of warning about unsolicited electronic junk mail ('spam'). The Federal Government has reacted to the spam epidemic by introducing legislation to outlaw spam. This legislation applies to email, SMS text messaging and multi-media/instant messaging. There are severe penalties for anyone who breaches the legislation, including fines up to $1.1 million. Some foreign jurisdictions have also introduced or have considered introducing anti-spam legislation in recent years.

Some organisations make use of 'self-help' remedies for spam. Organisations such as SPEWS (Spam Prevention Early Warning System) maintain blacklists of alleged spammers. System administrators can consult these black-lists and configure their systems to reject email from these sources.

Newsletters

A professionally produced newsletter can be an effective way of keeping customers aware of new products/services and other developments (such as recent awards, staff promotions, etc.). Your newsletter can also cover recent changes in law, tax or accounting which affect your industry, or trends from overseas.

Billboards, posters and public transport

There are many different types of posters/signs, including buses and taxis, bus shelters, outdoor posters, bumper stick-ers, sky-writing and sandwich boards.

To organise one of these you can contact the Outdoor

Advertising Association of Australia on (02) 9402 0660 or go to their web site: **www.oaaa.com.au**

PUBLICITY

There are a number of different events that you can use as the basis of a press release. Among them are:

- business launch
- opening of a new store
- involvement in community projects
- renovation of your premises
- new product launch
- staff appointments/promotions
- business awards
- change in ownership/management.

Publicity is free and impartial and often far more effective than advertising, as coverage may be seen as an endorsement by the relevant newspaper or journal.

A badly written press release will not be published. Editors receive many submissions each week and only the well-written and compelling ones get published. Something about your business must be newsworthy and of genuine interest to the community. There is no point in simply sending an advertisement to the editor dressed up as a press release as it will not get published and may jeopardise your chance of getting future stories published. Keep copies of any stories published and include these in a promotional kit for prospective clients.

When writing a press release, consider the following points:

- Give your press release an interesting, attention-grabbing headline. Avoid using your business name as the headline as people are more likely to be attracted by the benefits you offer rather than your business name.

- The newspaper will only publish your press release if it is newsworthy – don't bother sending them what is really just an advertisement.
- Use simple words, short sentences and keep the press release to about one page.
- Cover your most important message first. People often do not read past the first paragraph of a newspaper article.
- Ensure you highlight the newsworthy aspects early in the release. What is the special aspect of your release which makes it worth printing?
- A personal quote from the CEO of the business is a useful way of promoting the business.
- If possible tell your staff about the press release before you send it out. Ensure that they are ready to handle any increase in enquiries from customers as a result.
- Do not use jargon or technical terminology.
- Consider including a photo with the release.
- Ensure that your name and telephone number are printed at the bottom of the release.

Richard Branson is famous for his publicity stunts, such as round-the-world hot-air ballooning attempts. So is Dick Smith, who has successfully used publicity stunts throughout his career. Some of his more colourful stunts include towing an iceberg from Antarctica into Sydney Harbour, jumping over a row of motorcycles in a bus and flying his helicopter around the world.

When he launched his peanut-butter brand, Dick Smith took out an ad for $50 challenging someone to spend 43 days in a Himalayan cave with nothing to eat but his peanut butter. Smith values the free publicity from this stunt at $100 000 worth of TV, radio and newspaper articles.

Sponsorship

Another way of gaining publicity is to sponsor a community or sporting event. Sponsorship can be a direct contribution of money or the provision of your services or products. If you are sponsoring a specific event, you will need to work closely with the event manager to ensure you get appropriate acknowledgement in handouts, advertising, press releases, programs and posters/banners. Before signing up to the sponsorship, it is important to check whether the event manager has a good track record. Also ensure that the event you sponsor is directly compatible with your business and your image. You should check that:

- the audience of the event directly matches your target market
- you receive guaranteed exposure in terms of signage, advertising, programs, etc.
- you are either the main sponsor or, if not, your logo will not get lost in a sea of other sponsors.

CASE STUDY:
Richard Branson – Virgin

Richard Branson was born in 1950 and attended the Stowe School where, at the age of 16, he established a national magazine entitled *Student*.

At 17, with the aim of helping young people, he set up a student advisory service. At 20, he founded *Virgin* as a mail-order record retailer before opening his first record shop in Oxford Street, London.

Virgin Records' first album, 'Tubular Bells', recorded in 1972 by Mike Oldfield, sold more than five million copies. At 27, Richard signed the Sex Pistols to the Virgin Records label after the group was turned down by every other label in Great Britain.

From this early stage in business, Richard recognised the power of publicity, good or bad, and knew there was no better publicity machine in the business than the Sex Pistols. Richard proceeded to encourage their outlandishness and, although this went close to being offensive on occasions, the publicity led to plenty of record sales.

Over the years, he signed many superstar names including Steve Winwood, Paula Abdul, Belinda Carlisle, Genesis, Phil Collins, Peter Gabriel, Simple Minds, The Human League, Bryan Ferry, Culture Club, Janet Jackson and the Rolling Stones. By the early 1980s, Virgin Records was one of the top six record companies in the world. In 1992, the Virgin Music Group – record labels, music publishing and recording studios – was sold to Thorn EMI in a US$1 billion deal.

The Virgin Group has since expanded into international 'megastore' music retailing, book and software publishing, film and video editing facilities, and clubs and hotels, with 100 companies in fifteen countries.

Virgin Atlantic Airways, started in 1984, was founded on the idea of competitive and high quality first-class and economy services. People thought Richard was crazy when he first started the airline. Today, it is the second largest British long-haul international airline and holds many major awards. It recently earned 'Airline of the Year Award' for the third consecutive year. It operates a fleet of Boeing 747 aircrafts to New York, Miami, Los Angeles, Orlando, Boston, San Francisco, Washington, Dallas and Tokyo.

In 1993, the combined sales of Virgin Group Companies exceeded US$1 billion. In addition to his own business activities, Richard is a trustee of several charities, including the Healthcare Foundation.

Richard is widely recognised as the master of the 'branding' strategy. He believes that if the brand is strong enough, people will buy any product sold under its name. If publicity of the brand is imperative, then any publicity is good publicity, irrespective of whether or not it is related to his products.

Accordingly, Richard has indulged his adventurous personality and has been involved in a number of record-breaking land and air speed and distance attempts. In 1986, his boat 'Virgin Atlantic Challenger II' rekindled the spirit of the Blue Riband by crossing the Atlantic Ocean in the fastest recorded time ever.

His adventures in hot-air balloons have earned him and the Virgin brand much publicity. He became the first person to cross the Atlantic Ocean in his balloon 'Virgin Atlantic Flyer'. The balloon was the largest ever flown and reached speeds in excess of 200 kilometres per hour. In 1991, Richard crossed the Pacific Ocean from Japan to Arctic Canada, again breaking all existing records with speeds of up to 390 kilometres per hour. Importantly, in all of these adventures, Richard ensured that the Virgin brand was being mentioned throughout the world.

Richard Branson epitomises innovation and out-of-the-box thinking. Creating something you are proud of, rather than going into business purely to make money, is fundamental to Richard. His interest in life comes from setting seemingly impossible challenges and trying to rise above them. He continually attempts to push the boundaries of what is thought achievable at any point in time. The ingredients of success are being out there and giving it a go, having a good team around you, hitting the ground running, and more than your fair share of luck.

It could be argued that such publicity is not easily found and that Richard is one of a kind. However, even though not everyone is as charismatic as Richard (and that is why not everyone owns small islands) the lesson is still pertinent: a strong brand is of immense power and a business needs to be aware of its brand and position in the marketplace if it is to grow and succeed.

HOW TO WRITE AN ADVERTISEMENT
Good advertisements should follow the AIDA formula – Attention, Interest, Desire, Action.

Attention

Most people scan advertisements without paying much attention. You need to stop this browsing with something that grabs their attention. Clever use of colours, graphics or headlines can achieve this. Use an enticing headline to grab the reader's attention. Research shows that you can dramatically increase response rates by merely changing an advertisement's headline. A headline is most effective when it shows how your product satisfies your customer's basic buying motives.

Research shows that effective words to include in headlines are: free, guarantee, discount. A headline could use 'How to . . .' to entice its reader to find a practical solution, such as 'How to invest wisely', 'How to play golf better', 'How to look like a supermodel'. Another effective headline poses the reader a question, such as 'Would you like to be a millionaire?', 'Do you hate paying rent?', 'Are you always tired?'.

Interest

The next step is to gain their attention long enough to convey the core message – how your product or service satisfies their needs. Try to do it in a simple but interesting way. Don't make the mistake of creating an advertisement that is confusing and boring by trying to communicate too much – focus on the most powerful message. Ensure you communicate your competitive advantage. For example, if you offer a guarantee that is twice as long as your competitors, include that in your advertisement.

Desire

If you have managed to capture the audience's attention long enough and the message is powerful enough, then the potential customer should feel the need to purchase the product.

Action

The advertisement should encourage the customer to visit you and make the purchase. Many advertisements seek to do this by using such phrases as limited offer, half price, while stocks last, free trial, and so on. Others offer discount coupons or encourage the potential customer to give them a telephone call. Others make a statement of limited quantities, or the announcement of a specific time period for the promotion or impending event.

Before you send out your advertising copy, consider the following issues:

- Does the headline describe the main benefit of your product or service?
- Have you included your logo?
- Does the copy contain enough information to explain your product or service?
- Does it include your basic details such as location, opening hours, web site and telephone number?
- Is the layout of the advertisement such that it is easy to read?
- Does the advertisement explain how you satisfy your customers' basic buying motives?
- Does the advertisement stimulate the reader to take action?

Ensure your advertising campaigns project a consistent image and message. Some ways of keeping your advertisements consistent are to use:

- a distinctive logo
- a distinctive art style
- a distinctive typeface, border or advertisement shape.

This will not only make your advertisements instantly recognisable but will also build your brand name and reinforce your image.

HOW MUCH SHOULD YOU SPEND?

The amount you should spend on advertising will vary enormously depending on:

- the objectives of your marketing plan
- the scale of your operations
- the stage of your business life cycle.

As a rule of thumb, you should spend around 3 to 5 per cent of gross sales on advertising and marketing. When you are launching your business you will need to spend more on advertising than once you are established. If you are competing against a larger or more established business then you will need to spend a greater percentage of sales (say 7–10 per cent). Similarly, if you are launching a new product line, opening a new store, making a significant change in your image, or if there is a product line in which you are overstocked, then you will need to spend a higher percentage of sales.

List the various types of marketing media available and rank them according to estimated cost and estimated effectiveness of each medium. This will aid you in choosing the most cost-effective form. Weigh the costs of these against your budget to get the most effective campaign you can afford.

KEEPING TRACK OF YOUR CAMPAIGN

You can measure the effectiveness of your advertisements in a number of ways:

- Keep records of the number of visits to your web site, phone inquiries and visits to your premises.
- Carefully track sales before and after a marketing campaign.
- Use a special phone number for responses to advertising.
- Offer a discount to customers who mention your advertisement or send in a coupon.

- Ask your customers where or how they heard about the business.
- Include a survey or questionnaire in mailings to your customers.
- Consider inserting a code into advertisements and asking customers to quote the number.

Once you have analysed the results of your marketing campaign, you can modify your future strategy.

THE *TRADE PRACTICES ACT*

Before embarking on any marketing campaign you need to understand the prohibitions contained in the *Trade Practices Act 1974*, because their contravention can lead to heavy fines. The Act applies to all forms of advertisements, including television, radio and magazine advertising, brochures, billboards and other signs.

The *Trade Practices Act* prohibits any advertising that is 'misleading or deceptive'. This includes:

- the use of symbols or abbreviations not generally understood by the public
- claims based on a statistical survey that have been distorted
- offers of credit or finance that do not disclose the source or terms
- prices that do not show additional charges that the consumer must pay, such as delivery
- direct mail that implies that the reader has been especially selected to receive a limited offer, when in reality the offer is freely available
- claims of savings that would not be achieved by an average user except in unusual circumstances
- misrepresentations that goods or services are of a particular standard or quality

- offers of gifts, prizes or other free items with the intention of not providing them as offered
- advertising discounted goods or services that do not exist in reasonable quantities
- representations that goods or services have sponsorship, approval, performance characteristics, accessories, uses or benefits that they in fact do not have
- artificially inflated regular price when advertising a lower sale price.

14. LAUNCHING A WEB SITE

- **Research**
- **Web site planning**
- **Building a web site**
- **Domain names**
- **Internet Service Providers (ISPs)**
- **Marketing your web site**
- **Online business**

The Internet is a worldwide network of literally millions of computers. They are linked together using international and domestic telephone systems. The main uses of the Internet are for communication via email, research, news, education and e-business. In simple terms, host computers are run by Internet Service Providers (ISPs), which are connected to the Internet twenty-four hours a day. Through them you can have your web page accessed by your customers at any time, day or night.

RESEARCH

Before designing your web site, spend some time looking at the web sites of businesses that are similar to yours. Make notes of the features you like or do not like. For each site, note the function, content, look and feel, and whether it is easy to navigate.

Function

Ask yourself whether your competitor's site adds value for that business, and if so, how. Also consider which functions are most useful and which are not useful at all. Are there any features not offered by the site?

Content

Assess whether the content is up-to-date and relevant, and whether it is sufficiently detailed.

Look and feel

Graphics and logos need to be consistent with the corporate identity of a business. Do your competitors achieve this? Does the look and feel of their sites help to promote the objectives they are trying to achieve? Do the graphics and layout dominate the site or complement its useability? How is the site affected by banner ads? Are there too many?

Navigation

Sites need to be easy to navigate. Assess whether your competitor's site is easy to move around. Can tell where you are on the site?

WEB SITE PLANNING

A web site should match the information needs and sophistication of its audience. Additionally, it is important to consider whether your audience will want to spend a lot of time on the site or will visit briefly. Some audiences, including potential customers, employees and investors, will judge the quality of an organisation or its products by the quality of its web site.

A web site plan should fit into your business plan. It is

important to understand the role that the web site will play in achieving the company's business objectives. It is a good idea to focus on one or two major benefits that need to be delivered under the business plan. Consider what visitors to the site will take away. Visitors could be suppliers, customers or people seeking employment. There are four main things that a web site should achieve.

- **Reduce information costs** – by distributing it online. This information can include technical manuals, frequently asked questions or archived information. The information might be extremely helpful or needed frequently, but time-consuming to retrieve through traditional means.
- **Reduce transaction costs** – by automating the processing of transactions between yourself and your customers or suppliers. There are a lot of third-party products that you can use to do this. This sort of integration is expensive, but can be a big advantage to your business.
- **Increase the number of customers** – by providing marketing information or shipping to locations that would otherwise be outside the company's geographical reach.
- **Increase sales to existing customers** – by customising their interaction with your business and making it more convenient to do business.

Managing a web site can be a full-time job for one or more highly skilled people, even after the site is up and running. Most of the cost and effort involved with an information system is incurred in maintenance.

BUILDING A WEB SITE

Most businesses employ a professional web design consultant to build their web site. The programming involved in even a basic web site can be quite complex and time-consuming. If you want a site that allows secure credit-card transactions, order forms, order tracking or database functionality, then the programming required is substantial.

Before signing up a consultant, ensure you:

- get three quotes
- look at other sites they have built
- do a reference check by speaking to their old customers
- get them to sign a web-development contract which confirms the cost of the project and the deadline, and contains an acknowledgement from the developer that you own the intellectual property.

Some companies produce simple, easy-to-implement web solutions for businesses. These can be especially useful if your business is not big enough to justify an in-house web developer. There are also software packages available that allow you to put together a web site with a minimum of effort. In deciding whether to use an out-of-the-box solution consider whether:

- you can implement your web site plan with that solution at an appropriate quality level
- the out-of-the-box solution delivers enough in terms of savings, flexibility and ongoing maintenance to be more effective than an alternative solution.

Design considerations

One of the key things to bear in mind when building your site is the balance between speed and use of graphics. If it takes too long to download your site, your customers will quickly become frustrated and go elsewhere. On the other hand, if your site is dull, users will become bored and move on to more stimulating sites.

Spend time getting the layout of your site well structured.

Avoid cluttering the page with reams of text set out to fill the screen from top to bottom and left to right.

To maximise your chances of launching a successful site, try to give it a sense of 'community'. Make your site interactive by allowing your users to send emails, join 'chat rooms', win prizes and customise your site. The more your customers can interact with your site, the more likely they are to come back and also to tell their friends about it. This is sometimes called 'net equity'.

To keep people coming back ensure you change the content and look/feel of the site regularly. If it changes weekly (or daily) you're more likely to stimulate repeat visits.

A good site for tips on web design is **www.killersites.com**

CASE STUDY:
Bill Gates – Microsoft

Bill Gates is chairman and chief software architect of Microsoft Corporation, the worldwide leader in software, services and Internet technologies for personal and business computing. Microsoft has revenues of more than US$40 billion and employs more than 60 000 people in eighty-five countries and regions.

In seventh grade, Bill entered Seattle's exclusive Lakeside School, where he met Paul Allen. Gates was first introduced to computers and programming languages in eighth grade. He quickly discovered his passion for software and began programming computers, aged 13.

Soon afterward, Gates, Allen and other students convinced a local computer company to give them free access to its PDP-10, a new minicomputer made by Digital Equipment Corporation. In exchange for the computer time, the students tried to find flaws in the system. Gates spent much of his free time on the PDP-10, learning programming languages such as BASIC, FORTRAN and LISP. In 1972, Gates and Allen founded Traf-O-Data, a company that designed and built computerised car-counting machines for traffic analysis. The project introduced them to the programmable 8008 microprocessor from Intel Corporation.

In 1973, Gates entered Harvard University and met Steve Ballmer, now Microsoft's chief executive officer. While at Harvard, Gates developed a version of the programming language BASIC for the first microcomputer – the MITS Altair.

Gates left Harvard in his junior year to devote his energies to Microsoft, a company he had co-founded in 1975 with his childhood friend Paul Allen. Guided by a belief that the computer would be a valuable tool on every office desktop and in every home, they began developing software for personal computers. Gates' foresight and vision for personal computing have been central to the success of Microsoft and the software industry.

In the early 1980s, Gates led Microsoft's evolution from a developer of programming languages to a diversified software company producing operating systems and applications software as well as programming tools. This transition began with Microsoft's introduction of MS-DOS, the operating system for the IBM PC (the new personal computer from International Business Machines Corporation or IBM). Gates persuaded other computer manufacturers to standardise on MS-DOS. The effect was to fuel software compatibility and computer industry growth. Gates' vision saw him push Microsoft to introduce application software, such as the Microsoft Word word-processing software.

Microsoft expanded rapidly in the 1980s and 1990s, driven by the success of its applications software and operating systems. The company's Windows operating system, which employed a graphical user interface, became the most widely used operating system for PCs. As the company grew, the value of its stock boomed. In 1987, aged 31, Gates – who then owned about 40 per cent of the company's stock – became the youngest self-made billionaire in American history. He became the wealthiest individual in the world by 1999, amassing a personal fortune in excess of $80 billion.

Under Gates' leadership, Microsoft's mission has been to continually advance and improve software technology and to make it easier, more cost-effective and more enjoyable for people to use computers. The company is committed to a long-term view, reflected in its investment of billions of dollars on research and development each year.

In 1999, Gates wrote *Business @ the Speed of Thought*, a book that shows how computer technology can solve business problems in fundamentally new ways. The book was published in 25 languages and is available in more than 60 countries. *Business @ the Speed of Thought* has received wide critical acclaim and was listed on the bestseller lists of the *New York Times, USA Today*, the *Wall Street Journal* and Amazon.com. Gates' previous book, *The Road Ahead*, published in 1995, held the number one spot on the *New York Times'* bestseller list for seven weeks.

Microsoft's success made Gates one of the most influential figures in the computer industry and, eventually, the wealthiest person in the world. To his credit, Gates has proceeded to give something back to society, donating proceeds of both his books to non-profit organisations that support the use of technology in education and skills development. Philanthropy is an important aspect of Gates' life. He and his wife, Melinda, identified health and learning as critical areas which we should strive to make available to more people. They contributed $30 billion to a foundation to support philanthropic initiatives in the areas of global health and learning. To date, the Bill and Melinda Gates Foundation has committed more than $10 billion to global health organisations and to programs that improve learning opportunities, including the Gates Library Initiative to bring computers, Internet access and training to public libraries in low-income communities in the United States and Canada.

In addition to his love of computers and software, Gates has broad interests in quasi-computer fields such as biotechnology, telecommunications, art and photography. He has used his immense wealth and position to invest and assist many corporations in these fields. In 1998 Gates relinquished his role of guiding the day-to-day business operations of Microsoft when he appointed an executive vice-president of the company, Steve Ballmer, to the position of president. In 2000 Gates transferred the title of chief executive officer to Ballmer, a change that allowed Gates to focus on the development of new products and technologies.

Gates' success is largely due to brilliant foresight and an ability to pursue his ideas aggressively whilst persuading others of the merits of those ideas.

DOMAIN NAMES

Each web site has an address on the World Wide Web called a unique resource locator or URL. A domain name is split up into different sections, each separated by a full stop known as a dot, hence the dot.com references. A domain name represents the name of the organisation, the type of organisation, and the country code. For example:

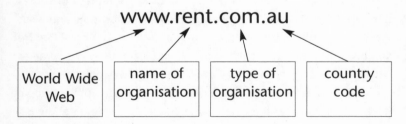

There are five basic types of organisation classes for domain names. In Australia and USA the following codes are used:

.com   commercial
.edu   education
.org   non-profit organisation

.net   Internet service providers

.gov   government

The UK and NZ use the following codes for different types of organisations:

.co   commercial

.ac   education

.govt   government

Every country has a different country code. For example:

.au   Australia

.nz   New Zealand

.uk   United Kingdom

.to   Tonga

Most US businesses simply end at the .com part of the name rather than using the country level .us domain.

Visitors to a web site will perceive a .com.au business as one with an Australian focus, and a .org domain as a non-profit organisation. Companies who want to be perceived as internationally oriented tend to choose .com domain names.

Registering a domain name

Domain names in Australia are registered by Melbourne IT, which is the Australian commercial domain name registrar. When registering a .com.au domain, there are a few things you need to bear in mind:

- Domain names are for commercial organisations. To register one, you must have an ACN (Australian Company Number), ABN (Australian Business Number) or a registered business name.
- The domain name must be able to be derived from the company name or business name.
- A domain name must be constructed of alphanumeric

characters in the same order as they appear in the registered name.

- Domain names are registered on a first-come, first-served basis.
- You can only register one domain name per company name and one domain name per business name owned by that organisation.
- A domain name must not be a place name, service type, industry sector, good, organisation type or other generic descriptor.
- A domain name must not conflict with another firm's registered trademark.

A detailed description of the .com.au domain name policy can be found on Melbourne IT's web site (**www.melbourneit.com.au**). Name registration for two years costs $140.

Before you register, ensure no-one else has a right to that name. There are two ways in which your proposed domain name could already be taken. Another business may currently be operating under the name you wish to register. To see if this is the case, search the Australian register of business names and company names for names that are similar to yours (see **www.asic.gov.au**). Another business may have registered a trademark, which gives them certain rights to use that name exclusively. To see if anyone has done this, search the registry of Australian trademarks (a searching service can be found at **www.ipaustralia.gov.au**).

In addition to searching for your exact domain name using these services, you should also search for a few names which are similar to that name. If one of your searches does reveal a similar name, there may be a risk of conflict with the business name or trademark owner.

INTERNET SERVICE PROVIDERS (ISPs)

To connect to the Internet, you will need an account with an ISP. You can find ISPs in the Yellow Pages and in specialist magazines such as the *Australian Net Guide* or the *Australian Net Directory*. In addition to renting web space on the ISP's host computer they can provide your business with email and web browsing access. Once you have a domain name, the ISP will set up their computers for you and tell you how to install your newly-built site onto them.

When choosing an ISP, you should consider the following points:

- **Cost** – the cost of their services and how payment is structured.
- **Length of the contract** – the Internet industry will change almost beyond recognition every twelve months. If you have a contract that lasts longer than this, you could be locked into inappropriate terms.
- **Speed** – check the quality of the ISP's link to the Internet. This is important as it determines how fast people can access your site, and how fast you can access the Internet. Always get an ISP with a 'big pipe' so people can access your site quickly.
- **Flexibility** – the contract should be sufficiently flexible to meet the needs of a growing business, without imposing any undue cost.
- **Stability of the ISP** – it may be worth paying a little more for an ISP which is reliable, and which will still be around when your contract expires. Customers and suppliers tend to blame a company for faults with its web site, whether or not those faults were caused by the ISP.
- **Tracking** – make sure the ISP can track the volume of hits to your web site and provide detailed reports of where

visitors went and the time spent there.
- **Services** – whether they support the services you need, such as credit-card processing, secure ordering and forms. On the other hand, are you paying for services you will never use?
- **POP** – the number of Points of Presence the ISP has, as this is important if the business is in several non-metropolitan locations.
- **Technical support** – the quality of their technical support. Ask other users whether they have found the support to be timely and helpful.
- **Space** – the amount of web server space included in the price.

ISPs offer a huge variety of different plans, each of which varies significantly in terms of the considerations set out above. It is also important to remember that a plan that is suitable now may not be suitable in the future – the industry changes very quickly as will your business needs.

MARKETING YOUR WEB SITE

Any marketing effort for a web site should begin with the business plan and the web site plan. As with every other aspect of the web site creation process, the marketing effort should be driven by what the business expects to gain from having a web site.

There are several techniques for marketing your business online, including reciprocal links and referrals, search engines and directories, online forums, banner advertising, loyalty programs and email promotion.

Reciprocal links and referrals

Links from other web sites may have more credibility than paid advertising. In addition to being free, they are targeted at people who are already interested in the product.

Many web site operators are willing to exchange links. A good way to do this is to find sites that you feel your customers are likely to visit and approach the webmasters of those sites with an offer to exchange links. If they agree, that site will post a link to your web site in exchange for you posting a link to theirs.

Depending on your goals for the web site, consider setting up a bookmarks or links section on the site.

Search engines and directories

Some people may arrive at your site via Internet search engines. It is possible to announce a site to search engines so that your site will appear when people search for a certain term or in a given category. Most web search engines have an 'Add URL' link from their home page, which allows registration of a site.

Many traditional search engines mechanically search the text of a web page. However, more advanced engines, such as LookSmart, generate results based on people's reviews. Sites such as Google and Yahoo generate results based on the number of sites which link to a particular site. Some search-engine operators are beginning to charge fees for priority in the search order. Understanding how results are generated will help you make sure that your site appears on the right searches.

Some search engines to visit include:

- **yahoo.com.au**
- **excite.com**
- **lycos.com**
- **google.com**
- **infoseek.go.com**

- **altavista.com**
- **looksmart.com.au**
- **webcrawler.com**

Online forums

Newsgroups, mailing lists and forums can all be used to disseminate information about your business. You will need to consider which forums reach your target audience, the general mood of the particular forum and how people on that forum view commercial posts.

There is a considerable amount of netiquette in posting to online forums, and an inaccurate or inappropriate post can be worse than none at all.

Advertising

Many web sites carry advertising in the form of banner graphics at the top or bottom of their web pages (or both). A lot of money is spent on banner advertising, and space on a popular site can be very expensive. Alternatively, you can swap advertisements with other sites in a no-cash exchange.

The proportion of people who actually click onto sites behind banner advertising is relatively small. Even of those who do, the evidence suggests that as few as 8 per cent subsequently buy online. In addition, technology is appearing which has the ability to block banner ads altogether.

Loyalty programs

The online environment gives businesses the opportunity to track their clients quite closely. This personal touch allows the business to offer loyalty program benefits, such as special pricing, discounts for referrals, and so on.

Email promotion

Email is a good way to keep interested customers up to speed on your marketing initiatives, via the following means:

- email update services, which inform site visitors of new content/products
- email newsletters, which should provide readers with useful information and include advertorial content.

New legislation has been introduced that prohibits unsolicited email (also known as spam). See chapter thirteen for more details on the anti-spam legislation.

ONLINE BUSINESS

There are a number of issues to consider when conducting business online.

- **Payment options** – research indicates that most people who read about a product online expect to be able to purchase online rather than having to make a phone call or send a fax. People who cannot pay using their preferred method are also likely to turn away without making a purchase. Try to offer as many different payment options as you possibly can.

- **Security** – despite evidence showing that online credit-card fraud is no more common than any other type of fraud, many people do not feel comfortable using their credit card online. In order to make your customers comfortable buying from you online, you should also clearly post a policy on use of credit cards.

   It is important to have very strict credit-card security. You should make sure that you enforce strict privacy standards, and avoid storing credit-card details on a web server where they can potentially be hacked.

- **Automating credit-card payments** – under an automated payment system, payments are automatically credited to your account as soon as they are made. There are different service models – some providers charge a large upfront fee and low per-transaction costs, whereas others charge no set-up fees but as much as 15 per cent of each transaction.

CASE STUDY:
Michael Dell – Dell Computer Corporation

In 1984, with $1000 and an idea, Michael Dell founded the Dell Computer Corporation. Today he is chairman and chief executive officer of one of the fastest-growing computer systems businesses in the world.

From the outset, Michael used direct marketing as his strategy to get his custom-built personal computers to the customer first-hand, bypassing the middlemen such as retailers and wholesalers, who he believed added a lot to the end price but very little to the value of a product.

The direct-marketing approach and the pioneering of the industry's first service and support programs were instrumental in Dell Computer Corporation becoming one of the top vendors of PCs worldwide.

By 1999, the company's sales had skyrocketed from $6 million in its first year of operations to $23.6 billion. Dell had opened sales offices in over thirty-four countries, and employed over 33 000 people in over 170 countries and territories all over the world.

Michael did not become complacent with the success in the direct marketing of PCs. His innovation earned him leadership on the World Wide Web, with Dell now recognised as the largest online commercial seller of computer systems, amassing an average of over $30 million per day in online sales. The company is also redefining the role of the Web in delivering faster and more efficient service to customers.

Most of the companies in the *Fortune 500* list of the top-performing American companies are Michael's clients, with Dell Computer Corporation being added to the list in 1992.

The value of Dell's stock has risen almost 70 000 per cent over the past decade and, in 1999, *The Wall Street Journal* named Dell Computers number one in total returns to investors over the past three, five and ten years.

In reflecting upon the business in its formative years, Michael is the first to admit that he and his team made all kinds of mistakes. However, the inherent value in what they were doing masked many of the mistakes and, importantly, very few of them were ever repeated. Michael and his team learned from the mistakes and figured out how to progress. He points to the core principles of the company as the key to success. From the beginning, there was a strong ethic around the customers and how to best serve them. The fundamental philosophy of the company is that they do what is right and treat people right.

Michael is quick to point out, however, that a customer-oriented philosophy does not mean that he gives every customer everything he or she wants. Rather, Dell provides the level of service that the customer is willing to pay for and makes available tiered services tied to the demands of the marketplace and their willingness to pay.

While customer service is tiered at Dell, management is not. From the beginning, management structure did not have many layers. In order for a flat management structure to be effective, Michael and his entire management team all need to understand the business model, to be result-oriented and speedy, and to set aggressive goals. The team also needs the ability to be self-critical and to talk about problems openly. Driving for results and eliminating bureaucracy are hallmarks of the management style at Dell.

The extraordinary achievement of the company has seen Michael receive a string of the most prestigious awards in business. In 1999, he wrote the bestselling book *Direct From Dell: Strategies That Revolutionized an Industry*, which describes the rise of Dell Computer Corporation and the strategies he has refined that apply to all corporations.

15. INSURANCE

- **Policies for consideration**
- **Evaluating insurance policies**
- **Insurance brokers**
- **Additions and deletions**
- **Insurance for home-based businesses**

Insurance provides you with protection against a broad range of liabilities such as injury to staff, theft, fire and other disasters. In simple terms, an insurance policy is when you pay a fee or premium to an insurance company in return for which they promise to pay you compensation if a pre-defined loss arises.

There are a large number of different types of insurance. In addition to the well-known insurances, such as contents and car insurance, there is a wide range of different insurance policies available, from general policies – public liability and worker's compensation insurance, for instance – to industry-specific insurances – professional indemnity insurance for businesses that provide professional services, for instance.

In deciding which types of insurance you need, you will have to consider the nature of the risks your business is exposed to and the maximum amount of coverage required.

POLICIES FOR CONSIDERATION

Fire and disaster – covers the building and its contents against fire and other disasters (such as lightning, explosion, riots, earthquakes, aircraft or other vehicles crashing, storms and malicious damage). It covers items of property, such as stock, equipment, fixtures and fittings. Note that most policies do not cover flood damage caused by the overflow of a river or creek.

Burglary – covers theft of property and the damage to doors/windows caused by a break-in. The theft requires forcible entry and does not cover shoplifting or theft by staff.

Money – covers loss of cash while on your premises or in transit to the bank.

Glass – covers breakage of glass, such as shop windows, display cases, doors and counter tops.

Business interruption – also known as loss of profit insurance. It provides cover if your business is interrupted through damage to assets by fire or other disasters. While fire and disaster insurance will arrange for new equipment and a refurbishment of the premises, it will not cover you for the loss of profits while your business is inoperative.

Motor vehicles – there are a number of different types of car insurance, ranging from compulsory third-party insurance (which forms part of the requirements when registering your vehicle) and third-party property (which covers damages caused by you against other cars/property) to third-party fire and theft, and comprehensive insurance (the most extensive type of insurance covering third-party property and damage to your own car).

Transit – covers financial loss incurred while goods are being transported or shipped. This can be arranged for specific shipments or on an ongoing basis.

Fidelity – covers loss resulting from misappropriation or embezzlement of cash or stock by employees. The policy can be written to cover a particular group of employees, such as the accounts division, an individual person (e.g. accounts clerk) or all your employees.

Public liability – covers your business against damage to property, and injury or illness caused to a member of the general public on your premises. As a business owner you owe a duty of care to your customers and other people who enter your premises, such as suppliers or even trespassers. If they suffer an injury while on your premises due to neglect by yourself or your employees, you may be sued for significant sums of money. Public liability insurance covers injuries to people on your premises, including those caused by use of vehicles or equipment on your premises, and damage to third-party property.

Product liability – covers your business in the event that a product you have manufactured or sold injures or damages property of your customers. Goods are considered defective if there is inadequate safety caused by:

- inadequate labelling, warnings or instructions
- poor design or structure of the goods
- marketing which promotes inappropriate use.

Workers' compensation – compulsory for all businesses that employ staff. It covers any accident or illness that occurs as a result of workplace conditions. Claims can be made for any harm an employee suffers while working for you – even if they are not on your premises. This insurance will only cover claims up to a statutory limit – ask your broker if it is adequate to cover your business. There are penalties against employers who fail to take out worker's compensation insurance. Premiums vary depending on the size of your payroll and the industry in which you operate – service industry premiums are generally low while manufacturing and building premiums are much higher.

Personal disabilities – if you are self-employed or a subcontractor you may not be protected by workers' compensation insurance. Personal disability insurance will compensate you for loss of income due to illness or accident.

Key person – a life-insurance policy which pays the company a lump sum if a key person dies or is disabled. If you have key staff or executives whom you cannot afford to lose you should arrange for key person insurance.

Professional indemnity – if your business provides expert advice, this policy can cover you against claims from your clients. In some occupations this insurance is compulsory (e.g. lawyers, stockbrokers and insurance brokers).

D & O insurance – directors and officers insurance covers the officers of a company against claims for negligence or breach of duty.

Employment practices liability (EPL) – covers a company and its directors, officers and employees against employment-related claims. An employment practice breach can include:
- unfair dismissal
- breach of contract
- unfair contract
- misleading and deceptive conduct
- sexual harassment
- workplace harassment
- interference with privacy
- alleged/committed discrimination or victimisation.

Credit insurance – protects your cash flow in the event of bad debts through your customers' insolvency or default. Cash flow is the lifeblood of any business and bad debts can undermine your ability to meet your own creditor commitments. Benefits of credit insurance generally include:
- underpinning your growth
- reduction in bad debt provisions
- providing security on your current assets.

Package policies – in line with modern business practices, some insurers now offer package policies (a number of covers combined into one) for specialised applications. These include:

- industrial special risks – available for most medium to large industrial concerns
- office pack policies – especially designed to cover small professional or commercial offices
- shop or retail pack – designed for small to medium premises.

EVALUATING INSURANCE POLICIES

Before you choose a policy you should consider the following:

- **Shop around** – get at least three quotes.
- **Rates** – compare the premiums, the no-claim bonuses and other discounts available.
- **Exclusions** – check carefully what is and is not covered – read the wording and definitions closely as most policies will expressly exclude certain types of losses.
- **Commencement** – check when the policy commences.
- **Reference checks** – ask others in similar businesses what their experience has been with an insurer. Were the claims procedures straightforward and prompt?
- **Limitations** – how much coverage does the policy provide? Most policies place a cap or ceiling on the amount you can claim.
- **Disclosure** – if you fail to disclose information about your business to the insurer, your policy may be void.
- **Cover** – is it adequate? Do not underinsure – make sure the policy is adequate to cover the replacement cost of your assets (if in doubt as to the value of the assets, engage a qualified valuer to make an assessment).
- **GST** – if you are registered for GST and take out business insurance you may be entitled to claim GST input tax credits.

- **Tax liability** – if you successfully make a claim under an insurance policy for an asset that has been destroyed or stolen there may be certain capital gains tax consequences. Ask your tax adviser for advice.
- **Claims occurring or claims made** – most insurance policies in Australia (except D & O insurance, professional indemnity and employment practices liability, which are usually claims made policies) are claims occurring policies. A claims made policy will, in effect, indemnify you when a claim is made against you and notified to the insurer during the period of insurance. In contrast, a claims occurring policy means that the claim (event/incident) has to occur during the period of insurance.

INSURANCE BROKERS

In addition to buying insurance from an insurance company or their agent, you can seek advice from an insurance broker. Brokers are independent and have a duty to find you the best insurance at the best price. The brokers will shop around the different insurance companies to find the most suitable policies for your business. They will also assist you in applying for the policy, advise which policies are most appropriate and help if you need to make a claim. Because they must always act in your interests, they are valuable people to have onside rather than dealing directly with insurance companies or their agents, who act in their own interests. Brokers can advise you of the range of policies available and the amount of coverage required.

ADDITIONS AND DELETIONS

All insurance policies are capable of being altered (endorsed) to suit your individual requirements and you should consult an expert in the field to assist you in determining the coverage you require. For example, your fire policy can be extended to include such risks as lightning, explosion, aircraft, earthquake, storm, flood and water damage. Cover should also include your firm's stock in trade, work-in-progress and raw materials. Numerous other extensions and alterations may be made to a fire policy. Those mentioned above are only a sample.

You should ensure that the indemnity period of your consequential loss policy is of sufficient length to allow your business turnover to reach the same figure it was prior to the fire or loss occurring. All other policies can be altered to suit your special needs.

INSURANCE FOR HOME-BASED BUSINESSES

Many people who work from home are not aware of the fact that home contents insurance does not cover their home office. Even if the home computer is used for both domestic and for business purposes, it will be classified as a business asset and will require a separate policy.

Another hidden cost to be aware of is meeting the security standards required by the insurance policy. The insurance policy for your home office might stipulate an upgrade of security before coverage commences, and require deadlocks on doors and windows, smoke alarms and external lighting. If you fail to comply with these requirements you might find that the policy doesn't cover you in the case of theft or fire.

16. INTELLECTUAL PROPERTY

- **What is intellectual property?**
- **Trade secrets**
- **Patents**
- **Trademarks**
- **Registered designs**
- **Copyright**
- **International protection**
- **Licensing**
- **IP audits**
- **IP strategy**

WHAT IS INTELLECTUAL PROPERTY?

Intellectual property (IP) represents the property of your mind or intellect. In business terms, this means your proprietary knowledge. It can be a complex area but if you fail to develop appropriate strategies before you make your IP public, you could lose the IP rights and your creative effort could be wasted. For instance, if you tell someone about your ideas or sell unpatented products, your competitors can use them. Then, you cannot obtain a patent because your products are no longer considered new. Nor can you protect your products from being copied.

You should be aware that most of the registration and protection processes outlined in this chapter are reasonably complicated and may take some time to achieve. You should ensure that you obtain the advice and assistance of an IP professional such as a lawyer or patent attorney when using any of these registration and protection processes.

Protecting your proprietary knowledge

It is vital to protect your IP, and there are various ways to do this – patents, registered designs, trademarks, trade secrets, copyright. These are designed to maximise your protection and the potential of your business. You can protect your IP by using one or a combination of the following strategies:

Commercial strategies – include trade secrets to keep processes or formulas secret; confidentiality agreements to protect proprietary knowledge; rapid development and production for products with a short life span; and appropriate licensing arrangements with suppliers of IP to both your business and your customers.

Registered rights – include patents for inventions of new or improved technology; trademarks for distinguishing a brand for goods and services; and registered design for the appearance of articles.

Unregistered rights – include copyright for works of art, literature, music, films, broadcasts and computer programs; circuit layout rights for integrated circuits; and common law rights regarding unregistered trademarks.

IP is a business asset and, like other business assets, it should be identified and an appropriate value placed on it. Valuing your IP may help you obtain better access to finance and will almost certainly increase the value of your business.

This means you must be diligent in safeguarding and maintaining secrecy, communicating your legal rights and, if necessary, defending your rights through legal action. Legal protection will help safeguard your intellectual investment and ensure that only you can turn your ideas into a commercial reality.

Ownership

Confidential information, patents, registered designs, trademarks, copyright, circuit layout rights and plant breeders' rights are all legally classified as IP rights. Ownership of these rights is the legal recognition and reward you receive for your creative effort. You can own, sell, license or bequeath IP in much the same way as a building or a block of land. Smart companies list their IP as part of their assets.

Ownership of those aspects of your IP that are covered by copyright and circuit layout rights is automatic. Patent, trademark, design and plant breeders' rights vary in the protection they provide and in the length of time for which protection is available. Often, more than one may be necessary to fully protect your creation.

Patent, registered trademark, registered design or plant breeders' rights are not automatic. For these, you must register your IP with the relevant government organisation. In Australia, patents, trademarks, designs and copyright have been Commonwealth functions since Federation. Some IP rights are automatic while others are granted only after application and examination against the appropriate criteria by relevant agencies.

Note that unregistered trademarks do not automatically create rights. An unregistered mark or common law mark requires use in trade and commerce to attract legal protection.

The different bodies that register IP are:

- The Attorney-General's Department administers the legislation for automatic rights to copyright and circuit layout rights.

- IP Australia administers patents, trademarks and design rights with an examination and registration process. Visit **www.ipaustralia.com.au**
- Plant Breeders' Rights Australia in the Department of Primary Industries and Energy administers plant breeders' rights and also has a registration and examination process.

You can take legal action under common law for infringement of trade secrets, passing off trademarks and breach of confidentiality agreements. It is your responsibility to defend your rights and to make sure others are aware of them. Most disputes over rights are settled by negotiation. Litigation may be expensive, particularly if a settlement cannot be agreed and the matter is taken to court.

TRADE SECRETS

A trade secret can provide effective protection for some technologies, know-how and other forms of IP. Ideally, however, it should be backed up by signed confidentiality agreements with every person who has knowledge of the secret. This will give you further evidence of what is agreed and protection through the law if this agreement is breached.

Confidentiality agreements

A confidentiality agreement is often used to stop employees from revealing your secret or proprietary knowledge during and after their employment or association with your business. Contractors and employees are often asked to provide written undertakings not to compete with your business after they leave. It is often much easier to prove this than to prove breach of confidentiality. These undertakings are difficult to enforce and need to be prepared by your legal adviser.

Third parties It is particularly important to ensure that third parties who have access to your confidential information enter into confidentiality agreements. These include your contractors, suppliers, competitors and customers. While your employees can generally be bound by at least an implied obligation to keep your trade secrets confidential, these third parties may not be.

When to use Relying on trade secrets is useful when the IP is unlikely to result in registrable rights or you wish to retain exclusive use beyond the term of a patent. A trade secret strategy is appropriate when it's difficult to copy the construction, manufacturing process or formulation from the product itself – that is, when reverse engineering is difficult.

Reliance on trade secrets can also be very useful when combined with rapid product change and development of products with a short life span. They may be new products or refinements of existing ones. Innovative companies and those operating in a fast-moving industry often adopt this strategy.

These companies keep ahead of their competitors with rolling plans for future innovation, enthusiastic and loyal workers, strong commercial skills and a bit of luck. For them, secrecy is critical during the production stage but not later. It's a very effective strategy for products with a quick turnover and limited research and development requirements.

Risks Secrecy, however, does not stop anyone else from inventing the same product or process independently and exploiting it commercially. It does not give you exclusive rights and you are vulnerable when employees with this knowledge leave your firm. As well, trade secrets are difficult to maintain over longer periods or when a larger number of people are made privy to the secret. Secrecy is harder to enforce and protecting it is potentially more costly than registered rights because it relies on the complexity of proving a breach of confidence under common law.

Brand loyalty Building brand loyalty, usually with a trademark, is a useful adjunct to a rapid production and development strategy because once your product is in the market you can do nothing to prevent others copying it.

For products with a longer development and production cycle and higher research and development costs, a patent is more suitable.

PATENTS

An Australian patent gives you the right to stop others from manufacturing, using and/or selling your invention in Australia. It may be used to license someone else to manufacture your invention on agreed terms.

A patent is a legally enforceable right and if you've invented new technology with the potential for substantial commercial gain, it's a very effective protection strategy.

Protecting your product

Registration Patent protection is not automatic. You must file an application with the patents office within IP Australia, which will assess whether or not it is new and meets legislative requirements. Patents cover, generally, any device, substance, method or process that is new, inventive and useful. Artistic creations, mathematical models, plans, business schemes or other purely mental processes cannot be patented.

Application   Your patent application must describe accurately and broadly the characteristics of your invention and state the scope of the patent rights sought. It must also be new and unique. You cannot obtain a patent for things that have already been patented, or which are already available in the market. Thorough searching and careful drafting of your application is necessary and we recommend you consult a qualified patent attorney before you apply.

Disclosure   Do not publicly disclose your invention before you file a patent application. If you demonstrate, sell or discuss your invention in public before you file, you cannot get a patent. You may talk to employees, business partners or advisers about your invention but only on a confidential basis. Written confidentiality agreements with these people are advisable.

Publication   Patent applications are published and join a library of over thirty million patent documents worldwide. More than 70 per cent of technical information is published exclusively on this database, which makes it an extremely valuable source of commercial information. For those involved in research and development, or those who want to keep an eye on their competitors' activities, or are simply interested in the latest technological trends, the patents database is a unique resource.

Overseas   Most countries have patent systems similar to the Australian system and obtaining patents overseas helps you protect your valuable export markets. Australia is party to a number of international agreements which can reduce the complexity of applying overseas. For example, the filing date of an Australian patent application can usually be used to establish priority for corresponding patent applications made overseas within the following twelve months.

Term An Australian standard patent lasts for twenty years although annual maintenance fees are payable from its third year. You can find out more about patents, patent applications and searching patent information in *The Patents Guide* published by IP Australia.

TRADEMARKS

A trademark can be a letter, number, word, phrase, sound, smell, colour, shape, logo, picture, aspect of packaging or any combination of these. It is a sign used to distinguish goods and services of one trade from another, and therefore must not be a sign that other traders may wish to use to promote or describe their goods and services. This means you can't register a trademark that directly describes your goods (e.g. radios) and services (e.g. electrician). While it is very difficult to register a geographic name or surname, someone who has used one extensively for a considerable period of time may be able to achieve registration.

Protecting your business identity

The identity of your goods and services is a major business investment and it's worth protecting. Once you register a trademark, you normally have the exclusive legal right to use, license or sell it within Australia for the goods and services for which it is registered.

Unregistered marks You don't have to register your trademark in order to use it. There is protection against misrepresentation under the trade practices or fair trading legislation and it is possible to take action under common law. Registration is advisable, however, because it's an expensive and time-consuming exercise to take action under the common law without it, and you must also demonstrate that you have been using the trademark for a period of time and built up a sufficient amount of goodwill associated with that mark.

Registration To register your trademark, you need to apply to the Trade Marks Office in IP Australia. This office will examine your application to see if your trademark meets legislative requirements. Trademark rights are legally enforceable and a letter from your lawyer or patent attorney is sometimes all that is needed to deter infringers. It is also possible to register a local trademark overseas, under international treaties.

It is wise to search existing trademarks before using a mark or applying for registration. IP Australia officers can show you how to do this or a patent attorney, trademark attorney, trademark agent or professional search firm will search for you. You may find yourself the subject of legal action if the mark is already registered or in use by someone else.

Trademark registration differs from registration of a company or business name, which does not give you the right to use that name as a trademark. Check the Trade Marks Register before registering a business name to avoid infringing someone's trademark.

Term Initial registration of a trademark lasts for ten years. After that time you can continue to renew your registration for successive periods of ten years on payment of the appropriate fee. A trademark can therefore have an infinite life representing significant business value. However, you must use your mark in a bona fide way to avoid it becoming vulnerable to removal on the grounds of non-use.

REGISTERED DESIGNS

Registered designs are used to protect the appearance of manufactured products. A registered design gives you a legally enforceable right to use your product's design to gain a marketing edge. It also prevents others from using the design without your agreement.

To be registered, your design must be new and original. New means not known or previously used in Australia. Original means it has never been applied to your type of product, although it may have been applied to another type of product.

When seeking design registration you need to be aware that:

- it is intended to protect designs that are applied industrially rather than a single artistic work (in the latter case copyright protection would apply);
- the protection you receive is only for the appearance of the article and not how it works.

To seek registration you must apply to the Designs Office of IP Australia, which can provide more detailed information. A patent attorney can also give you advice about protecting your industrial design. Initially the registration is for a period of twelve months but can be extended to a total period of sixteen years.

COPYRIGHT

Copyright protects the original expression of ideas, not the ideas themselves. It is free and automatically safeguards your original works of art, literature, music, films, broadcasts, computer programs and web sites from copying and certain other uses.

Protecting your expression of ideas

Nature of rights   Material is protected from the time it is first written down, painted or drawn, filmed or taped. Copyright owners from most other countries are also protected. Copyright protection is provided under the *Copyright Act 1968* and gives exclusive rights to license others in regard to copying the work, performing it in public, broadcasting it, publishing it and making an adaptation of it. Rights for artistic works, for instance, are different from those for literary and musical works.

Extent of protection   Although making copies of copyright material can infringe exclusive rights, a certain amount of copying is permissible under the fair dealing provisions of the legislation. Copyright doesn't protect you against independent creation of a similar work. Legal actions against infringement are complicated by the fact that a number of different copyrights may exist in some works – particularly films, broadcasts and multimedia products.

Copyright notice   A copyright notice, with the owner's name and date, can help prove matters in Australia and is essential to establish copyright overseas. It is worthwhile to note that copyright is lost if the owner applies three-dimensional artistic work industrially. In such a case, it is necessary to register the design if protection is required.

Term   Time limit of protection varies according to the nature of the work and whether or not it has been published. Depending on the material, copyright for artistic, literary, dramatic and musical works generally lasts seventy years from the year of the author's death or from the year of their first publication for anonymous works. For broadcasts, copyright generally lasts fifty years from the year in which they were made, and for sound recordings and cinematograph films, seventy years from the year in which they were published.

INTERNATIONAL PROTECTION

Registering your application for patents, trademarks and designs in Australia does not give you international protection. International agreements are in place which make it easier to obtain rights in other countries, but you need to seek protection in each country according to the laws and conventions of that country. This is a costly process, particularly when it involves the translation of applications into other languages.

It is particularly important that, when disclosing or marketing your invention or design in Australia, you do not invalidate a future patent or design in another country. Under international conventions, once you apply for protection in other member countries, it is provided within the following time limits:

- patents – twelve months from the date of the first application in a member country
- designs and trademarks – six months from the date of the first application in a member country.

This gives you the opportunity to obtain exclusive rights to your IP in overseas markets. Your applications in those countries will have a 'priority date', which is the filing date of your original application. While you can apply outside these time limits, you cannot obtain the benefit of the international convention and any earlier disclosure of your invention or design may invalidate your rights in those countries.

Some countries are not members of the convention and any publication or use can prevent you obtaining protection in those countries. It is best to seek advice from an IP professional before you publish or use your invention.

LICENSING

Licensing arrangements are a fairly common method of exploiting copyright, patents, design and trademarks and can be exclusive and non-exclusive. They give the licensee the right to use, but not own, the copyright, patent, trademark or design.

The owner of the rights will usually get payments in the form of royalties for its use. The value of these rights is a commercial agreement based largely on the IP of the creation or invention.

Quite often you will be required to give third parties access to your IP in the course of conducting your business. For example, your customers may need knowledge of a patent to be able to use your products. For these relationships, it is important to ensure that you have appropriate licensing arrangements in place to protect your IP. Typically, these third parties may be permitted to use such material under a licence agreement, which should clearly set out the rights of the parties to use such materials. It is advisable for a lawyer to review any such licensing documentation to ensure that it adequately protects your rights in your IP.

Licensing your IP to another party can be an effective way to exploit IP, particularly if you don't have the resources or experience to develop and market your product or service. As with all other aspects of commercialising your IP, licensing needs to fit in with your business strategy and practices.

Another approach is to take out a licence on someone else's IP. You may have a good idea but find someone else has already thought of it. Taking out a licence is a cost-effective alternative to investing in development which has already been done.

If you think licensing is for you, you should seek the advice of a lawyer to help you ensure that where you are receiving IP you have adequate rights to use and exploit that IP within your business, and that where you are licensing IP your rights are adequately protected.

IP AUDITS

Most businesses are not aware of the full extent of their generation or use of IP. As this chapter has demonstrated, this is a complex area, and businesses should ensure that they have taken all practicable steps to protect their own IP, and ensure that they are not using someone else's IP in an unauthorised manner. One way that businesses can evaluate their use of IP is through an IP audit, conducted by an IP professional such as a lawyer. An IP audit is not only useful for the management of IP within a business, but may also demonstrate to potential investors and shareholders the valuable IP assets that the business owns.

IP STRATEGY

Developing an IP strategy is important to protect your rights. Consider the following practices when developing an IP strategy:

- Search patent and trademark databases as well as other literature and the Internet to ensure your ideas are new and to avoid infringing the rights of others. You can also search for new business opportunities and keep a tab on what your competition is doing.
- Maintain secrecy and be first to market your product or service.
- Develop an infringement strategy.

- Educate your staff as to their obligations and, where necessary, have key staff sign confidentiality agreements.
- Be sure whether or not you actually own the IP you think you do.
- Consider ways you can use the IP system in your overall business strategy.
- Identify and value your IP assets and ensure that they are itemised in your business plan. You may wish to conduct an IP audit as part of this process. Regularly review your IP inventory.
- Ensure that you have appropriate licensing arrangements in place.
- Nominate an employee to be responsible for IP issues.

17. INCUBATORS, AWARDS AND GRANTS

- **Business incubators**
- **Industry awards**
- **Government programs**

BUSINESS INCUBATORS

Incubators nurture young businesses, helping them to survive and grow during the startup period when they are most vulnerable. Incubators provide access to experienced management and to financing, and co-ordinate exposure to key business and technical support services. They also offer access to shared office space and equipment.

Incubators are designed to assist startup companies by providing an environment where many of their day-to-day needs are met. These needs could include:

- office space at subsidised rates and flexible 'easy-in and easy-out' lease terms
- access to office facilities, such as laser printers, photocopiers and facsimile machines
- access to a range of business advisers at free or reduced rates.

A key advantage of an incubator is being surrounded by like-minded entrepreneurs and skilled professionals. This environment fosters idea generation, cross-disciplinary learning and business networking, which are all critical to the launch of successful ventures. A key cause of business failure is lack of management skills. To overcome this, incubators typically have access to a number of experienced business mentors. There may also be a panel of tax, legal and accounting professionals who offer their services at discounted rates.

Incubators are also called technology parks, science parks or business enterprise centres. Many incubators are operated or funded directly by the federal or state government. A number of incubators have also been established by universities and private non-profit organisations. In more recent times a number of independent for-profit centres have also been established.

Incubators impose rigorous selection criteria upon prospective companies, and usually concentrate on industry niches such as technology, manufacturing or life sciences.

There are around eighty business incubators in Australia, hosting more than 1200 companies. On average, each incubator will house between twelve and eighteen startups, who stay between one and three years before graduating. To obtain more information about the different incubators, contact Business Innovation and Incubation Australia (BIIA). This is the peak association of business incubators in Australia and New Zealand. Their web site includes information on BIIA membership and locations of incubators throughout Australasia and can be found at **www.businessincubation.com.au**

The following describes some of the key Australian incubators.

Australian Distributed Incubator   Australian Distributed Incubator (ADI) is dedicated to assisting entrepreneurs build and develop technology companies. It specialises in supporting new concepts that have unique offerings or global potential. ADI offers two programs to help entrepreneurs:

- The Business Readiness Program is an innovative mix of mentoring, consulting and support services designed for early stage businesses. Even just an idea can be taken to ADI for consideration in this program.
- The Investment Program is a less hands-on program designed for more developed businesses.

ADI has recently been acquired by Business Strategies International (BSI), a Melbourne-based private investment firm. Their web site is **www.bsi.com.au/adi**

Australian Technology Park (Sydney)   The Australian Technology Park at Eveleigh is a non-profit company backed by the University of New South Wales, the University of Sydney and the University of Technology, Sydney. It has a number of incubators within the National Innovation Centre and International Business Centre. These include:

- IT&T and advanced Internet incubator
- Biomedical/biotechnology incubator
- Environmental incubator
- Telecommunications and software development incubator.

Sydney Business Enterprise Centre (BEC)   Sydney BEC delivers a range of services for startups and small businesses, including:

- advice and consulting across all areas of business including business planning, marketing, operational systems, finance and compliance
- seminars and training, for business owners
- Business Village – an incubator providing low-cost, serviced offices for short or longer terms
- Business Resource Centre, providing access to demographic

profiling and industry benchmarking data
- Innovations Advisory Centre, to help your invention become a reality – information on protecting your idea, market research, and industry and government assistance
- referrals and networking opportunities, to help you develop links, alliances and friendships with other businesses across a broad spectrum of industries
- business startup kits and books.

Sydney BEC and Parramatta BEC are supported by the NSW Department of State and Regional Development and are part of the WorkVentures Group.

Greenhill Enterprise Centre This centre is located within the Ballarat Technology Park and is intended to provide a nurturing environment for small IT businesses involved primarily in information technology research and development. Contact them through their web site: **www.ballarattechnologypark.com**

Interactive Information Institute (I-cubed) I-cubed is a collaborative venture between RMIT University, commercial partners and the Victorian Government. It employs multidisciplinary teams to develop sustainable products and services in all aspects of interactive media. Their web site is **www.iii.rmit.edu.au**

Enterprise Network for Young Australians (ENYA) ENYA is an organisation that has been established to promote the participation of young people in enterprise. It is targeted at 18 to 30-year-olds who have a new business or social enterprise, and concentrates on general business skills rather than specific industry information. The main services offered are a virtual business incubator and a mentoring program. The concept of a virtual business incubator is derived from traditional business incubators, but the emphasis is on the 'virtual' services that can be provided, such as a free advice line, shared meeting spaces and assistance with financial planning. For more information see their web site: **www.enya.org.au**

The contact details for other incubators are:

- RedCentre: **www.redc.com.au**
- National Business Incubators Association (USA): **www.nbia.org**

INDUSTRY AWARDS

There are a number of awards/programs sponsored by industry. In summary the main awards are:

- New Enterprise Incentive Scheme
- Yellow Pages Business Ideas Grants
- Micro Business of the Year Awards
- Nescafé Big Break Award
- Australian Technology Award
- Telstra Small Business Awards
- Quality in Business Awards
- Ernst & Young Entrepreneur of the Year Awards
- Deloitte Technology Fast 50.

New Enterprise Incentive Scheme

This scheme provides a free business planning course for unemployed people. If your plan is considered viable you may be granted over $10 000 in living allowances. For more information contract Centrelink on 13 28 50 or visit their web site (go to **www.centrelink.gov.au/internet/internet.nsf** and search the site for 'NEIS').

Yellow Pages Business Ideas Grants

The Yellow Pages Business Ideas Grants aim to recognise, assist and reward Australia's small businesses with great ideas. The scheme has been in operation for over ten years and in 2003 provided almost $300 000 in prizes including $150 000 in cash grants to successful applicants. The scheme has a particular emphasis on advertising and promoting innovative ideas of Australia's small businesses to the wider Australian community and in turn developing these ideas into commercial successes. There are three categories of awards:

- Best Idea Concept Stage – open to businesses that have an idea, and have identified a target market and the resources necessary to exploit the idea, but have not developed the concept any further.
- Best Idea Product Development Stage – open to businesses in the prototype/testing stage, where a business plan has been prepared and the resources have begun to come together.
- Best Idea Business Development Stage – open to businesses that have implemented a business plan and commenced trading.

Winners are selected from each state in each of these categories, with one national winner in each category. Call the Yellow Pages Business Ideas Grants information line on 1800 886 680 or visit their web site: **www.sensis.com.au/big/**

Micro Business of the Year Awards

These awards are open to all businesses throughout Australia who employ five or fewer full-time or part-time employees. For details see the web site: **www.mbn.com.au**

Nescafé Big Break Award

This award is open to young Australians between sixteen and twenty-one who have an idea and need some cash (up to $20 000) to get it going. Entry forms can be obtained by calling 1800 630 630, or can be downloaded from the Nescafé Big Break web site: **www.nescafebigbreak.com.au**

Telstra Business Awards

These awards were introduced in 1992 to acknowledge the extent and diversity of successful small businesses around Australia and to provide a vehicle for recognising and promoting these enterprises as role models. Developed by Telstra and managed in conjunction with the respective state and federal governments, the awards run in each state and territory. An overall state/territory winner is selected along with state/territory winners in each of the following categories:

- Commonwealth Government Micro-Business Award – open to businesses with five employees or fewer
- MYOB Business Award – open to businesses with more than five employees but less than or equal to twenty employees
- Panasonic Australia Business Award – open to businesses with more than twenty employees but less than or equal to fifty employees
- Hudson Business Award – open to businesses with more than fifty employees but less than or equal to one hundred employees
- AMP Innovation Award – open to businesses that have successfully introduced an innovation.

The state/territory winners then go on to compete at a national level which culminates in a national presentation and awards night where the national category winners and the overall Telstra National Business of the Year are announced.

Sponsored by Hudson, MYOB, Panasonic, AMP and the various government partners, the state winners generally receive prizes and grants ranging in value from $7000 to $10 000. National winners receive additional grants in similar amounts and the overall winner receives a third grant of $10 000.

All types of small business which have been in operation for at least two years are eligible to enter the awards. Key management decisions must be made by the owners of the business. Your business must not be a non-profit organisation or a listed company and must be registered in the state/territory of application. Details can be found on their web site: **www.telstrabusinessawards.com**

Ernst & Young Entrepreneur of the Year Award

These awards have been established to recognise the achievement of individual entrepreneurs who demonstrate keen entrepreneurial spirit, innovation and personal integrity as well as achieving successful financial performance, strategic direction and making a national or global impact for their business. Winners are selected in the following categories at both a regional and national level:

- Retail, consumer and industrial products
- Services including financial business and property
- Technology, communications and life sciences
- Master entrepreneur – for those who have made a sustained contribution to the success of one or more businesses over a period of more than ten years
- Young entrepreneur – for individuals under 35 years of age
- Entrepreneurship in a social, community or not-for-profit enterprise.

Overall winners are also selected for each region and nationally, with the national winner going on to compete at the Ernst & Young World Entrepreneur of the Year awards in the following year.

Deloitte Technology Fast 50

These awards go to the 50 fastest growing technology companies in Australia. The business must have been in operation for at least three years, be Australian-owned and have a turnover of greater than $100 000 in the first year of calculation and greater than $1 000 000 by the third year of calculation. If your business does not meet this criteria you may still apply for a Rising Star award under the same program. Although no prizes are awarded in this scheme, there are substantial benefits in profile raising, access to industry experts and networking, as all 50 companies are invited to various functions including a global Fast 500 summit of similar companies in America. More information can be found on their web site: **www.tech50.com.au**

GOVERNMENT PROGRAMS

There are a large number of government programs, concessions and grants available to people starting or developing their own business. They can represent an important source of assistance for small-business owners. The main sources of government assistance can be found through:

- Business Entry Point
- AusIndustry
- R&D Start Program
- R&D Tax Concession
- Austrade.

Business Entry Point (BEP)

The Business Entry Point provides small business and its advisers with access to comprehensive information on business-related matters and allows for a range of commercial transactions to be carried out. Through BEP you can also access AusIndustry's Business Information Service, industry associations and chambers of commerce, and the Business Licence Information Service which provides information on all licences and permits required in the running of a business. The BEP provides an extensive search facility through the hundreds of different government programs. See their web site: **www.business.gov.au**

AusIndustry

AusIndustry is the Commonwealth Government's central point for business assistance and information. Through AusIndustry, the Commonwealth Government provides a number of assistance programs to help Australian businesses become more successful and internationally competitive. The AusIndustry Hotline (13 28 46) provides access to information on over 800 assistance programs offered by commonwealth, state and territory governments and industry associations and chambers of commerce. See their web site: **www.ausindustry.gov.au**

A recent program introduced by AusIndustry is COMET (Commercialising Emerging Technologies). It can provide, in its own right and through associations with venture capital funds or other investors, for funding (agreed activities such as strategic planning, market research, establishing a sound management team and building a working prototype) to implement commercialisation activities. It can also provide up to $5000 to cover half the cost of a management skills course.

R&D Start Program

The Research and Development (R&D) Start Program is a competitive, merit-based program which to June 2011 will provide grants and loans totalling about $1 billion to assist companies to undertake industry R&D and related activities. The R&D Start program was suspended for six months in 2002 due to unprecedented demand for grant funds. However, changes have been made to program management to ensure that there will be no further interruptions to new applications.

The R&D Start Program has five separate elements of funding – Core Start, Start Plus, Start Premium, Start Graduate and concessional loans.

- Core Start provides grants of up to 50 per cent of the project costs of smaller Australian companies (turnover of up to $50 million over previous three years) for the early commercialisation of technological innovation.
- Start Plus provides grants of up to 20 per cent of eligible project costs to Australian companies with a group turnover of more than $50 million to undertake R&D projects.
- Start Premium offers additional assistance to industry for high-quality projects. This program offers all companies an additional repayable amount that tops up either Core Start or Start Plus to a maximum of 56.25 per cent of eligible project costs.
- Start Graduate grants are available, on a competitive basis, for companies with turnover of less than $50 million to engage a graduate on a specific R&D-related project that is undertaken in collaboration with a research institution. Projects can extend for up to a two-year period. The maximum grant is $100 000 or 50 per cent of eligible project costs.

- Concessional loans are also available to organisations employing fewer than 100 persons for the commercialisation of technological innovation.

All applications for financial assistance under R&D Start are assessed on a competitive basis by the Industry Research and Development Board. The merit criteria include management capability of the applicant, commercial potential of the project, technical strength of the project and of the company, national benefit of the project, and the need for R&D Start funding for the project. The company must also demonstrate its ability to obtain sufficient funding for the project from financial institutions. For more information on R&D Start, telephone 13 28 46, contact your nearest state office of the Department of Industry, Tourism and Resources or visit their web site: **www.ausindustry.gov.au**

R&D Tax Concession

The R&D Tax Concession aims to encourage increased investment in R&D by Australian companies to make them more innovative and internationally competitive. The tax benefit derived from the concession provides companies with the opportunity to reinvest resulting tax savings in their future. Support for business innovation is available through the base 125 per cent tax concession for research and development (R&D) and the 175 per cent Premium R&D Tax Concession for additional labour-related R&D expenditure. The concession is broad-based and market-driven and supports much of the industry R&D spending in Australia. It is a permanent provision to enhance and increase the level of R&D being conducted.

The tax concession enables companies to deduct up to the base 125 per cent of eligible expenditure incurred on R&D

activities from assessable income when lodging their tax returns. The tax benefit provides companies with more money to invest in their future, while the new and improved products and services developed can increase competitiveness.

An important recent development is the ability for small companies to obtain a cash rebate for their R&D deductions, if they have an annual turnover of less than $5 million and R&D of up to $1 million.

Companies incorporated in Australia or public trading trusts can seek the deduction. They must register with the Industry Research and Development Board in order to claim the concession, within ten months of the end of the year of income in which the R&D expenditure was incurred.

For copies of registration forms or for more information on the R&D tax concession, telephone 13 28 46, contact your nearest state office of the Department of Industry, Tourism and Resources or visit their web site: **www.ausindustry.gov.au**

Austrade

Austrade is the Federal Government's export and investment facilitation agency, which aims to encourage Australians to win export business and generate inward and outward investment. Austrade helps companies determine whether they are ready to export and provides initial advice and general market information which then helps in deciding how best to proceed. Austrade also provides advice to companies on which overseas markets hold the highest sales potential for their product, how they can build a presence in these markets, and what sort of practical and financial help is available.

Relevant information can include detailed market intelligence such as competition, prospects, cultural considerations, distribution systems and government regulations. Many of Austrade's services are free or partially subsidised by the government. When the preparatory work is done, Austrade's overseas offices can contribute to a successful market visit. Austrade also co-ordinates international trade fairs, which can be an effective way of promoting your products and services to targeted buyers and users overseas. Contact Austrade on 13 28 78 or visit their web site: **www.austrade.gov.au**

Export Market Development Grants
For information on these grants, refer to chapter twenty.

18. BUYING AN EXISTING BUSINESS

- **Weighing up the pros and cons**
- **Finding a business for sale**
- **Assessing experience and skills**
- **Signing a terms sheet**
- **Undertaking due diligence**
- **Doing a valuation**
- **Organising finance**
- **Negotiating and signing legal contracts**
- **Checklist before buying**

WEIGHING UP THE PROS AND CONS

The main advantages of buying an existing business are:

- You will save the time and effort required to build the business and eliminate any teething problems (including purchase of equipment such as desks and computers, recruitment of staff and securing suitable premises).
- It is lower risk as supplier relationships have already been established.
- Existing clientele should mean that you are not exposed to a long set-up period without incoming revenue.
- It will be considerably easier to obtain finance for a business with a track record than for a startup.

The main disadvantages of buying an existing business are:

- Starting from scratch can be cheaper, as you are not paying for goodwill.

- You may overvalue the business if you are too optimistic about the future earnings potential of the business.
- The previous owner may have had poor relationships with employees, customers or strategic partners. This feeling of ill will may be difficult to overcome.
- The seller may have misstated the value of the assets or the business's financial statements.
- You may inherit prior mismanagement such as holdings of obsolete stock or software which is antiquated. However, this may be reflected in a discount to the purchase price.

FINDING A BUSINESS FOR SALE

Finding suitable businesses for sale is a challenging task. The main sources of leads are:
- business brokers, corporate advisory firms and merchant banks
- metropolitan newspapers
- newsletters and magazines
- word of mouth
- cold-calling
- the Internet.

Business brokers, corporate advisory firms and merchant banks

You will need to contact a range of intermediaries (including corporate advisory firms, business brokers and merchant banks) to register your interest in acquiring a business in a certain price range, industry sector and geographical area.

A business broker matches people who want to buy a business with people who are selling one. Brokers typically deal in smaller businesses (under $2 million) such as retail, manufacturing, hospitality and professional practices.

Corporate advisers and merchant banks tend to act in larger deals (over $5 million) and generally play a more active role in the transaction than a business broker – actively finding buyers, preparing information memorandums, setting the terms and pricing. Advisers charge the seller a success fee ranging from 1 to 3 per cent.

One of the benefits of buying a business through corporate advisers (or to a lesser extent brokers) is that they will generally screen the businesses for sale to determine if there are major problems and will also help set a realistic price. There is, however, no substitute for personal due diligence.

The adviser and broker will guide the seller through the process of selling, ensuring a more streamlined and professional process. However, the agent's fee to sell the business will probably result in a higher sales price for you, even if the seller is the one who is nominally paying this commission.

Metropolitan newspapers

Classified advertisements in local and metropolitan newspapers remain a good way of locating businesses for sale, especially businesses priced under $1 million. You will need to scan the listings regularly to locate a business that is attractive to you. Unfortunately, many good businesses for sale never make it into the classified advertisements because of sellers' concern that their staff and customers will learn that their business is for sale, which could ruin staff morale (fears of redundancy) and jeopardise sales.

One way of using the classified advertisements is to advertise yourself as 'seeking a business for sale' and detail the characteristics of the business that you want. Some business owners who are contemplating selling their business will scan the classifieds to get an idea of which businesses are available for sale and what the asking prices are for similar businesses. By advertising yourself as a buyer, you may be able to find business opportunities before the general market hears about them.

Newsletters and magazines

There are various newsletters and magazines that list businesses for sale (such as in-house brokerage publications, and regional and national independent publications). These newsletters and magazines are good sources of up-to-date listings on a broad array of businesses for sale, especially for those priced under $1 million. Unfortunately there is not a strong national multiple listing service of businesses for sale (as there is for residential and commercial real estate).

These newsletters are in a variety of forms:

- **Local broker newsletters** – published by individual brokers and list only the businesses they have been engaged to sell
- **Coalition business brokers' newsletters** – a group of brokers combines their listings within a specific market area
- **Regional and national newsletters** – combine many listings in a range of categories across regional and national markets
- **Magazines and periodicals** – usually national in scope with long lead times for advertising and publishing (so listings are sometimes out of date).

Word of mouth

Word of mouth is an important way to find out about a business for sale. You cannot just sit back and let sellers come to you. You should 'spread the word' among your advisers (such as legal and accounting) and through your network (including business, social and industry circles) that you are interested in purchasing a business. If there are serious sellers in these groups, you may not otherwise know because of the need for confidentiality regarding a business for sale.

Cold-calling

You do not have to limit your search to businesses that have been listed for sale. If you find a business that you would like to own, tell the owner you would like to buy it and make an offer (subject of course to contract, finance and due diligence). The worst that can happen is that the owner will say 'no'. It is important, however, to make sure your approach is professional and courteous – you do not want it known in the market that you are a time-waster.

Internet

The Internet has become a good source of listing information for businesses under $1 million. To find information about businesses for sale just go to your favourite search engine, such as **Google.com.au** or **Yahoo.com.au**, and conduct a key word search. The best key words are, 'businesses for sale', 'buy business', 'sell business' or 'buy sell business'. It is usually best to use the advanced search capability on the search engines to better target the results you want, for example by seller or region.

Some business broker web sites include:

- **www.barclays.com.au**
- **www.realcommercial.com.au**
- **www.businessforsale.com.au**
- **www.practice4sale.com.au**
- **www.macquarie.com.au**
- **www.lloydsbus.com.au**

- www.bsale.com.au
- www.businessfind.com.au
- www.v-capital.com

Other sources

If you know what type of business you are looking for, trade and industry associations may be a good place to start your search. If you are looking for a business in a particular area, contact the local chamber of commerce to see if they can provide any assistance. Venture capital funds may also be a good source of businesses for sale. They will be looking for liquidity in deals they did three or four years earlier.

Before you ask . . .

Spend as much time as possible researching the industry sector you are interested in. Many people know that they want to buy a business but do not know what *type* of business they want to buy.

The larger the deal the more the seller will expect of the buyer in terms of having the necessary resources and credibility to close the deal. Don't expect to get past the first phone call unless you can answer the following questions from the seller:

- How much cash do you have?
- Who is backing you?
- Who is the management team?
- What is your plan for the company?

ASSESSING EXPERIENCE AND SKILLS
Self-assessment

One of the first steps in buying a business is a thorough personal assessment of your risk profile, motives and the seriousness of your search. You also need to assess realistically the size of the financial/professional resources to which you have access. Another key assessment is to determine how closely the business matches your personal skills and interests. Business ownership requires a huge time input and the closer the match, the better your chance of success.

An important aspect of self-assessment is tactical. During your search and analysis for businesses for sale you will deal with numerous sellers and advisers. Unless they sense a degree of commitment and clarity from you they may not treat your enquiry as serious.

Experience and skills

The next step is to ensure that you have the necessary experience and skills to operate the business. In addition to general business skills (finance, marketing and operations as discussed in chapter one) you will need experience and expertise in running a business of that magnitude and in that particular industry. You must ensure that you have the myriad business and management skills required (it is not enough to have simply worked in a business in the same industry). You should also join the relevant industry association and consider undertaking a short course of study.

In some cases you may be able to work in the business for a short period of time before committing to purchase that business. The seller may also agree to a 'handover period', where they stay on in the business after you have purchased it to show you the ropes.

Qualifications

Some industries also require business operators to have special qualifications. For example, you may need a suitable degree or diploma and relevant industry experience to hold the necessary licences or permits.

You may also be required to obtain a government permit or licence to operate a business. The Business Licence Information Service (BLIS) provides information about all business licences required in each state, and also those required by the Commonwealth Government (see chapter six).

SIGNING A TERMS SHEET

Before you spend significant time conducting due diligence, you should consider signing a terms sheet with the seller. Do not sign a fully binding terms sheet unless it is conditional upon the satisfactory completion of due diligence, raising of finance and execution of legal documentation. You should also seek legal advice before signing a terms sheet.

A terms sheet summarises the intentions of the parties and describes the general terms and conditions of the transaction. The terms sheet should deal with:

- the purchase price and how it is to be calculated (for example, $2 million plus stock at value)
- whether the sale is by shares or assets
- the assets and liabilities to be transferred (and excluded).

Terms sheets are usually non-binding; however, the 'no-shop' or 'exclusivity' clause and the confidentiality provisions should be binding. The no-shop clause protects the buyer by stating that the seller will not negotiate with other potential buyers for a period of time – anywhere from two weeks to two months.

Advantages of a terms sheet

A terms sheet demonstrates that the parties are serious about moving forward and encourages them to negotiate in good faith. Another benefit is that it clarifies the major issues before the parties begin drafting the definitive documents – a time-consuming and expensive task. The terms sheet should be drafted simply and with minimal back and forth between lawyers.

Disadvantages of a terms sheet

A terms sheet is a legal document and, even if expressed to be a 'letter of intent and non-binding', you may inadvertently make it binding and commit to something before you know all the facts. It may also tip your hand in negotiations; it is hard to change something once it is in the terms sheet.

A terms sheet can slow down the process. It is one more thing to negotiate and can take a significant amount of time to agree – time you should be spending on due diligence.

Tips for drafting

The key issues to bear in mind when drafting a terms sheet are:

- Typically, the terms sheet is drafted by the buyer.
- It is better if the first draft is prepared by the principals, rather than the lawyers.
- Focus on the major points; do not go into the details.
- The letter should be short – three or four pages at most; if it is longer, you are including too much detail.
- State expressly which terms are meant to be legally binding and which are not.
- Specify what conditions must be satisfied before the transaction is completed.
- State expressly that the investment, sale or purchase depends upon the execution of a definitive agreement.

UNDERTAKING DUE DILIGENCE

The legal adage of *caveat emptor* or 'let the buyer beware' applies when you purchase a business. Before you buy the business, you must satisfy yourself as to the prospects and viability of the business. You should undertake extensive due diligence (or investigations) into the business you are purchasing. A consistent and methodical process is crucial so that you can compare different proposals with each other. You should also seek appropriate professional advice from legal, tax and financial advisers.

Before commencing the detailed due diligence you should also consider some broader macro-economic issues. It will be important to understand the industry and its competitive dynamics in order to assess the viability of the business. It will also be useful at this point to consider the best structure to achieve your objectives: should you buy the business, invest in the business, consider a joint venture with the business or make some other arrangements?

Your investigations should focus on the following issues:

- What are the maintainable earnings of the business?
- Is there potential to improve sales/earnings?
- Is the asking price justified by the value of the assets and the past and potential profits?
- Is there sufficient working capital to operate the business (i.e. will additional funding be required)?
- Will the potential profits provide you with an adequate salary plus a return on your capital?
- Is the cash flow predictable?
- Are the sales and revenues growing, stagnant or declining?
- Have adequate financial records been kept over the life of the business?
- Is there any capacity to reduce the level of overheads?

- Are key personnel 'locked in'?
- Ensure you (and your lawyers) review all major contracts (with customers, suppliers and personnel). You should ensure that there are no termination provisions which are triggered by a change of control or assignment, that proper arrangements are in place for fees payments, and that there is no excessive exposure to liability or indemnities. Note any key performance indicators which must be met and assess if they are achievable. Ensure that there are no other unusual or material provisions.
- How long has the business been on the market? Clearly, the longer it has been for sale the more bargaining power you are likely to have.

In addition to the responses you will receive from the seller, it will also be useful to discuss these issues with key customers, key suppliers and the employees to obtain a full picture of the business's operations.

Why are the owners selling?

Part of your due diligence enquiries should be to establish why the current owners are selling. Some corporations will sell off a division which is non-core so they can focus on their main operations. On the other hand, are they simply getting out before the business goes into insolvency? If they assure you that the business is a goldmine, why are they selling?

Most sellers will offer a range of seemingly valid reasons for disposal. An individual seller may be sick or planning to retire. A corporate seller may explain the division is no longer part of the overall group's strategic focus or no longer has support from head office.

You need to find out the *real* reason they are selling. An analysis of external threats (factors outside their control which pose significant risks to the business) may highlight the real reason. For example:

- **Demographics** – changing demographics in the market may mean the long-term prospects of the business are not viable.
- **Regulation** – the government may be planning to introduce new legislation which will hamper the industry. The local council may be planning to rezone the area, restricting your ability to carry on the business, or it may be planning to change regulations such as traffic flow or parking which may also be detrimental to the business.
- **Competition** – a new well-funded competitor may be launching. Consider the impact of the introduction of Toys R Us on small toy-retailers. Is a similar change about to occur in your industry? Trade and industry associations are good places to gain intelligence on new competitors.
- **Obsolescence** – are the products or services sold by the business about to become obsolete through the introduction of new technology? (For example, CDs have made vinyl records obsolete; will Internet movies make DVDs obsolete?)

It is also worth checking on the seller's intentions after the sale. Are they simply moving down the road to a more prominent location or cheaper premises? A restraint of trade provision is important in any business purchase.

Review the financial statements

Obtain the business's financial information (profit and loss statements, balance sheets, budgets, audit working papers and tax returns) for the past three years. Note, however, that most businesses will be reluctant to give you forecasts of future revenues and, if forecasts are provided, you should assume that these will be optimistic and not necessarily likely to reflect the true potential of the business. It is important that you make your own forecasts based on the existing accounts. See chapter eleven for further assistance in analysing financial statements.

When reviewing the past accounts, bear in mind:

- Accounting treatment and preparation of accounts may vary between businesses.
- The accuracy of accounts depends on the honesty and precision of the previous owner.
- There is no guarantee that the business will continue to generate similar or higher revenues in the future.
- The business may be driven by the past owner's personal reputation.

You should obtain a profile of the returns of similar businesses in the same industry. Publicly listed companies are required to disclose their financial position in detail, and reports can be downloaded from the Australian Stock Exchange web site (**www.asx.com.au**). Investment banks and stockbrokers (here and overseas) regularly publish research reports on different industries and companies. These reports will contain valuable intelligence on the state of the market as well as useful measurements of the performance of key players. Large proprietary companies must also lodge audited financial statements with ASIC (see **www.asic.gov.au**). Compare the seller's business to the industry standard (this is known as 'benchmarking'). Material differences (either positive or negative) are worth investigating.

Employees

An important part of due diligence is assessing the employees and senior management of the business. You will need to assess whether or not they have the necessary skills and expertise to conduct the business. You will also need to ensure there is a cultural fit between your management style and personality, and the rest of the employee team.

Find out whether there have been any industrial disputes or formal complaints made internally, such as equal opportunity or discrimination claims. You will need to check the occupational health and safety record of the business. If there has been a large number of claims there may well be an ingrained operating system which is creating unsafe work conditions.

Obtain detailed records of the employees and their salaries and superannuation, and other employee entitlements such as overtime, long-service leave and accrued sick leave. You will be inheriting these financial obligations when you purchase the business.

DOING A VALUATION

Although it may take many years to accumulate the financial resources necessary to buy a business, it could take only a few months to lose it. It is important that you do not buy a job, but rather a business that can meet your financial and personal goals. Understand what these goals are and be clear on what has to occur within the business to achieve these goals.

Valuation

Accordingly, do not simply accept the seller's own estimate of the worth of the business. Obtain the assistance of a qualified accountant to calculate a fair value. If part of the business includes real estate (either a long-term lease or freehold) you should obtain a report from a registered property valuer. It is critical that you evaluate what the maintainable earnings of the business are, and base your valuation on this amount. In particular, you should consider whether the assets are sufficient to generate such maintainable earnings. If there are any deficiencies in the asset base you will need to consider whether there are any synergies or other advantages that will come with your ownership that could sustain the earnings which you will require.

There are a number of different valuation methods (such as net present value calculations or earnings multiples based on industry averages), which are beyond the scope of this guide. For example, some companies are valued on the basis of a market-based pricing multiple such as a multiple of EBIT. Such market-based pricing may be useful as a rule of thumb, however you must still accurately assess a business on its own financial performance and prospects.

In many cases the future viability of a business purchase will come down to one single decision – the valuation paid for that business. If you pay too much for the business you will spend a disproportionate amount of your profits paying off principal and interest, and simply trying to recover your invested capital. Before completing the purchase you will need to make a number of sanity checks such as benchmarking the price to sales of similar businesses in the marketplace, comparing the forecast return on your investment against simply investing the money in blue-chip listed stocks, or comparing the purchase price to what it would cost to establish the business from scratch.

This section is primarily to aid buyers of existing businesses, but the principles also apply to decisions about establishing a new business or buying a franchise.

When valuing a business you will need to establish which assets are going to be purchased (such as stock, receivables, plant and equipment), any liabilities to be assumed (such as trade creditors) and the market value of each asset, and then add an amount which represents goodwill. If the business being purchased is part of another business, then it is also important to be aware of the costs and revenue allocated within the group. Once separation occurs, what costs and obligations will the business you are buying be left to bear?

The purchase price of a business is often divided into various components:

Total purchase price	$2 000 000
Assets	
Plant and equipment	700 000
Fixtures and fittings	200 000
Stock	400 000
Work-in-progress	50 000
Accounts receivable	50 000
Intellectual property	200 000
Less	
Employee entitlements	(25 000)
Trade creditors	(25 000)
Sub-total	$1 550 000
Goodwill	$450 000

The key steps in assessing the value of a business are to determine the value of the following:
- plant and equipment
- fixtures and fittings
- stock

- work-in-progress
- accounts receivable
- intellectual property
- liabilities
- goodwill.

Plant and equipment

Plant and equipment includes items such as machinery, tools, refrigeration, desks, chairs, photocopiers, fax machines and computers. Inspect all assets to ensure they are in good condition and working order, and carefully assess the remaining useful life of each item. Find out whether they are still covered by a manufacturer's warranty and make sure you get copies of the warranties when you buy the business. Check that there is no off-balance-sheet financing (in other words, hire-purchase or leasing arrangements which effectively mean the lessor still owns those assets) in relation to these items.

Plant and equipment can usually be valued relatively easily by comparing similar items for sale via wholesalers or through the sale of used items by public auction. Professional valuers are also listed in the Yellow Pages. In some cases, however, specialist equipment may be difficult to value as there is not a readily available market for it.

Check the condition of any motor vehicles to be purchased. Check with the Register of Encumbered Vehicles (REVS) in your state to find out if a motor vehicle is still under a finance lease arrangement (and thus the property of a financier and not the business).

Excluded assets Assets which may be excluded from the purchase may be cash at bank, debtors (also known as accounts receivable) and any non-core assets such as motor vehicles and real estate.

Fixtures and fittings

Fixtures and fittings are items such as air-conditioners, shelving, machinery and ovens which are connected to the premises; they cannot simply be moved by hand but must first be disconnected (by screws, bolts, plumbing or wiring). You must be careful with fittings and fixtures – at law, things connected to a building become part of the land and are the property of the landlord. If, however, a tenant installs equipment in leased premises to allow proper operation of that equipment it will remain their property and may be sold, removed or replaced.

Stock

In the case of stock you should perform a physical audit to ensure the stock is saleable and not obsolete, shopsoiled or in excesses of odd sizes. The value of stock on hand is usually in addition to the purchase price and is determined by a stock-take close to or on the date of settlement to avoid disputes relating to removal of stock. Payment for the stock will usually be required within seven days of completion. You may be able to engage an accountant with expertise in that particular industry, or other consultants, to conduct the stocktake and assess the stock's saleability.

A key issue in valuing stock is to determine which stock can be rejected by the buyer. Although the stock may be of good quality, it may be slow moving, out of date or simply out of fashion. Why pay full value for these items when there is no prospect of quick sale and recovery of full value on the open market?

Occasionally a business sale is on a 'walk-in/walk-out' basis – the value of the stock is included in the purchase price and accepted on its face by the buyer. In these circumstances it is important to have a special condition in the contract to prevent the seller from running down the stock below a particular level.

A buyer should ensure that:

- the seller does not sell or move any stock which is subject to the sale
- the valuation of stock on closing is performed by an independent valuer
- the valuation of stock is on a cost basis, verified against invoices from suppliers.

Work-in-progress

Where contracts are partially performed, whether for services or goods, a valuation will need to be placed on that work-in-progress. Typically it should be assessed in accordance with the customer contract and, if possible, any valuation agreed with that customer. The value of any work performed by the seller that will be invoiced by the buyer will normally be an adjustment to the purchase price in favour of the seller. When considering work-in-progress, it is important to bear in mind the risk of possible disputes over the quality of the work previously performed by the seller, and the risk of not recovering debts in relation to that work.

Accounts receivable

You need to assess carefully whether you want to purchase the accounts receivable of the business (net for an allowance for bad and doubtful debts). There is a risk that debtors will not be collectable. A bad debt relating to a debt assumed may not be deductible from your tax, as you did not actually make the sale that generated the debt. On the other hand, if you leave it to the seller to collect accounts receivable after the business has been sold, they may not be 'tactful' as they no longer have a vested interest in maintaining good relations with the customers of the business. A good compromise is for the seller to retain accounts receivable and for the buyer to act as an agent for the seller and collect accounts receivable for three months after the purchase (the buyer may wish to charge the seller a collection fee).

Intellectual property

Intellectual property is defined as the intangible assets of the business, including the rights and information protected by patent, design or trademark registration; domain names, business or company name registration; and copyright and confidentiality agreements. Goodwill is discussed below.

It is difficult to value intellectual property. Software that has been generated internally could, for example, be simply valued at the number of hours taken to develop the software multiplied by the employee's, or a consultant's, hourly rate. The true value of that software, however, may be considerably more or less than that figure. On one hand, the software may be out of date or require significant continual maintenance, making it far less valuable. On the other hand, this simple method of valuation does not take into account the profit-making potential of the software. An alternative method of valuing this type of intellectual property is to capitalise the forecast profits that the software will generate – for example through licence fees, direct sales revenue and even the cost-savings generated. Clearly all these decisions require considerable commercial analysis and judgment.

Liabilities

If possible you should avoid assuming the seller's liabilities. If you do, ensure that there is a corresponding reduction in the purchase price, that the nature of the liabilities you are assuming is tightly defined, and that the seller 'indemnifies' you for any liabilities not expressly assumed (ask your solicitor to advise). The seller should pay out all employee entitlements up to the settlement date (such as salary, superannuation and commissions). The purchase price should be reduced by the amount of any other benefits accrued but not paid (such as long-service leave and annual leave). Sick leave is not normally treated as an adjustment to the purchase price.

Goodwill

The seller usually asks for a premium, in addition to the market value of the assets of the business, which represents the intangible asset known as goodwill (i.e. purchase price less market value of assets). This represents the reputation of the business and the strength of its relationship with key stakeholders – employees, customers, strategic partners and suppliers. It is the ability of the business to earn a greater level of profits than the same business started from scratch.

In general, the younger a business is, the less likely it has goodwill. A business with a well-known brand name will carry a substantial goodwill premium. The amount of goodwill which you should pay will depend on the future profitability of the business. Accountants often use a multiple of past profits or revenues (such as one year's profit before tax).

When considering how much goodwill to pay, you should ensure that the business will generate sufficient net profit to provide you with not only a fair income but a reasonable return on capital invested in the business, and the ability to recover your invested capital including the goodwill component. Goodwill should not be excessive in relation to the profitability of that business.

Personal goodwill In assessing the value of goodwill, you should consider whether the goodwill can be transferred to the buyer. How much of the goodwill is reliant on the personality, qualifications and good name of the existing owner? A key risk in the purchase of a business where personal goodwill exists is that customers follow the seller to a new location and do not continue business with the buyer. Personal goodwill also exists where a partner in a business has some special permit, licence, qualification or skill which cannot be transferred to the buyer.

Personal goodwill is common in industries where the proprietors have a personal following, such as in professional practices (like medical, dental, architectural or legal practices), hospitality businesses (like hotels, restaurants or cafes) and personal services such as hairdressing.

The purchase price of the business should not include any component which reflects personal goodwill unless:

- the seller stays on in the business long enough to introduce customers to the buyer
- the seller agrees to a 'restraint of trade' clause in the contract of sale.

Local goodwill If the location of a business is important because of its accessibility, visibility, proximity of customers and suppliers or special-purpose buildings, then the location will be an important part of goodwill. There are a large range of businesses where the location is a vital part of the business's success, including many retail businesses, convenience stores, service stations, hotels and motels. It will be important when valuing the goodwill driven by location to ensure that there is security of tenure over those premises. Ensure that you have a long lease with options to renew; it may be that you make the purchase conditional upon the landlord giving consent to extending the term of the lease.

Economic life   Many people consider that they will be able to recover the goodwill component at a future date when they sell the business. It is important to consider that some businesses may not be able to be resold if, for example, major customers cancel their contracts, there is an increase in competition or the lease over the premises has expired. A combination of one or more of these factors may mean that the 'economic life' of the business is limited and, as such, the investment and goodwill should be carefully considered.

ORGANISING FINANCE

The next step is to arrange suitable finance for the purchase. The various types of finance available are discussed in detail in chapter five. In summary, you can obtain finance for business purchases from the following financiers:

- trading banks
- venture capitalists
- finance companies
- merchant banks.

The most common source of finance is from trading banks who offer bank overdrafts and term loans. Financiers usually require some 'security' for the loan in the form of:

- mortgage of land

- fixed or floating charge of company assets
- personal guarantee.

NEGOTIATING AND SIGNING LEGAL CONTRACTS

Before signing any legal documentation it is important that you seek advice from a solicitor and tax adviser who have experience in the type of business you are buying. Each party to the purchase should be separately represented.

Deposit

The deposit is generally 5 to 10 per cent of the purchase price (excluding the stock figure). If the deposit is less than 5 per cent it should be enough to show a bona fide commitment by the buyer to purchase the business.

The deposit is normally paid in full, on exchange of contracts, to the agent or the seller's solicitor as 'stakeholder', and deposited into a trust account. If the deposit is to be invested between exchange and completion, it should be clear where and how the deposit is to be invested and how the interest will be shared.

Do not pay the deposit directly to the seller, as you risk the seller defaulting under the contract and keeping your deposit.

Shares versus assets

Buying a business should be compared to buying a company or, more precisely, the shares of a company. Buying a company involves not only buying the business of the company but also taking on all the debts and liabilities owned by the company (such as loans, overdrafts, tax, trade creditors and litigation). On the other hand, buying shares incurs less stamp duty than buying a business. In general, shares can be transferred for stamp duty of only 0.3 per cent (in some states, such as Victoria, Tasmania and Western Australia, no stamp duty is payable on transfer of shares, unless the company owns land), whereas a business sale can incur up to 5.5 per cent. However, because the entire history of the company is 'inherited' by the new owners in a share purchase, more extensive due diligence will be required and it will be critical to assess the risk of any contingent liabilities. For example, if you were to buy a company that had failed to pay taxes for the previous financial year, the company would be liable for the unpaid tax (and you would have less profit to distribute to shareholders). You might be able to sue the sellers for breach of warranty and recover some of the undisclosed liability but you would be taking a credit risk on the sellers repaying you. If you buy a business, the sellers remain liable for any unpaid tax.

Negotiation issues

There will be tension between the buyer and seller around a number of issues (not just the purchase price).

	Buyer will want:	Seller will want:
Settlement date	delayed payment terms	settlement as soon as possible
Breadth of warranties	detailed warranties	buyer to rely on their own enquiries
Assumption of liabilities	to minimise the liabilities of the seller which they have to take on	buyer to take on the burden of existing liabilities

Tax implications	to allocate the purchase price to minimise stamp duty payable and to ensure maximum deductions from depreciable assets	to allocate the purchase price to minimise capital gains tax payable on any gains made
Competition restraint	to ensure the seller cannot compete against the business for a long period of time	to be able to launch a business in the same industry

Do not be afraid to walk away from a deal; there will always be plenty of other opportunities. Whilst disappointing, a failed purchase is not a total waste – you will have gained further experience about the industry which you can use in the next deal.

Competition restraint In practice, the most common way to protect goodwill is to require the seller (and other key people) to agree not to compete with the business within a particular geographic area and for a particular period of time after the sale. Such restraints need to be carefully drafted by your lawyer. Restraints which are unnecessarily wide, both in respect of area and time, may be unenforceable.

Legal searches
Before buying ensure your solicitor undertakes searches to ensure that:
• there are no mortgages or charges over the assets

- no litigation has been commenced
- business names and domain names have been properly registered
- any trademarks or patents are registered.

Warranties The contract should contain a number of 'warranties' from the seller. Warranties are statements of fact that the seller makes and upon which you rely. If they are proven to be incorrect after you have purchased the business, you may be able to sue the seller to recover part or all of the purchase price. Typical warranties are:

- that financial statements are properly prepared in accordance with accounting standards and give a true and accurate picture of the business
- that the seller owns all the business assets, free of any third-party interests (for example, the computers are owned outright and are not subject to a hire-purchase arrangement)
- that no litigation has been commenced or is pending against the business.

It will also be necessary to assess the credit risk of the seller. If there is a risk that they may be unable to meet any warranty claims, then you should consider withholding a retention amount from the purchase price. This amount could then be paid some time after completion, when your understanding of the risks in the business is better and you have had a chance to claim against any warranties which have been breached.

Warranties are no substitute for due diligence, just further protection in case anything unforeseen goes wrong. In an ideal transaction all such problems would be revealed in the due diligence process and rectified prior to completion.

Tax, GST and stamp duty

It is important to obtain tax advice on the tax implications of the purchase. Some of the key tax issues to consider are:

- Stamp duty may apply on the purchase of shares and assets. In relation to asset purchases, the allocation of the purchase price is crucial. Trading stock is not liable for stamp duty. Intellectual property created under Commonwealth legislation, but which is not situated entirely or predominantly in one state, may be liable only for nominal stamp duty. (In such cases it may be appropriate to apportion part of the goodwill to intellectual property to reduce stamp duty.)

- The purchase of a business as a 'going concern' is generally free of GST – otherwise a further 10 per cent may be payable.

- Recent changes to the tax laws may mean that if you purchase a subsidiary of another company and that subsidiary is part of a consolidated group for tax purposes you may become jointly and severally liable for the tax liabilities of other companies in that group.

CHECKLIST BEFORE BUYING

Ensure you answer the following questions before you buy an existing business.

Background

- Why is the seller selling the business?
- How long has the business been on the market?
- How important are the personality and talents of the seller?
- How long would it take to start this business from scratch?
- What is the cost of starting from scratch?
- How much risk is there in starting from scratch?

Finance

- Have you obtained disclosure of the business's financial information for at least the past three years?
- Is there sufficient working capital to operate the business?
- Are the actual and forecast profits of the business sufficient to repay your finance, pay you a market salary and give you suitable return on capital?
- Have you obtained finance to purchase the business?
- What is the sales trend (over at least the past three years)? When you subtract inflation from these figures what does the real trend look like?
- How do these sales figures compare with trends in this sector of business?
- How many years will the business take to pay for itself? (As a rule of thumb, the business should pay for itself in less than five years.)

Operations

- Have adequate records been kept?
- Is the location of the business suitable?
- Was the business well managed?
- Have you interviewed staff, customers and suppliers to assess their attitude to the business and its sale? (Ensure you obtain the seller's approval before doing this.)
- Have you assessed whether there are any external factors (such as competitors or new legislation) which may affect the financial viability of the business?
- Have you asked the seller to do a handover period?
- Have you locked in the valuable employees and executives with suitable service agreements?

Assets

- Has your lawyer obtained approval from the landlord for an assignment of the lease?
- Have you inspected all the assets of the business and ensured that they actually exist and are in good repair?
- Have you obtained a valuation of the business from a professional adviser?
- What value, if any, has been placed on goodwill?
- Are there any hidden costs to the purchase – for example, will you need to replace equipment which is out of date?
- Are you being sold all the assets you need to run the business?
- Is there any hidden value with excess assets? – for example, the seller may be valuing land and buildings in accordance with their original cost, when the market value is significantly higher, leaving the purchaser with a better deal than the seller thinks.

19. VENTURE CAPITAL

- **What is venture capital?**
- **Advantages and disadvantages**
- **The investment process**
- **Post-investment**
- **Raising funds in Silicon Valley**

WHAT IS VENTURE CAPITAL?

Venture capital involves the provision of funding, by way of an equity or debt investment, to rapidly growing companies. Venture capital investors provide capital and also offer value-added services in the form of providing strategic advice, introducing alliance networks and negotiating exit strategies.

The founder of a company agrees to trade a percentage of shares in their company in return for the venture capital funding. Venture capitalists tend to take a minority stake in a company and typically do not take control of the day-to-day affairs of the company.

Venture capital is often called 'patient capital' as it seeks a return not through immediate and regular payments of principal and interest but through long-term capital appreciation. Venture capitalists realise their investment when they sell their shares in the company. They do this by way of an Initial Public Offer (known as an IPO) on a stock exchange, like the Australian Stock Exchange (ASX), or a trade sale to a competitor, supplier or customer. This usually occurs between three and five years after the investment, although longer periods may be acceptable in biotech investments.

Industry focus

To compensate for the long-term commitment and a lack of liquidity and security, venture capitalists expect to receive very high returns for their investment. As such, they primarily invest in companies with high growth potential. Venture capital investments tend to have the following key characteristics:

- new marketing ideas, innovative technology or new product application potential
- a significant, although not necessarily controlling, participation by the venture capitalist in the company's management
- high-quality executives and employees who are energetic, focused and professional
- products that have passed through the early prototype stage and are adequately protected by patents, copyright or confidentiality arrangements
- businesses with the potential to mature within a few years to the point of an IPO or trade sale
- opportunities for the venture capitalist to make a contribution beyond the capital investment.

Examples of venture-backed public companies include LookSmart, Netscape, Yahoo! and Apple Computer.

Although information technology and life sciences have in the past attracted the majority of venture capital investment, venture capitalists invest in many different fields that have the potential to offer an optimal rate of return. Successful investments also occur in manufacturing, consumer products and new materials. Many venture firms typically avoid certain sectors, such as property, retail, mining and agriculture.

Comparison to debt

Startup companies often require large amounts of money to be spent early to establish the business before a revenue stream can be established. For this reason, traditional debt finance is usually unsuitable as the company may not be able to make the regular interest payments demanded by debt financiers and may not have the assets necessary to secure a loan. This is where venture capital may be a more suitable option. The following table sets out the relative differences between debt and venture capital financing from the investor's perspective.

DEBT VERSUS VENTURE CAPITAL

	Debt financing	Venture capital financing
Form of investment	The company borrows money which it has to repay later, with interest	In return for funds, the investor receives a percentage stake in the capital of the company
Investor's source of return	Interest	Growth in the value of the investor's shares
Return on investment	5–10 per cent per annum	An internal rate of return (IRR) of 35–40 per cent
Protection for investor	Mortgage over the assets of the company	Board seats, preferential shareholder rights
Risk	Low, as secured assets can be sold if company defaults	High to very high
Considerations for investor	Adequacy of collateral	Management team and market potential of company

Time before investor generates income	Usually one month	Typically two to six years
Means of exit for investor	Loan repayment	IPO or trade sale

ADVANTAGES AND DISADVANTAGES

Venture capital provides the funding that a company needs to expand its business. It also offers a number of value-added services.

- **Mentoring** – venture capitalists provide companies with ongoing strategic, operational and financial advice. They can act as your mentor, business coach and motivator. They will typically have nominee directors appointed to the company's board and often become intimately involved with the strategic direction of the company.

- **Alliances** – venture capitalists can introduce the company to an extensive network of strategic partners (including customers, suppliers, financiers and advisers), both domestically and internationally, and may also identify potential acquisition targets for the business and facilitate the acquisitions.

- **Facilitate exit** – venture capitalists are experienced in the process of preparing a company for an IPO of its shares

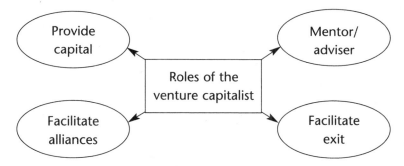

onto the ASX or overseas stock exchanges such as NAS-DAQ. They can also facilitate a trade sale.

On the downside, most venture capitalists seek to realise their investment in a company within three to five years. This means that if an entrepreneur's business plan contemplates a longer timetable before providing liquidity, venture capital may not be appropriate. Entrepreneurs should also consider that venture capitalists are:

- typically more sophisticated and may drive a harder bargain
- more likely to want to influence the strategic direction of the company
- more likely to be interested in taking control of the company if the management is unable to drive the business.

Tip from the trenches

Some entrepreneurs desperate for funding sell the proverbial family farm and give their financiers high equity stakes or unduly onerous protections. Always get advice from your lawyer before contemplating this and be wary of giving up too much equity or control.

THE INVESTMENT PROCESS

The venture capital investment process, from the perspective of the entrepreneur, occurs through a series of assessments and negotiations. The diagram on the next page summarises the typical venture capital investment process.

Venture capitalists receive hundreds of unsolicited business plans. Due to time constraints, very few of these plans are read thoroughly. A good way to approach a venture capitalist is to be introduced by a person who knows them. Friends or associates who have obtained venture capital financing and entities that license technology to venture-backed companies may have connections to venture capitalists. Accountants, lawyers and bankers who advise venture capital funds or venture-backed companies are also

THE VENTURE CAPITAL INVESTMENT PROCESS

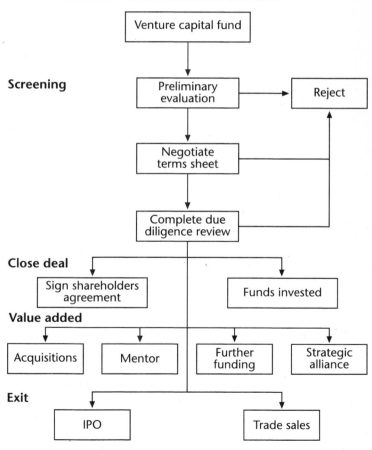

a good source, as well as superannuation fund managers, universities, and other entities involved in innovation and venture capital.

Selecting a venture capital fund

Your company should consider the investment preferences of the various funds, the quality of the relationship between the management team and the investors, and the ability of the fund to provide future funding. The following table highlights the points you need to take into account when selecting a venture capital fund.

SELECTING A VENTURE CAPITAL FUND

Investment preferences	You should look at the investment preferences of various venture capital funds, including the particular stages they invest in; the amount of money they invest; the industry sectors they prefer and their geographical location.
Communication	As the investment will typically last for a number of years and involve plenty of close negotiations/discussions, it is important that you select a fund with which you can build a strong and open relationship.
Experience	Other companies in your industry may have used particular funds and they could provide you with a track record of the venture capitalist.
Future funding	Check to see if the investor can provide further rounds of funding or introduce you into offshore finance markets.

Value-added services	The fund may offer industry-specific knowledge; financial and strategic planning; advice for key personnel; identification of business acquisitions; access to international markets and technology.
AVCAL	The fund should be a member of the Australian Venture Capital Association Limited (AVCAL). This association has adopted an industry Code of Conduct that establishes a minimum set of principles that members are to observe. (See **www.avcal.com.au** for a list of members and their contact details.)
Other investors	The venture capitalist may be willing to work alongside other investors or offer advice on other venture capital firms they think should be invited to co-invest into the deal.
Time horizon	You'll need to know what their exit time horizon is for their investment.

Submitting your business plan

Once you have selected a number of suitable venture capital funds, you should submit your business plan for evaluation. The venture capital fund will undertake a preliminary evaluation of the merits of your proposal, in particular:

- experience of the management team
- potential for exit
- profitability of the business
- outlook for the industry
- competitiveness of the product/services
- barriers to entry
- viable business model.

Most venture capitalists prefer business plans to be limited to no more than ten to fifteen pages. Anything that is not key to your company's message should be eliminated or attached as an appendix.

Your plan should also avoid calling for multiple opportunities simultaneously in multiple markets. Venture capitalists prefer companies with a focus on the greatest opportunity and with an objective of doing that well. Other opportunities can be discussed later or handled in a very brief section towards the back of your plan.

Once the venture capitalist has reviewed your business plan, there will be preliminary discussions and interviews to determine whether your company is suitable.

Valuation of the business

Negotiating valuations can be one of the most difficult issues in venture capital financing. Valuing a company is never easy, but it is especially difficult in the case of a startup with a limited operating history and this often involves intense negotiations.

Venture capitalists will often base their valuations on management's own projections and on other deals negotiated in the industry by other companies. Information about comparable companies which have received venture financing can be useful in setting benchmarks for valuation. The investor will want to ensure that the valuation is supported by financial and legal due diligence and that the company's forecasts are reasonable and based on sound assumptions.

Although valuation is of obvious importance, other issues, such as restrictions on the founder's shares and the investor's ability to introduce strategic partners, should be considered as well. These restrictions are discussed in more detail in the next section.

It is also good to remember that the venture capitalist willing to pay the highest price is not necessarily the best fund for the business. Another venture capitalist willing to pay a bit less may be a better partner for a dynamically growing business.

The terms sheet

Once a venture capital fund indicates its intention to invest in a company, there are a number of important issues to be negotiated. The terms sheet sets out the basic framework for the deal. Issues to be resolved at this stage include the form of the investment, protections to be given to the investors, rights of the investors to appoint board representatives, information rights and exit strategies. The terms sheet will govern the investment until such time as the parties negotiate the detailed legal agreements.

The following issues are likely to arise in the negotiations of the terms sheet. Venture capitalists:

- may invest in your company in the form of ordinary shares, preference shares or convertible notes. Venture capitalists generally want preference shares as they confer additional protection, such as preferential right to dividends, without leveraging the balance sheet.
- may wish to make their investment in stages or tranches with each tranche conditional upon the company achieving certain milestones (such as signing up key customers or achieving certain revenue rights).
- will want to oversee and control the progress of their investment. In order to do this, they will seek to appoint a certain number of directors to the board and tailor the matters that must be considered by the board.
- will require protection against dilution. There are two types

of anti-dilution protection – restructure and price protection. Restructures are protection against share dividends, share splits, consolidations and similar recapitalisations. Price protection is where a company issues shares at a discount to the shares bought by an investor.

- may seek the right to force the company to realise the value of the investment at some point in the future by requiring the company to buy back or redeem their shares if an IPO or trade sale has not occurred by a certain date.
- may also require a 'drag along' clause which compels all shareholders to sell their shares if more than a specified percentage of shareholders (usually 75 per cent) accept a third-party offer.
- may also require that the founding shareholders agree to a standstill provision which prevents them from selling their shares in the company for a period of time.
- may require that key executives sign appropriate executive service agreements.
- may want the right to receive certain information, such as monthly financial statements, annual audited financial statements, and the annual budget and business plan approved by the board.
- may require a pre-emptive right to invest in future issues of shares in preference to a third party.
- are driven by the need to realise the value of their investment and may seek to impose a provision enabling them to force a trade sale or IPO if such an event has not occurred within three or four years of the investment.
- may seek a period of exclusivity after the signing of the terms sheet, typically in the region of thirty to sixty days, where the venture capitalist has the right but not the obligation to invest.

Due diligence

Due diligence involves a detailed examination of the company. The due diligence process will run in parallel with the terms sheet negotiations. Generally, the venture capitalist and its lawyers will undertake the following due diligence:

- a review of the company's corporate structure
- a review of assets owned by the company
- verification of ownership of the intellectual property
- extensive review of the financial statements and accounts of the company
- a review of the company's key contractual relationships with suppliers and customers, licensing agreements and so on
- a review of the company's standard employment agreements, relationships with key employees, employee option plans.

Assuming the due diligence has not uncovered major issues relating to the prospects of the business, the parties will then prepare and sign formal documentation which sets out the detailed mechanics for the issues set out in the terms sheet.

POST-INVESTMENT

One of the main advantages of venture capital financing is that a good venture capitalist can continue to add value after the financing has been completed. This relationship is as much a part of venture capital financing as the funding. In order to gain the most out of the value-added services of the venture capitalist, the company should:

- hold regular meetings between the company's management and the venture capitalist. Keeping the venture capitalist well informed is the only way to ensure that the

company makes the best possible use of the venture capitalist's contacts and experience.
- ask the venture capitalist to introduce potential strategic partners and other organisations whose expertise could be valuable to the company.

RAISING FUNDS IN SILICON VALLEY

If you have a technology business which is 'born global' (has major customers overseas) and needs a significant injection of capital, it is worth considering raising funds in Silicon Valley. A number of Australian companies have successfully migrated to the US including LookSmart, Agrilink, Atmosphere Networks and webMethods. US venture capitalists tend to have far more capital available than their Australian counterparts and can also leverage their US networks to introduce key suppliers, customers and alliances and help with NASDAQ listing.

Before a US venture capitalist will invest in an Australian business they will require the following:

- **Migration to the US** – your company will need to become a US corporation. You will need to transfer the bulk of your IP into the new US corporation. You will also need to move your senior management to the US. It is typically acceptable to leave R&D in Australia (it may be preferable as the lower exchange rate and salary differentials mean Australian engineers/programmers are one-third the cost of their US counterparts).
- **Management team** – a strong, capable and experienced management team is crucial. Interestingly, past failure by the founders is seen as a positive in the US and gives you credibility (as you are less likely to make the same mistakes). In Australia, failure by an entrepreneur may

make it nearly impossible to raise funds in the future.

- **Large addressable market** – a product or service with potential sales of only $20 million a year is unlikely to draw interest. You need to be able to tap a big market (US$5 billion).
- **Interesting business model** – they are looking for a model that is able to be executed to seize an existing market failure or opportunity.
- **Frictionless investment** – venture capitalists in the US are suspicious of overly complex or unusual structures (which Australian entrepreneurs seem so fond of, such as a backdoor listing via a mining company or with a Bahamas IP company). Keep your structure as simple as possible.

20. EXPORT AND IMPORT BUSINESSES

- **Export businesses**
- **Import businesses**
- **Payment and trading terms**
- **International freight forwarders**
- **GST on exports and imports**
- **Government export grants and assistance**
- **Customs**
- **Australian Quarantine and Inspection Service**
- **Where to get help**

EXPORT BUSINESSES

Exporting is challenging and time-consuming, as you will not only have to run your normal business but also master the complexities of international trade (such as foreign exchange risk, quotas, tariffs, sales tax, Customs, freight forwarding) and the intricacies of foreign languages and cultures. Furthermore, the business basics which satisfy domestic customers may not apply, as international customers can be far more demanding.

Planning

Before embarking on a costly and time-consuming export program, it is important to undertake preliminary market research and planning. There is an enormous amount of work to do in preparing for exporting, and buying your airline ticket should be the *last* preparatory step. The key issues to consider in planning an export program are:

- Is there an overseas market for your goods and/or services?
- Is the product acceptable in its current form?
- Does your business have the right infrastructure to export?
- How will you distribute your product?
- How will you manage foreign exchange risk?

Is there an overseas market for your goods and/or services? In determining whether there is an overseas market, you must consider the 'who, where, when and why?' of your potential customers as well as other market forces such as potential competitors and regulatory issues. In particular, the following issues must be considered:

- **Customers** – who are your potential customers? Where are they? When will they buy? Why will they buy your product or service? How much will they buy? How often will they buy?
- **Market** – consider general economic conditions in that country. Is the economy stable? What is the nature of currency fluctuations? What are the trading preferences of that region (payment and trading terms)?
- **Regulatory** – are there any import duties, tariffs, quotas, local regulations or quarantine restrictions which will affect sales?
- **Competitors** – who are your existing or potential competitors in that market? What can you offer that is different from your competitors? How competitive are you in terms of price and quality?

Gathering this information will require extensive research. It can be obtained from a variety of sources including trade and industry associations, Austrade, freight forwarding agents,

Australian Bureau of Statistics, Customs brokers, chambers of commerce, government departments, trade journals, potential suppliers and even potential customers.

Is the product acceptable in its current form? It is important to consider the changes that might need to be made to your product before you can export (and the cost of those changes). They might include:

- labelling requirements
- foreign language requirements (instruction manuals, labels)
- safety regulations and other government regulations
- cultural factors
- electrical voltage.

Tastes and trends vary enormously between countries so it is vital that you factor in cultural differences. Make an effort to understand the local culture, otherwise you risk offending customers and distributors by using inappropriate language, branding, marketing or labels.

Does your business have the right infrastructure to export? Your plan should seek to answer the following questions:

- **Capacity** – what is the production capacity of your (or your supplier's) existing plant and equipment? Is it sufficient to cope with the increased volume which export orders are likely to generate? You may need to increase capacity, reconsider the efficiency of current plant layouts or find new suppliers.
- **Controls** – are quality control procedures effective? In particular do they account for foreign regulatory requirements?

- **Staff** – do you have enough personnel to manage the influx of new orders? Are they suitably trained and qualified to deal with the complexity of issues arising from foreign trade (such as sales tax, Customs clearance/duties, cultural issues, freight, etc.)?
- **Funding** – do you have working capital facilities in place to deal with the increased funds required? Manufacturing for export will require substantially more raw materials and updated equipment. Other expenses include overseas travel, freight, training of staff and holding costs caused by delays on the waterfront.
- **Supplies** – do you have access to sufficient raw materials? Exporting requires a great deal of time. If you already have a hectic schedule running your domestic business, how are you going to find the time to meet the demands of the export-related business, such as travelling overseas to meet potential customers and distributors?

How will you distribute your product? There are a number of different models for distributing your product overseas. You can appoint exclusive or non-exclusive distributors for different regions, or open branch offices. (An exclusive distributor is one who is the only distributor to a particular region. A non-exclusive distributor is one amongst a number appointed to the same region.) It is obviously far less risky to simply appoint distributors than to open a fully-fledged branch office. You will save the costs of hiring staff, leasing premises, buying plant and equipment, etc. On the downside, the distributor will take a significant cut of all sales in that region, and you will also lose control of the customer relationship.

How will you manage foreign exchange risk? It is important that you understand foreign exchange risk and implement a system for controlling it. In most cases, your customers will pay for your exported products in their local currency. You must understand the volatility of foreign exchange rate movements and the effect that they can have on your business. The Export Finance and Insurance Corporation (EFIC) may be able to assist you with this (see below).

Cultural issues

You need to explore the cultural features of the region, and take the time to understand the language requirements. Consider the following:

- Check what is the most appropriate greeting – in some regions, hugging or kissing is frowned upon, unless you know the person quite well. In Japan it is customary to bow; if the person you are bowing to is more senior, you bow lower than they do.
- Australians tend to address people by their first names immediately after an introduction; this may offend some Asian businesspeople.
- In cultures where family ties are important, you should get to know the family members of your foreign clients and suppliers. Bringing small gifts from Australia for their children will greatly strengthen your relationship.
- In most foreign countries, it will be well received if you or someone on your team can speak their language (even if it is simply at a social level, such as greetings).

Export quotation

A quotation is a formal offer and its acceptance constitutes a binding contract of sale. Take care when drafting quotations because, once accepted, they can be difficult to cancel or amend. To enable an importer to fully evaluate an offer, you must provide the following essential information:

- **Price** – the importer needs to know the price at which the goods are being offered, the currency in which the price is quoted and for how long the offered price will be held firm.
- **A detailed description of the goods** – to enable the importer to correctly classify the goods for Customs duty purposes.
- **Trading terms** – indicate what is (and what is not) included in the quoted price. The most commonly used trading terms are explained later in this chapter. For example: *Free On Board* or FOB includes all charges incurred in cartage and loading the goods on to the ship; *Cost and Freight* includes all FOB charges plus freight up to the port of discharge.
- **Packing specifications** – to enable the importer to calculate cartage, handling charges and freight, etc. on the imported cargo.
- **Payment terms** – indicate the method by which payment will be made to the exporter. There is a range of payment terms ranging from cash in advance (the most secure from an exporter's point of view), to payment after the goods have been received by the importer (the least secure). Payment terms are discussed later in the chapter.

The Export Finance and Insurance Corporation

The Export Finance and Insurance Corporation (EFIC) is Australia's official export credit agency and assists exporters with medium to long-term finance and insurance, where traditional sources are not available. EFIC supports several billion dollars' worth of exports every year to more than 150 countries.

Export Credit Insurance   In certain 'risky' countries, there are a range of economic, political and legal factors which are outside the direct control of your customers. So, even creditworthy customers with honourable intentions can sometimes fail to pay. There will also be times when normally 'safe' markets have problems; indeed more than half of EFIC's claims relate to North America and Europe.

EFIC's Export Credit Insurance provides cover for payments owed to Australian exporters by overseas buyers. The insurance provides cover for non-payment arising from particular commercial, political or legal events. This allows exporters to secure new export business by offering more attractive payment terms and to minimise balance-sheet risk and protect cashflows.

Finance products   EFIC also provides a range of products aimed primarily at supporting exports of capital goods including export finance, performance bonds and working capital guarantees.

- **Export finance** – helps overseas buyers to purchase Australian exports. EFIC also provides direct loans or an export finance guarantee which assists banks to provide finance to the overseas buyers.
- **Performance bonds and guarantees** – may be required of Australian exporters by overseas buyers of capital equipment as security for advance payments or in support of their performance obligations under a contract. EFIC will issue the bond directly to the overseas buyer or

will provide your bank with a guarantee and they will issue the bond.

- **Working Capital Guarantee** – can help exporters access finance when they have a large export order but cannot secure the working capital needed to complete it. EFIC provides a guarantee to your bank, which can then lend the funds.

The Export Finance and Insurance Corporation can be contacted via their web site: **www.efic.gov.au**

CASE STUDY:
Duncan MacGillivray – Two Dogs

From its humble beginnings in a casual joke with a mate over a beer, Two Dogs has become a worldwide beverage empire and is credited with creating an entirely new category of alcoholic drinks.

It started in 1991 when Adelaide publican and microbrewer Duncan MacGillivray had a drink with a friend who happened to have truckloads of unsellable lemons and nothing to do with them. With his experiences in the pub and a little bit of creativity, Duncan was able to discover a method of brewing them into a light and drinkable form of alcoholic lemonade. Before long, Two Dogs Lemon Brew (named after the punchline to a well-known joke) was on tap at many pubs throughout Adelaide and, soon after, in bottle shops around Australia. Only a few years later, Two Dogs was available throughout the world from North America to Europe and Asia.

Apart from having a novel idea, Duncan also recognised that there was a gap in the market for his product. There was an increasing demand for convenience; drinkers were becoming less content with buying large bottles of ingredients and mixing them at home. The 'ready-to-drink' phenomenon was reborn, but with entirely new products rather than premixed versions of the old favourites. Furthermore, with increased responsibility in the service of alcohol, a standardised drink with a prescribed alcohol content is considered by many drinkers and publicans to be more sensible. From an insignificant market share prior to the launch of Two Dogs, the ready-to-drink market now represents approximately 20 per cent of all liquor sales in Australia.

Beyond the product idea, the Two Dogs philosophy is simple: create a distinctive brand and advertise it internationally. This type of branding philosophy has been used to great effect by many other entrepreneurs throughout the world – probably none more successfully than Richard Branson with his Virgin products.

In addition to the branding component of the philosophy, Duncan made two crucial observations of potential limitations in his product right from the start: Two Dogs was a summer drink, and Australia has a small population. It was this recognition which led Duncan to his rapid expansion in exports.

The particular business model Duncan chose for his global expansion is also interesting, as it is not a straight-out export and distribution arrangement. Rather than deal with the hassles of operating a large company in a variety of different countries, all with different legal systems and market pressures, Duncan issued licences to local business to produce and distribute the product. By using this system, Two Dogs has been able to 'follow the sun' as the seasons change around the globe, without being lumbered with the logistical difficulties of organising an estimated 7000 people associated with Two Dogs into one company structure. According to Duncan, the primary caution in pursuing such an arrangement should be to ensure quality control by requiring that appropriate corporate standards are clearly set out in every licensing agreement.

Along the way, Duncan has collected a number of entrepreneurial awards including a Telstra Business Award in 1999, the Impact 'Hot Brand' Award in the USA in 2000 and the Rabobank Agribusiness 'Value Adding' Award in 2002, to name a few. These awards constitute recognition of the rapid success Duncan had in building his brand. In only a few years, he took Two Dogs from a concept to a multimillion-dollar, worldwide alcoholic beverage empire. It is an example of recognising a great idea and a gap in the market, acknowledging the strengths and weaknesses of the product, and capitalising on the idea by sticking with a simple branding strategy through international growth.

IMPORT BUSINESSES
Costing

While you may recognise a market opportunity for an imported product, it is difficult to assess the size of the market for the product until you have calculated the selling price, a key driver of which is the costings. The main cost components are:

- **The exporter's selling price** – what is the exporter's price, and which elements of the transport costs are included in that price?
- **Inland transport to the point of loading** – obtain this cost from either the exporter or importer's forwarding agent. This will often be included in the exporter's price.
- **Port charges at the point of discharge** – obtain from the forwarding agent, shipping company, airline or loadings Customs agent. Typically, port charges at both loading and discharge points are included in freight rates.
- **Freight from the point of loading to point of discharge** – obtain from the forwarding agent, shipping company or airline.
- **Clearing charges** – obtain a quotation from your Customs agent for the work involved in clearing the goods from Customs control.
- **Customs duty** – seek advice from your Customs agent

or ask Customs the rate of duty which would apply to the goods you wish to import.

- **Sales tax** – check with the Australia Taxation Office (or your Customs agent) whether sales tax is payable on the goods you intend to import. If goods are imported for retail sale, sales tax is payable at the time of importation. However, if goods are imported for wholesale they may be exempt from sales tax. Sales tax is then collected when the goods are re-sold to the retailer.
- **Fumigation/inspection charges** – obtain (if applicable) from your Customs agent.
- **Inland transport to importer's premises** – obtain this cost from the cartage company, forwarding agent or Customs agent.
- **Insurance against loss or damage** – this is arranged by most forwarding agents or through insurance underwriters or brokers.

If possible, obtain import quotations and invoices in Australian dollars to minimise exposure to fluctuations in foreign exchange rates. If this is not possible, consider arranging with your bank manager for a forward exchange contract.

Planning and research

You should study the Australian market to ensure there is sufficient demand for the product you are seeking to import. Consider:

- Is there a market for the product? How big is this market (revenue in dollars and unit sales)?
- Is the product currently being made in Australia or imported into Australia? If so, will your product be price-competitive?
- Who are your existing and/or potential customers? Where

are they? When will they buy? Why will they buy your product or service over alternatives? How much will they buy? How often will they buy?

- Are there any import duties, tariffs, quotas, local regulations or quarantine restrictions which will affect sales?

The fact that a product is already being imported into Australia does not necessarily mean that you will not also be able to successfully import it. In fact, it may be far easier to import and sell a product that is already on the market, rather than trying to create a new market.

If the product you intend to import is already on the Australian market, study the product and take note of presentation, packaging, labelling, quality and retail price.

Once you have established that there is a market for the product, bring a test sample into the country and approach your potential clients to gauge their interest in the product.

Finding products to import   Finding products for import used to be a time-consuming process that involved wading through dozens of brochures just to find the names of companies. Thankfully that exercise has been simplified, as chambers of commerce and Austrade now have computer databases listing not only the companies but the range of products they manufacture and contact names, numbers and email addresses.

Australian Bureau of Statistics   The Australian Bureau of Statistics may have statistics on the product you wish to import, including quantities currently being imported, total dollar values and individual unit prices. This data is invaluable in assessing the level of competition, and gives you a good feel for the level of market activity.

Further, it will help you to benchmark the price asked for by the overseas supplier.

Finding an overseas supplier

When importing, it is important to have reliable overseas suppliers. If they become insolvent, provide products late or supply poor-quality products, it is your reputation (and bottom line) which suffers.

You must ensure that your supplier is willing to comply with any special requirements that might be necessary, such as special labelling/packaging and any product modifications required to meet Australian standards or tastes.

When selecting a potential overseas supplier, ask for references from other importers who have dealt with them. Your lawyer may be able to organise a credit check to assess the supplier's financial stability. The advent of electronic commerce has made the threat of fraud ever-present. Do not simply rely on the Internet for all your market research. Remember that while a web site may take some time to create and look professional, it can disappear (with your money) instantly. You should also visit the supplier yourself.

Placing an order with a supplier

When placing an order with a supplier, ensure that the terms and conditions of the contract of sale are in writing and as detailed as possible, including:

- the product
- part or product numbers
- price per unit
- description and specifications
- quantity
- labelling, packaging and marking requirements

- embarkation point and destination
- trading terms
- payment terms
- shipping method
- required documentation.

Australia has many requirements for imported goods (see discussion on Customs, later in this chapter), so know the requirements before placing an order.

Upon arrival, the goods received should be thoroughly examined for quality, quantity and condition. If the quantity and quality of the goods is inadequate you must contact the supplier immediately. If the goods have been damaged in transit, you will need to contact your insurance company.

Financing your order

A key part of the transaction is how you will finance the purchase of the goods. An importer will often be required to make payment to their suppliers before receipt of payment from the ultimate buyers. Importers need to manage this mismatch in cash flows by:

- negotiating trading terms with suppliers and buyers that will more closely match the timing of payments against expected receipts; and
- seeking financing from financial institutions (see chapter five for more details).

PAYMENT AND TRADING TERMS
Payment terms

These will always be the subject of some negotiation between exporter and importer. Consult your bank manager or accountant for assistance in selecting the method of payment. Common methods of payment in import/export transactions are:

- **Cash in advance** – payment by the importer *prior* to shipment
- **Letter of credit** – an undertaking given by a bank (on behalf of the importer) to pay an exporter an amount of money at sight or at a determinable future date provided that certain terms and conditions are fulfilled. A confirmed irrevocable letter of credit cannot be cancelled or amended without the consent of the beneficiary.
- **Bill of exchange** – the shipping documents under cover of a bill of exchange are either drawn at sight or at a fixed or determinable date (e.g. 15 April or 30, 60 or 90 days after sight) and are delivered by the exporter to their bank, who transfers them to the importer's bank. The importer's bank will surrender the documents to the importer upon payment of the face value of the bill of exchange or an undertaking (usually in the form of an endorsement on the reverse of the bill) to pay when the bill matures.
- **Open account** – the exporter sends the documents directly to the importer who makes payment by means of cheque, telegraphic transfer, etc.

Trading terms

Common trading terms are:

- **ex-works** – the price quoted only covers supply of goods at the exporter's warehouse and does not include any element of the cost of transportation or insurance
- **FOW (free on wharf)** – includes cartage to wharf but excludes wharfage
- **FAS (free alongside ship)** – includes cartage and wharfage but not the cost of loading on board the vessel
- **FOB (free on board)** – includes all charges incurred in cartage and loading the goods on board the vessel

- **CFR (cost and freight)** – includes all FOB charges plus freight up to the port of discharge
- **CIF (cost insurance freight)** – includes all charges including freight and insurance up to the port of discharge
- **CIFC (cost insurance freight and commission)** – includes the CIF price plus a commission payable to the exporter's agent
- **FIS (free into store)** – includes all charges incurred in delivering the goods to the importer's premises, including wharfage duty and inland cartage.

INTERNATIONAL FREIGHT FORWARDERS

International freight forwarders organise the movement of cargo from one location to another and have a network of offices (or agents) in a number of international locations.

They can assist exporters and importers in a number of ways:

- **Booking space** – making the necessary bookings with shipping companies or airlines to ensure that the cargo is transported with the minimum amount of delay
- **Freight savings** – making regular 'block bookings' of space on ships and aircraft, enabling them to consolidate the cargo from a number of small exporters and pass on the savings achieved to their clients in the form of reduced freight rates
- **Costing** – assisting exporters and importers in calculating the cost involved in exporting goods to a particular destination, and advising on the most economical means of transport, (i.e. air versus sea or a combination of both)
- **Cargo monitoring** – monitoring the movement of particular cargo from the time it leaves the exporter's premises to the time it arrives at the importer's premises

- **Documentation** – producing documents which comply with the regulatory requirements in the importer's country and in letters of credit, etc.
- **Storage** – having the facility to store outgoing and incoming cargo (this facility usually extends to a bonded warehouse, which allows goods to be held in Customs – see section on GST below). They are also able to arrange inspection by Australian Customs Service or other agencies if this cannot be accomplished conveniently at the exporter's premises.
- **Information** – providing clients with information about market conditions, duty rates, etc.

GST ON EXPORTS AND IMPORTS

In general exports of goods and services from Australia are GST-free. Exporters are entitled, however, to claim input-tax credits on the materials and supplies required to produce the goods and services exported. Ask your solicitor or tax adviser for more details.

Most imported goods are subject to GST, calculated at 10 per cent of the value of the taxable importation. This value is not simply the purchase price but is the sum of the Customs value, Customs duty, the amount paid to transport the goods to Australia and transit insurance.

The goods are subject to GST at the time of entry through Customs and, as such, input credits relating to imported goods are claimable in the tax period in which GST was paid.

To manage your GST, consider:

- bringing the bulk of your imports through Customs at the end of your tax period or attempting to sell the goods at the beginning of your tax period so you can fund the GST

- minimising stock on hand by importing only when sales have been secure
- using a bonded warehouse, which allows goods to be held at Customs (GST would not be payable until the goods are released and entered through Customs).

GOVERNMENT EXPORT GRANTS AND ASSISTANCE

There are a number of different programs available to assist exporters.

Austrade

Austrade is the Federal Government's export assistance agency. It is represented in 140 locations in 60 countries, including an extensive domestic network throughout Australia. Austrade offers the following services:

Advisory services   Austrade offers market intelligence, practical advice and ongoing support (including financial) to Australian businesses looking to develop international markets:

- **Market intelligence** – Austrade can assist with detailed information on competition, prospects, cultural considerations, distribution systems and government regulations.
- **Advice** – Austrade can help businesses determine whether they are ready to export; identify potential distributors, buyers or agents around the world; provide advice on which overseas markets hold the highest sales potential for their product; and pass on specific business opportunities as they arise.
- **On-the-ground support** – in overseas countries, Austrade offices can assist with a number of services including arranging appointments with distributors or other useful

contacts; organising interpreters; attending meetings to help overcome language or cultural barriers; and organising product launches and promotional material.
- **Investment opportunities** – Austrade also provides advice and guidance on overseas investment and joint-venture opportunities, and helps put Australian businesses in contact with potential overseas investors.

New exporter services – TradeStart Austrade and TradeStart offer a package of free services, designed to assist small- and medium-sized Australian companies with launching and developing their businesses overseas. The table below sets out the range of services offered:

Service offered	Process
Assess your export capability	• review your export capability and export readiness • identify target markets • provide advice on management issues
Prepare for your selected market	• advise on your marketing strategies and marketing plan • evaluate the suitability of your service/product for target markets and any changes required • provide feedback on promotional material/ brochures • update you on socioeconomic conditions and commercial practices

In your selected market	• arrange appointments with selected business contacts
	• provide briefings on local practices and culture by Austrade staff in-market
	• if necessary, arrange interpreters or translation of documents
Follow-through by your export adviser	• assess the outcomes of your visit
	• assist you to achieve maximum impact from the visit

Source: Austrade, 2006

To be eligible for TradeStart, your business must have:
- a current Australian Business Number (ABN)
- Australia as its main place of business
- not completed TradeStart, the former Export Access program, or received Austrade's new exporter services, during the last three years (some exceptions apply)
- no recurrent export revenue in the same market over the last three years.

Trade shows   Austrade can also advise businesses of the dates and details of overseas trade shows and expos. By visiting trade shows and fairs, you are able to measure reaction to your goods immediately and determine whether to move into that market. You may be able to share the costs of a stand with another Australian business. While there you will have the opportunity of networking with experienced exporters from around the world who can provide valuable tips.

Austrade can be contacted by phone on 13 28 78 or their web site is at **www.austrade.gov.au**

Export Market Development Grant

Austrade offers exporters financial assistance through the annual $150 million Export Market Development Grant (EMDG) scheme. EMDG is targeted at small- to medium-sized exporting enterprises, who spend at least $15 000 every year on export marketing. To be eligible your firm must have a total business turnover of less than $30 million.

Before a business can qualify for a grant, it must spend $15 000 of its own money on export promotional activities and marketing. Your first EMDG claim can combine two years of expenses. Eligible marketing expenses include:

• visiting overseas markets
• producing product samples
• trade fairs, brochures and advertising
• hiring consultants
• communication costs.

Grants are calculated at 50 per cent of eligible expenses (less the first $15 000). Grants up to $150 000 are paid in a single full payment.

Assistance in a single export market is limited to eight years. Extensions are available for three years for each new market entered. First-time applicants must register with Austrade by 30 June and lodge applications between 1 July and 30 November.

Export Access

Export Access assists small- and medium-sized enterprises to become sustainable exporters. Since 1991 some 3000 companies have used the program to achieve more than

$230 million in export sales. Export Access is ideal for companies with no (or limited) export experience. While the program offers no direct financial assistance, it provides experienced project managers to coach businesses entering their first overseas market or developing their business in an existing market.

Selected companies work through the following program with their project manager:

- assessment of the company to define export potential
- identification of export markets most suitable for the business's product/service
- preparation of a company profile and marketing materials
- development of a specific export marketing strategy
- examination of finance options
- planning of an overseas market visit
- follow-up on overseas market visit and help in identifying export leads
- referral to Austrade for assistance in developing subsequent markets.

Firms from all industry sectors can apply for Export Access assistance. To be eligible for Export Access your business must have:

- an annual turnover of more than $300 000 and less than $20 million;
- export sales of less than $3 million over the last three years and less than $1 million in the last year; and
- a business track record of at least twelve months, with Australia as its main place of business.

Australian Agency for International Development (AusAID)

The Australian Agency for International Development has $10 million to fund joint ventures in the Asia-Pacific region in the following industry sectors:

- environmental or waste management
- information technology
- human resources and training.

They will reimburse up to half of the costs of training an applicant's overseas partners in Australia, up to a total of $50 000.

The Australian Agency for International Development can be contacted by phone on (02) 6206 4000.

CUSTOMS
Australian Customs Service

In general, most goods exported from Australia must be declared to the Australian Customs Service. The key exceptions are unaccompanied personal/household effects, consignments leaving Australia valued at $2000 or less and goods that have been temporarily imported into Australia. Customs Information Centres are able to advise of any export restrictions, permits or regulatory requirements for commodities being exported from Australia.

All goods imported into Australia (whether by air, sea or post) must be cleared by Customs. While imports of low value will generally be released by Customs for delivery direct to consignees, importers are responsible for obtaining Customs clearance for consignments of goods valued at $1000 or more.

Customs carries out testing on goods that must meet specified requirements and all testing is charged to the importer. In recent times, these charges have increased dramatically. However, if overseas certificates are available and are accepted by Customs you may be exempt from testing. Obtain these certificates in advance and present them at the time of importation to ensure unnecessary testing is not carried out.

Duty

Rates of duty payable by an importer are determined by the classification of goods within the Australian Customs Tariff. In some circumstances, anti-dumping (where goods sold into Australia are cheaper than in the home country) results in additional rates of duty.

Regulations

The following goods are subject to import control:
- certain drugs and goods containing those drugs
- hazardous and health-related manufactured articles and substances
- animals and animal products
- food and plant imports
- firearms and other weapons
- protected wildlife and related products
- protected cultural heritage
- motor vehicles.

Permission to import must always be obtained *prior* to the goods arriving in Australia. Failure to do so may result in the forfeiture or destruction of the goods.

The *Commerce (Trade Descriptions) Act 1905* details all the information and requirements for the correct marking of trade descriptions on imported goods. Customs officers may examine and inspect goods to ensure that they comply with the requirements of this Act. Goods that do not comply with the Act's requirements will not be released until the problem is rectified. Some goods may have to be destroyed or re-exported if the problem cannot be corrected. As a general rule, trade descriptions must be in English, in legible characters and on a principal label attached to the goods in a prominent position and in a manner as permanent as is practicable. The Act also requires importers to retain commercial documents relating to a transaction for five years from the date of entry.

Customs brokers

Customs brokers can assist you with the myriad of complex import and tax regulations. The broker will also arrange the pick-up and delivery of cargo to an importer's store.

The broker will process Customs entries using the documentation received from the importer. They will check the documents for accuracy and ensure that what is said to have been shipped has actually been shipped, so that duty is neither overpaid nor underpaid.

Brokers will collect the documents directly from the freight forwarder and pay the relevant charges such as:
- freight
- international terminal fee
- airline documentation and handling fees
- air cargo automation fee.

When choosing a broker, ensure they are a member of the Customs Brokers and Forwarders Council of Australia – members are required to hold professional indemnity insurance.

The Customs Brokers and Forwarders Council of Australia can be contacted by phone on (07) 3252 1348 or their web site is at **www.cbfca.org.au**

Duty Drawback

You may be eligible for a refund (known as Duty Drawback) of Customs duty and sales tax paid on imported goods if they are subsequently exported from Australia. It can be claimed if the goods are exported in the same form as they were imported or if they have been incorporated into another product. For example, duty paid on imported fabric can be claimed when shirts, blouses and other garments produced from that fabric are exported.

Contact the Australian Customs Service on their National Information Line (1300 363 263) or view their web site at **www.customs.gov.au**

AUSTRALIAN QUARANTINE AND INSPECTION SERVICE

Consider whether you need to obtain clearance from the Australian Quarantine and Inspection Service (AQIS). Certain products are not allowed into Australia.

If you intend to import animals, food, plants or associated products, you will need to apply to AQIS for an import permit, to ensure that the threat of bringing in pests or other disease risks is minimised.

AQIS establishes import conditions and modifies them appropriately when necessary (for example, when new information on a pest or disease becomes available). A review may be prompted by interested parties presenting information that justifies further risk analysis. Alternatively, AQIS may decide to initiate an analysis on the basis of information gathered from its own sources.

There is a provision within AQIS for appeal on the decision-making process following a determination on whether or not an item is allowed to be imported.

The Australian Quarantine and Inspection Service can be contacted by phone on (02) 6272 3933 or 1800 020 504, or their web site is at **www.affa.gov.au** (click on 'AQIS').

WHERE TO GET HELP

Below are phone numbers and web site addresses for some key organisations which assist importers and exporters.

ACT and Region Chamber of Commerce and Industry
(02) 6283 5200
www.actchamber.com.au

Australian Business Ltd
13 26 96
www.australianbusiness.com.au

Business SA
(08) 8300 0000
www.business-sa.com

Chamber of Commerce and Industry WA
(08) 9365 7555
www.cciwa.com

Chamber of Commerce Northern Territory
(08) 8936 3100
www.chambernt.com.au

Northern Territory Chamber of Commerce and Industry
(08) 8936 3100
www.ntcci.com.au

State Chamber of Commerce (NSW)
1300 137 153
www.thechamber.com.au

Tasmanian Chamber of Commerce and Industry
(03) 6236 3600
www.tcci.com.au

Queensland Chamber of Commerce and Industry
(07) 3842 2244
www.qcci.com.au

Victorian Employers' Chamber of Commerce and Industry
(03) 8662 5333
www.vecci.org.au

21. FRANCHISING

- **History of franchising**
- **Franchising in Australia**
- **What is franchising?**
- **Advantages and disadvantages**
- **Financial aspects**
- **Franchise documentation**
- **Regulation of franchising**
- **Evaluating the franchise opportunity**
- **Suitability as franchisee**
- **Selling the franchise**

HISTORY OF FRANCHISING

Isaac Singer, the founder of the Singer Sewing Machine Company, is generally credited as the founder of franchising. In the 1850s the Singer company sought 'regional agents' who would pay a fee for regional territorial rights to sell, demonstrate and repair Singer sewing machines. This new method of distribution allowed the Singer company to penetrate the US market quickly with limited capital.

Manufacturers and suppliers such as motor-vehicle manufacturers, soft-drink companies and oil companies have traditionally used franchising as their primary distribution method, and franchising still remains the dominant business method in those industries.

'Business format' franchising (the concept which is commonly associated with franchising today) was developed in the United States in the 1950s by some of the well-known US fast-food chains. This method was introduced into the Australian market in the early 1970s when fast-food retailer McDonald's opened its first stores. Since its introduction, business format franchising has transformed this method of distribution into a highly competitive, innovative vehicle for expansion for virtually any industry or sector where goods or services are sold to consumers via a network.

Below is a list of well-known companies that use franchising techniques in their businesses.

Franchise type	Examples
Fast-food retailer	Burger King
	Hungry Jack's
	KFC
	McDonald's
	Boost Juice
Bulky goods retailer	Forty Winks
	Freedom
	Harvey Norman
Book retailer	Angus & Robertson
	Dymocks
Automotive retailer	Autobarn
	Bob Jane T-Marts
	Midas
Baker	Bakers Delight
	Brumby's
	Michel's Patisserie
Printing and signage company	Kwik Kopy
	SIGN-A-RAMA
	Snap Printing
Health industry operator	OPSM
	Terry White Chemist
	Priceline Pharmacy

Utility	AGL (Australian Gas Light Company)
	Energex
Service business	Fastway Couriers
	Jim's Mowing
	VIP Home Services
	ANZ Mortgage Solutions
	Mortgage Choice
	Fernwood
Real-estate firm	Raine and Horne
	PRD Nationwide
	Ray White Real Estate
Car-rental company	Budget
	Europcar
	Thrifty
Route trade operator	Dairy Farmers
	Nudie Foods
Oil company	Caltex

FRANCHISING IN AUSTRALIA

Franchising is a well-established and credible business method in Australia. There are more franchise systems in Australia per capita than in any other country, and at least three times as many franchise systems per head of population than in the United States.

The *Franchising Australia 2004 Survey* illustrates how the franchise sector in Australia is continuing to mature and consolidate, and is fast becoming more professional operationally.

Some of the key findings of the *Franchising Australia 2004 Survey* are:

- There are approximately 850 different business format franchise systems, over 92 per cent of which are home-grown Australian systems.

- There are approximately 54 000 franchised outlets.
- Approximately 507 000 people are employed in business format franchise organisations.
- The majority of franchising takes place in the retail (non-food) industry (30 per cent), with property (24 per cent) and business services (21 per cent) the next largest sections.
- Franchising exists in all regions of Australia, with New South Wales containing 31 per cent of all franchises in Australia, and both Victoria and Queensland containing 22 per cent.
- The majority of franchisors expect their franchisees to be hands-on operators involved in all aspects of the business.
- Single-unit franchise ownership is the norm, although the number of multi-unit franchise owners is growing.
- Most franchised outlets are operated by couples (50.7 per cent), with male sole ownership representing 28.4 per cent and female sole ownership 10.5 per cent.
- A high proportion (72 per cent) of franchisees are in the 31–50 age group.
- The growth rate in franchised systems from 2002 (the date on the previous survey) to 2004 is 14 per cent.

WHAT IS FRANCHISING?

There are two main categories of franchise arrangements – product franchises and business format franchises.

Product franchises

Typically, product franchises are arrangements where a manufacturer (the franchisor) grants to another (the franchisee) the right to distribute the manufacturer's product with the use of the manufacturer's trade name. Generally a territory or specific location is allocated to the franchisee.

The franchisee will usually pay the manufacturer fees or royalties based on sales. Motor-vehicle distributors, petroleum retailers and soft-drink bottlers are traditional examples of product franchises.

Business format franchises

Business format franchises comprise a more sophisticated business relationship. They are characterised by a system or method of business that the franchisor has developed, and which the franchisor permits the franchisee to use, in a controlled fashion, in the operation of the franchisee's independently owned business. Most business format franchises involve a franchisor who has a valuable trademark, image, reputation and business format, who grants to a franchisee – in exchange for initial and ongoing fees – the right to carry on business using the franchisor's trademark, image and business format for a specified period and on certain terms and conditions.

The phenomenal success of health food and beverage chain Boost Juice is an example of how an innovative idea can rapidly expand using franchising techniques. The first Boost Juice store was opened in South Australia in July 2000. In May 2002 the first franchised store was opened. Over the next twelve months, over 50 new stores were established across all states in Australia. The network is continuing to expand using a mix of franchised and corporate-owned stores, and by acquiring other juice businesses.

Under a business format franchise, the franchisor takes on responsibility for managing and developing the franchise network. Franchisors will often centrally manage activities such as product procurement and marketing, and provide a range of services to the franchisees. Stock may be supplied by the franchisor or sourced through third-party arrangements established by the franchisor.

An effective business format franchise will allow the franchisees to focus on operating their businesses. Usually the franchisees will own the equipment, vehicles, fixtures and fittings used in the business and will hold the stock. Employees involved in the business will generally be either principals or employees of the franchisee. The franchisee will handle most dealings with customers.

A business format franchisor will inevitably exercise a considerable amount of control over the operation of its franchisees' businesses. The purpose of the control is to regulate the quality and consistency of the products and services provided through the network. A 'rogue' franchisee could potentially have an adverse effect, not only on the franchisor, but on the franchise chain as a whole.

The franchisor's business format, which sets out the various controls, standards and procedures to be followed when operating the business, will usually be set out comprehensively in the franchisor's operations manuals and business handbooks. Most business format franchisors would regard it as critical that the franchisee strictly comply with the business format to ensure consistency and quality throughout the franchise network. A failure to comply with the standards of the system can result in a dispute and could potentially result in termination of the franchise arrangement.

ADVANTAGES AND DISADVANTAGES

Buying a franchise is not a guarantee for business success. However, for those looking at owning a small business, there are numerous advantages in buying a franchised business.

A franchise allows the business owner to operate his or her

own independent business, but with the benefits of an established and proven concept, and an existing network of similar businesses. For these reasons, a franchised business is generally regarded as carrying a lower risk of failure than other small businesses.

However, it is important to recognise that as a franchisee you are taking on a business risk. All business undertakings involve risk and a franchised business is no exception. The level of return that a franchisee can expect from the franchised business will depend largely on the ability and efforts of the franchisee. Those businesspeople that are able to use their own entrepreneurial skills and make the most of business opportunities will generally perform well and be able to maximise the return on their investment of capital and labour in the business. Those who expect the franchised business to run by itself and who fail to comply with the franchisor's business format are less likely to have a successful franchised business.

Also, it is sometimes the case that, despite the franchisee's best efforts and commitment, the franchised business fails. Failure can occur for reasons that are beyond the control of the franchisee or the franchisor, such as a downturn in the economy, withdrawal of an important source of products, or an aggressive competitor. It is vital that a prospective franchisee carefully evaluates the franchise and business opportunity before making the purchasing decision.

Advantages

A franchisee who purchases a franchise in an established business format franchise network would typically expect to enjoy some or all of the following advantages:

• an established and recognisable brand name

- the benefit of the franchisor's trademarks, trade secrets, formulas and patents
- a proven retail system developed over a period of time by the franchisor
- operations and procedure manuals and training programs to assist with running every aspect of the franchised business
- comprehensive advertising campaigns
- training and support from management across a wide range of areas including methods of accounting, business controls, marketing, promotions and merchandising
- the benefit of group-buying arrangements and negotiating power
- assistance with property issues such as site selection, rental, complying with planning (zoning) laws, rent reviews, relocations and shop fit-out
- assistance in calculating the correct level and mix of stock, and in the launch of the business
- assistance with equipment, fixtures and fittings
- the benefit of the franchisor's continuous research and development, designed to improve the business and keep it up-to-date and competitive
- guidance in obtaining finance for the establishment of the business.

Disadvantages

Franchising also has its disadvantages. Some of the criticisms often raised by franchisees include:

- the extent of control exercised by the franchisor
- the ongoing financial commitment required to be made to the franchisor
- difficulties with assessing the quality of the franchisor and the franchise system

- the franchisor's inability or failure to provide or maintain continuity of services to the franchisee
- the franchisor's restrictions against the sale or transfer of the franchised business
- decisions or innovations by the franchisor that turn out to be unsuccessful or detrimental to the franchisee
- having to work long hours
- lack of flexibility
- pressure to perform
- the risk of business failure and loss of other assets.

CASE STUDY:
Jim Penman – the Jim's Group

After a failed attempt to earn his PhD in history, Jim Penman was 30 years old, broke and, apart from research, only knew how to earn a living mowing lawns. Starting out with some gardening equipment and flyers for advertisement, he launched Jim's Mowing and managed to earn $600 per week, working six days. Soon the demand for his services increased to a point where Jim was unable to handle all of the work himself, so he started employing subcontractors and selling lawnmowing rounds. This was the informal beginning of the franchising concept for his business.

The sale of lawnmowing rounds was growing but in a disorganised, random way. Competition, in the form of an organised home-services business, provided the impetus for Jim to design a formal franchise system and contract.

Jim adopted certain principles in setting up his franchise. He was determined to put the franchisee first as he appreciated that satisfied franchisees would translate into satisfied customers. He was careful not to limit the size of a franchisee's business; it was up to them how large a business they built. Another fundamental principle was that Jim would go to any length to keep his customers satisfied. Jim believes that most businesses do not look after their customers and that the main reason for this is that they are not even aware of their inadequate service. Success in business is all about service. Jim serves his franchisees well and his franchisees serve the customers well.

Today the Jim's Group is made up of over 20 different divisions, including fencing, dog washing, paving, cleaning, computer services and book keeping. Entrepreneurs came up with the idea of diversifying beyond the mowing division, which proved to be a success. In order to diversify beyond his own sphere of expertise, Jim came to rely on the franchisees to provide the technical, on-the-job expertise, while the Jim's Group would provide the franchising expertise.

The key to successful franchising is quality people. Putting unsuitable people into franchises is a cardinal mistake. You must have the discipline to refuse to sign up someone who should not be a franchisee, even though they may have the money. The other common mistake is to have one-sided franchisee contracts which charge excessive royalty fees and impose restrictions on the growth of the franchisee's business.

The success of Jim Penman is best illustrated by the numbers. In 17 years, the Jim's Group has gone from zero to more than 2600 franchisees in Australia, New Zealand, Canada and the UK.

FINANCIAL ASPECTS

In terms of the financial commitment, franchise systems vary considerably. Generally it is common for the franchisor to charge an upfront franchise fee, an ongoing franchise fee and other specific fees for activities such as advertising, marketing and technology. Many franchise systems (especially those in retail) also fit out the premises and charge the franchisee for the cost. Some product franchise systems do not have an ongoing franchise fee per se. In those cases an ongoing fee is commonly factored into the price charged by the franchisor for the goods.

The initial financial commitment – usually comprising of the upfront fee, premises fit-out, equipment, trading stock, lease costs, bonds, professional fees and so on – can be significant. A franchisee must carefully consider all of the costs payable and plan appropriately.

The initial startup costs for a franchise vary considerably between franchise systems. Retail franchises require significant infrastructure and therefore the average startup cost is considerably higher than a mobile/home-based franchise.

The *Franchising Australia 2004 Survey* indicates the following ranges for total startup costs for a new franchised unit (excluding GST).

Item	Average cost	Range
Initial franchise fee	$35 000	$0–400 000
Inventories	$5000	$0–300 000
Fit-out costs	$21 737	$0–700 000
Training costs	–	$0–40 000
Other costs	–	$0–300 000
Total	$120 000	$2500–870 000

In addition to the initial financial investment, there is an ongoing financial commitment. Typically franchisees are required to pay ongoing fees for the services and support provided by the franchisor and for the privilege of using the franchisor's tried and tested business method. Ongoing franchise fees are usually either a fixed amount or an amount calculated as a percentage of turnover of the franchisee's business. Fixed range from $50 to thousands of dollars per month for more elaborate franchise formats that generate a higher turnover. Percentage fees may range from 2 per cent to as high as 20 per cent.

Often, marketing or advertising levies are also charged, and should be applied by the franchisor to the costs of group marketing. Again, the amount payable may be a fixed amount or an amount calculated as a percentage of turnover of the franchisee's business. The *Franchising Code of Conduct* prescribed under the *Trade Practices Act 1974* requires franchisors to account fully to the franchisees for all monies received as marketing or advertising levies.

There are a variety of other fees that may be payable to the franchisor. Many franchise systems have training fees, franchise agreement renewal fees, documentation fees, franchise transfer fees, site selection fees, fees for technology/Internet services and so on.

The majority of franchisors (especially mature systems) will consider the franchisee's working capital as part of the initial approval process. It is not uncommon for franchisors to make it a condition of the franchise that the franchisee have a debt to equity ratio of 1:1.

A prospective franchisee for a franchised business needs to establish clearly what their total investment will be, what that investment buys and what return can be made on that investment.

FRANCHISE DOCUMENTATION
The franchise agreement

The franchise agreement is the cornerstone of the contractual relationship and should set out the rights, duties and obligations of both the franchisee and the franchisor.

The franchise agreement is a legally enforceable contract

and, except in limited cases, the parties will be bound by each and every provision of the franchise agreement. This is the case even if the franchisee decides not to read the franchise agreement before signing it.

There is no 'standard' form of franchise agreement. As the relationship between the parties will vary between franchise systems, the contract that regulates that relationship will also vary.

The franchise agreement is usually prepared by the franchisor. A franchisee should ensure that the franchise agreement accurately documents the commitment made by the franchisor, and is fair and balanced.

A typical franchise agreement will cover the following aspects of the franchise relationship:

- the parties to the franchise relationship
- any preconditions to the commencement of the franchise, such as satisfactory completion of training by the franchisee's manager and key personnel
- the length of the term of the franchise and any renewal terms
- the extent of exclusivity granted to the franchisee
- the fees to be paid to the franchisor, including when payment is due and how payment is to be made
- the franchisee's obligations in connection with the use of the franchisor's trademarks, patents, copyright and other intellectual property
- the franchisee's obligations in connection with the premises (or mobile vehicle/home office) used to conduct the business, including fit-out, layout and signage
- the franchisee's obligations in connection with purchase of stock, products and services for use and sale through the franchised business
- the franchisee's obligation to comply with the franchisor's

operations manual, as well as with the franchisor's business format and system generally
- the franchisee's responsibilities to customers
- the franchisee's general business obligations
- the franchisee's reporting and accounting obligations
- the franchisor's obligations, such as to provide training to the franchisee
- the conduct of promotions and advertising, and payments to any central marketing fund
- required insurances
- procedures for assignment or transfer of the franchised business
- covenants restricting the franchisee's ability to operate competing businesses
- the grounds for terminating the franchise agreement
- the consequences of expiration or termination of the franchise agreement
- procedures for resolution of disputes between the parties
- liability for costs, stamp duty and registration fees.

The operations manual

There are many detailed issues that need to be regulated to ensure uniformity throughout a franchise network. It is generally not possible, and also inappropriate, to attempt to include every item in the franchise agreement. Also, much of the detail will change from time to time as the marketplace and the business change and develop.

Many of the key operating procedures required for carrying on a franchised business will be set out in the franchisor's 'operations manual'. Operations manuals are typically hard-copy manuals or electronic manuals accessed through the franchisor's Intranet. They range from being general to very comprehensive, dealing with each and every aspect of the business. Because of the nature of the information that it contains, the operations manual is regarded by the franchisor as a commercially valuable and confidential document.

The franchise agreement will normally include a provision requiring the franchisee to comply strictly with the operations manual. It will also normally allow the franchisor to amend or modify the operations manual from time to time, to reflect changes to the business and market trends. Provided that the process for amendment is clear and the franchisor is not unilaterally making a fundamental change to the nature of the franchised business, the franchisee will usually be obliged to comply with the revised operations manual.

Other legal documentation

The *Franchising Code of Conduct* obliges a franchisor to provide to prospective franchisees a comprehensive disclosure document prior to the franchisee entering into the franchise agreement. This is discussed in more detail below.

Other legal documents that the franchisee may be asked to execute include:
- a lease/sub-lease or licence agreement giving the franchisee the right to occupy the premises
- a trademark licence agreement or other documentation dealing with the use of the franchisor's intellectual property
- a confidentiality agreement, protecting the franchisor's confidential information such as the operations manual
- an equipment lease
- a guarantee and indemnity
- trading documentation, such as terms of trade
- a restraint of trade/restrictive covenant deed

- security or finance documentation if the franchisor provides finance
- a contract of sale for the business (if the franchisee is purchasing an existing business).

REGULATION OF FRANCHISING
The Franchising Code of Conduct

On 1 July 1998 the Australian Government enacted specific franchising legislation. This legislation is the *Franchising Code of Conduct* ('the Code'). The purpose of the Code is to regulate the franchise industry and otherwise assist franchisees to make an informed decision prior to entering into a franchise agreement. Compliance with the Code is mandatory. Failure to comply with the Code gives rise to the remedies available under the *Trade Practices Act*.

The Code regulates all those arrangements that fall within the scope of a 'franchise agreement', as defined under the Code. The definition of a 'franchise agreement' under the Code is expansive, and captures virtually all business format franchises and most tradename franchises, as well as some distribution, management and trademark licences and agency agreements.

The provision of a disclosure document

A key requirement of the Code is that franchisors provide a detailed disclosure document to its franchisees. The purpose of the disclosure document is to give a prospective franchisee information to help them make a reasonably informed decision about the franchise, including information that is material to establishing and operating the franchised business.

The franchisor must provide a disclosure document to prospective franchisees at least 14 days prior to the franchisee signing the franchise agreement or paying any non-refundable money to the franchisor. The obligation to disclose is a continuing obligation.

In the disclosure document the franchisor is required to disclose approximately 250 items of information listed under twenty-three categories. The type of information that a franchisor needs to disclose includes details of:

- the franchisor company and corporate associates of that company
- the business experience of the franchisor
- any current litigation and court proceedings against the franchisor
- current franchised businesses, including terminations and renewals of franchise agreements over the past three years
- all trademarks, logos, brands and any patent, design or copyright relevant to the business
- the franchisor's requirements for supply of goods or services to the franchisee
- the franchisor's requirements for supply of goods or services by the franchisee to consumers
- marketing or other common funds
- all the payments to be made by the franchisee in connection with the business
- any financing arrangements between the franchisor and the franchisee
- all the franchisor's obligations under the franchise agreement
- all the franchisee's obligations under the franchise agreement
- any other agreements that the franchisee may be required to sign.

Requirements of the Code   Some of the other requirements set out in the Code include:

- **Copy of the Code** – the franchisor must provide a copy of the Code to the franchisee with the disclosure document and give the franchisee the opportunity to read the Code.
- **Cooling-off period** – the Code allows a seven-day 'cooling off' period for franchisees. This means that if the franchisee terminates the franchise agreement within seven days of signing it, the franchisor is obliged to accept that termination and refund all monies paid to them by the franchisee (less the franchisor's reasonable costs).
- **Advice before entering into a franchise agreement** – franchisees are strongly encouraged to seek independent legal, business and accounting advice. Indeed before a franchise agreement is signed, the Code requires the franchisor to obtain from the prospective franchisee signed statements that the franchisee has been given advice, or has been told to seek advice but has decided not to seek it.
- **Provisions of franchise agreement** – the Code requires that franchise agreements include provisions regulating assignment, termination and dispute resolution.
- **Marketing and other cooperative funds** – the franchisor is required to provide financial statements for any marketing or other cooperative funds to which franchisees have made financial contributions.

Compliance with laws generally

There are many laws which are relevant to operating a business. The fact that the business is a franchised business does not diminish the franchisee's responsibility to ensure that it complies with the law. Most franchise agreements include a provision that specifically obliges the franchisee to comply with all relevant laws. A failure to comply may give the franchisor the right to terminate the franchise agreement for breach of its terms.

Franchisees need to consider the application of the laws in a range of areas including:

- employment
- corporate governance
- environment
- insurance
- occupational health and safety
- privacy
- tax and superannuation
- trade practices (anti-competition, fair trading and consumer protection.

EVALUATING THE FRANCHISE OPPORTUNITY
General considerations

A prospective franchisee should not rely solely on the information provided by the franchisor (or an agent of the franchisor). It is important that the prospective franchisee makes their own enquiries and assessment of the business opportunity.

A franchisee should not look to a franchisor to guarantee the success of their business and must bear their own business risk.

The evaluation of the franchise requires a consideration of the franchisor, the terms of the franchise, and the distinctive elements of branding and intellectual property which give the franchise its value in connection with the business to be operated by the franchisee.

A useful starting point is the franchise agreement and the disclosure document provided by the franchisor. These documents should contain much of the information a franchisee will require to commence investigations.

The evaluation of the business requires consideration of the longevity of appeal of the goods and services sold in the franchised business, demographic factors relevant to any proposed location or territory, any exclusivity, and pricing and product supply issues.

The franchisee should consider premises issues such as location, fit-out, rent, rent review, outgoings and any other special covenants.

The products or services sold as part of the business should be examined for their quality and pricing to ensure both are competitive. In addition, the franchisee should examine the opportunities for obtaining alternative supply, and the cost of doing so.

Matters such as finance, wages, sustainability of the business if marketing is not undertaken, the presence of competitors in the market, and the performance of non-franchised competitors should also be examined.

Tips from the trenches

Verify that the franchisor has substantial systems and a sound underlying business. There must be a proven business format, not just a good idea! Beware if the business seems to be a fad, or if there is too great a reliance on advertising to sustain the business. Ensure that the franchisor provides sufficient training to allow you to operate the business in accordance with the system.

Considerable industry information is available from the Australian Bureau of Statistics showing relevant margins and expense details, which can be benchmarked against the business opportunity.

In summary, when considering a franchised business you should:

- undertake due diligence in relation to the franchisor, especially where the franchise system is new to Australia.
- consider the likely impact of economic factors on the business. Ask specific questions concerning support and training – who? when? how often?
- look at the likely impact of competition on your business.
- check out the financials. Verify independently any financial information you have been given, and do your own 'worst case' forecasts. Do not borrow too much despite the tax deductions. Be wary of large upfront fees with little ongoing support.
- ensure any premises are well located, with long lease terms and reasonable rental.
- investigate the franchisor through the Franchise Council of Australia (FCA), the Franchise Association of New Zealand (if relevant), Consumer Affairs and industry experts. Ask for and read carefully the prior disclosure materials. Also read other franchising publications.
- ensure any claimed economies of scale actually apply.
- speak to existing franchisees and ask them about their experiences.
- obtain advice from professionals (lawyers, accountants and business advisors) who have franchising speciality.

SUITABILITY AS FRANCHISEE

A prospective franchisee needs to assess himself or herself critically, before entering into a franchise agreement.

Franchisors require adherence to systems and procedures.

A person who is not prepared to accept guidance and direction should not acquire a franchise. If the franchisee does not enjoy dealing with people in a retail environment, it is inappropriate to acquire a franchise where every sale is dependent upon the franchisee's selling skills. Franchised businesses often require franchisees to work long hours, which could have a substantial impact on health, family, lifestyle and social activities.

Anecdotally, less than 5 per cent of initial enquiries actually result in a franchise agreement, and the franchise application process can take from four weeks to four months from the initial enquiry through to signing the agreement.

Franchisors typically look for the following characteristics in their franchisees:

- consistency between their vision and the goals and aspirations of the franchisor
- the required level of capital for the business
- a sales focus with the ability to communicate the benefits of the products and services to customers
- a desire to work within the relevant industry
- a desire to seek continuous improvement
- the ability to work hard and operate successfully within a team environment
- a desire to participate actively in the franchise network
- a background which showcases their ability to successfully operate a business.

In addition to personal factors, a franchisee must honestly assess and disclose to the franchisor his or her current financial position. An applicant for a franchise should take care to ensure that all information they provide is true and accurate. Where a franchisor is induced to enter into a franchise agreement as a result of a misrepresentation by the franchisee, the franchisor may at law bring an action for damages, provided the franchisor can show that the statement was made fraudulently. More importantly, the misrepresentation will be likely to constitute misleading or deceptive conduct in breach of section 52 of the *Trade Practices Act*.

While innocent and careless misrepresentation will not provide the franchisor with an action for damages, they may give the franchisor grounds for terminating the franchise agreement. A franchisor will stipulate that it is a condition of the franchise agreement that the information provided in the application is true, accurate and not in any way misleading.

SELLING THE FRANCHISE

Franchise resales are a common occurrence in most if not all franchise systems. The Franchising Australia 2002 survey confirmed previous surveys in finding that the significant majority of 'franchisee exits' (franchisees leaving a franchise system) are brought about not by expiration or termination but by the sale of the franchised business.

Exit Method	Per cent
Term expired	6.0
Sale to another franchisee	72.1
Sale to franchisor	1.8
Termination by franchisor	4.3
Termination by franchisee	7.1
Termination by mutual agreement	5.1
Other reason	3.6
Total	**100.0**

Apart from continuing to operate the franchised business, the franchisee's only opportunity to profit from their investment of capital and human resources is by selling the franchised business to a third party.

Many franchisees will purchase a franchised business with the objective of using the business as a source of income and employment in the short term, but with the equally important objective of building a valuable asset to be sold at a later time.

Some franchisees also enter into a franchise relationship not knowing whether the business, lifestyle or role as a franchisee is going to suit them. Knowing that they can exit by selling the franchised business offers some comfort.

Whatever the motive for exiting the relationship, the ability to exit the franchised business at a time that suits the franchisee and in a manner that allows them to maximise the sale price, is an important factor for many franchisees.

The parties to a franchise agreement may choose to exit from the franchise agreement in a number of ways. The rights and obligations may be surrendered, sold, transferred, subcontracted, leased, licensed, subdivided or otherwise dealt with. The transaction may relate to some or all of the rights under the franchise agreement, and may also involve other assets, rights or obligations.

A franchisee's options will depend upon the nature of the franchised business and the rights granted by the franchise agreement. A franchisee may be able to:

- **Sell the business and assign the franchise rights** – the normal arrangement in the case of business format franchise businesses. The underlying business and the franchise are closely linked, and the sale value is maximised if they are both sold together.
- **Retain the business, but relinquish or assign the franchise rights** – common in the case of participation franchises such as cooperatives.

- **Sub-franchise some of the franchisee's rights** – may be appropriate where the franchisee has a large territory, or new opportunities arise within a territory.
- **Sell part of the business** – can apply in the service sectors where the business is customer-based rather than territory-based. Some networks actively encourage sale of customers. Indeed in the lawnmowing and home-services sector some systems have a specific formula to calculate the value of customers sold or repurchased by the franchisor.
- **Sell the business and sublicense or sub-franchise the rights under the franchise.**
- **Transfer or assign an interest in its issued shares to a person other than an existing shareholder.**
- **Issue new shares to a person other than an existing shareholder.**
- **Where the franchisee is a unit trust, dispose of units in the trust.**

Prior to the introduction of the *Franchising Code of Conduct* in 1998, franchisees had no inherent right to assign their franchise agreement. A franchise agreement could expressly provide that the rights granted were personal to the franchisee and could not be assigned. The Code now provides that franchise agreements must allow the franchisee to assign the franchise with the franchisor's consent, which must not be unreasonably withheld.

The introduction of the mandatory Code makes it difficult for a franchisor to refuse consent to an assignment by a franchisee except for legitimate commercial reasons. Clause 20 of the Code provides that a franchisor must not unreasonably withhold consent to any written request for transfer and sets out a non-exhaustive list of circumstances where a refusal for consent is reasonable. These include circumstances such as where the proposed transferee is unlikely to meet the financial obligations and does not meet the selection criteria of the franchisor.

Franchising Disputes

The level of disputes in the Australian franchising sector remains low, despite the perception that is sometimes given in the media. The majority of formal disputes are resolved through mediation, rather than formal litigation. The Franchising Code of Conduct sets out a process for mediation that all franchisors and franchisees must follow.

The most common franchisor-instigated disputes relate to non-payment of fees and failure to comply with the system. For franchisees, the most common disputes arise out of the franchisor's failure to deliver the system and on 'promises' made prior to the purchase of the franchise.

The *Franchising Australia 2004 Survey* indicated that over a period of 12 months, less than 2 per cent of all franchisees had a dispute with their franchisor.

22. PROTECTING AGAINST FRAUD AND THEFT

- **Contributing factors**
- **Fraud types**
- **Detecting fraud and corruption**
- **Australian standards in fraud and competition control**
- **Internal controls**
- **Physical security**
- **Security issues for retailers**
- **Checklist for prevention**

Fraud is, unfortunately, common in the Australian economy – and growing. It can take many forms, from a fraudulent application for a personal loan to the embezzlement of many millions of dollars by a senior employee.

Statistics collated by the Australian Institute of Criminology since 1953 show a ninefold increase in the level of fraud reported to the Australian police services over the last fifty years.

Fraud The person most likely to commit fraud against Australian business in the early twenty-first century is a longstanding and apparently loyal middle-level manager who is motivated by a compulsive gambling habit involving electronic gaming machines, casinos or some form of online gambling. His or her crime will most likely involve the manipulation of the purchasing process in some way and the preparation of false invoices for goods or services not supplied or supplied at inflated prices. He or she is unlikely to collude with any other person in committing the fraud.

Corruption The person most likely to become involved in corrupt behaviour is again a middle-level manager. He or she will have significant involvement in the procurement function and most likely will have the power to award contracts on behalf of the company. His or her motivation will most likely be lifestyle and there will often be a direct link between the services he or she acquires on behalf of the company and the improvement in his or her lifestyle; often bribes will be paid by the provision of free services to the employee concerned (quite often building-related services).

Manipulation of financial statements Also on the rise in recent years has been the incidence of financial statement manipulation. There has been an increased focus on this kind of fraudulent activity since the collapse of Enron. In a typical case, a senior manager or executive, motivated by his or her performance-based remuneration, will bring forward sales, create fake sales, capitalise expenses or fail to write down the value of receivables that are not recoverable in order to make it appear that the business unit concerned is meeting its performance goals.

Organised crime In recent years the Australian economy has been exposed to highly mobile and organised criminal gangs who are able to recruit large numbers of experienced criminals from Asia. These 'runners' are enticed to enter

Australia on a false passport, are provided with a 'fraud kit' including false drivers' licences and fraudulent credit cards, a mobile telephone and a map of shopping centres in which to operate. The credit cards they use have been manufactured in Taiwan or Hong Kong, normally using details 'skimmed' from credit cards tendered in restaurants, service stations, taxis and many other businesses by the unsuspecting cardholder.

Did you know that . . .

- fraud costs the Australian economy more than $3 billion each year?
- around 70 per cent of fraud against Australian entities is committed by the organisation's own personnel?
- statistically, the employee most likely to defraud his or her employer is a long-standing and trusted middle-level manager?
- in more than one-third of cases, early warning signs are ignored by the victim organisation?
- the most important factor in allowing fraud to occur is poor internal control?
- the most common method of detection is through the perpetrator's fellow employees?

CONTRIBUTING FACTORS

What factors contribute to the incidence of fraud, corruption and other crimes against business? What lessons can we learn from the mistakes of the past and present that can be applied in better safeguarding the assets of Australian business against future attack?

Certainly an increasing reliance on computerised systems has also had a significant impact. In many organisations the introduction of computerised purchasing, payment and payroll systems has resulted in many manual internal controls being replaced by a relatively ineffective system of controls that have a reduced focus on business risk, and the risks of fraud and corruption in particular.

Along with new computerised business systems have come new electronic payment channels. Electronic Funds Transfer, EFTPOS, online business banking and personal Internet banking have created new opportunities for the modern commercial criminal, who is now able to steal on a scale not dreamt of twenty-five years ago.

Many businesses have been caught flat-footed on these issues. Their major focus has been on implementing new systems while minimising the expenditure of resources on managing risks which are dismissed as irrelevant to the entity simply because it has had no previous experience of them.

Many Australian organisations are also striving for ever-greater operating efficiencies. This generally means reduction of staff at middle-level management, where internal control systems have traditionally been enforced.

Market pressures and the pace of business have also had an impact on the typical organisation's capacity to control the risks of fraud and corruption, while greatly improved educational standards – the mobility of the general populace and other demographic factors – have played a significant part in creating the right conditions for crime against business.

Another significant factor in the increasing incidence of fraud involving the manipulation of accounting records is recent and ongoing changes in remuneration structures, whereby a person's income is more dependent on strong financial performance than ever before.

A model of fraud and crime against business

In seeking a better understanding of the issues around the increase in the rate of fraud, it is useful to consider commercial crime in the context of a four-element model as set out in the following diagram:

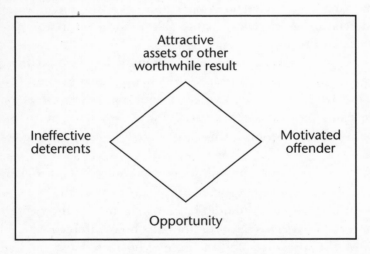

The model applies to internal fraud and corruption as well as other crimes against business.

The change in these factors within Australian business in recent years has been dramatic and is discussed briefly below.

The increasing value and accessibility of attractive assets held by Australian business Funds held by business in increasingly complex banking arrangements are becoming more accessible to staff in their everyday work. This greater accessibility is driven by the business needs of the entity, but in many ways it also makes the funds more accessible to would-be fraudsters.

Changing motivations The motivation of people who would commit fraud has also undergone fundamental change in recent years. Social pressure to attain or maintain a certain lifestyle; an addiction to illicit drugs; ebbs and flows in economic conditions resulting in personal financial crisis; and accessibility to gambling have all contributed to raising the level of motivation to commit fraud or theft against Australian business.

A worrying trend has been the increasing incidence of gambling addicts stealing from their employers in order to repay the money they've borrowed to fund their gambling – this money often comes from dubious sources who charge grossly excessive rates of interest. In one recent case, interest demanded by a 'loan shark' who lent money to an addicted gambler was 10 per cent for every twelve hours the money was outstanding.

Increased opportunity As they try to achieve the right balance between cost and benefit in maintaining tight security over their assets, many Australian businesses have left themselves exposed to the losses of fraud, corruption and theft. Many Australian entities across a range of sectors build a certain level of fraud 'tolerance' into their business planning on the basis that the costs of controlling the risk of fraud are greater than the loss that would be suffered if fraud occurred.

One form of fraud that has increased markedly in recent years is unauthorised use of corporate credit cards. The issue of corporate credit cards to senior employees – and in many organisations to almost all operational employees – is appealing to many organisations as a means of reducing the cost of the entity's procurement function. Until the introduction of a corporate credit card, most transactions with suppliers were processed through a cumbersome accounts-payable system.

Deterrence Many entities' response to detected fraud is weak or unclear, sending a confusing message to management and the workforce. There have been many cases where the employee concerned has been allowed to resign rather than management suffering the embarrassment of having detected a fraud within their business unit.

Sometimes, it goes beyond merely allowing an employee fraudster to resign. In one case, a middle-level manager with twenty-five years' service who admitted stealing $15 000 by raising false invoices and processing them through the entity's accounts-payable system, offered to resign quietly if he was given a redundancy package totalling more than $50 000. His proposal was agreed to! The result – outrage among his former workplace colleagues who were not offered redundancy.

In addition to sending a confusing message to the remaining employees, there are a growing number of reports of employees committing fraud in one organisation, being allowed to resign after having admitted their guilt, being provided with a glowing reference and then committing the same fraud at their next employer, who took the reference at face value. In one recent case, an employee committed a combined accounts-payable/payroll fraud with losses totalling almost $800 000. She was allowed to resign from her position, was provided with a favourable reference by a manager who did not know the circumstances of her departure, and took up a similar role with a new employer where she committed a $40 000 fraud with precisely the same *modus operandi* before being detected a second time.

Organisations need to have a strong policy which is invariably followed when fraud or corruption is detected. This policy should, in appropriate circumstances, include reporting the matter to the police and taking action for recovery of the proceeds of the illegal activity.

FRAUD TYPES
Common reported crimes

The most commonly reported crime against Australian business for which statistics are maintained is fraud against the banking sector involving the misuse of stolen credit cards, credit-card numbers or credit-card merchant facilities. Theft of inventory within the manufacturing and distribution sector may be more common, but it is difficult to assess the impact of this kind of fraud on the victim entities.

Each year, tens of thousands of fraudulent credit-card transactions are processed by Australian banks, unaware until after the transaction that the cards have been stolen, the number of a card issued by the bank has been copied or a fictitious but apparently authentic card number has been generated.

Other types of external attack on the banking system include lending fraud, cheque fraud and, more recently, ATM/EFTPOS fraud and Internet banking fraud where the card number and personal identification number (PIN) are obtained from the victim in increasingly sophisticated ways.

Card numbers are relatively easily obtained by organised

crime; numbers are skimmed at the point of sale before being sold in bulk over the Internet. PINs are now being obtained by the use of pinhole cameras installed into ATMs, dummy ATMs and even transparent plastic sheets laid over the top of ATM number pads that are capable of sending keystrokes electronically to the organised crime gang, who monitor the activity on the ATM from their vehicle a few hundred metres away. While we know this kind of sophisticated and highly organised criminal activity is going on within the Australian economy, getting the evidence to gain a conviction is very difficult for the police.

Tip from the trenches

Common fraud types in Australia:

- Credit-card abuse (theft of credit cards or credit-card numbers and later fraudulent use)
- Theft of plant and inventory by employees
- Lending fraud – fraudulent loan application by bank employee or external party
- Unauthorised use of corporate credit cards by employees
- False invoicing (creating a false invoice as an employee or supplier)
- Payroll fraud (ghosting of fictitious or former employees)
- Accounts receivable fraud (diversion of remittances received by the entity)
- Theft of funds (including EFT)
- Sale of confidential information
- Cheque theft (manipulation of cheques stolen from the mail)
- Falsification of financial statements at corporate or business-unit level

The dark cloud of corruption

It is difficult to make an accurate estimate of the extent of corruption in the Australian economy. As a crime, it is more difficult to detect than fraud. While prosecutions for employee fraud are numerous, prosecutions for employee corruption are relatively rare. The infrequency of corruption prosecutions involving private-sector organisations can result in the misconception that this kind of activity is uncommon within Australian business.

Recent work by Transparency International has shown that Australia is not, as some might believe, 'squeaky-clean' relative to other developed economies. Australia ranked 11th out of 102 countries in the 2002 Corruption Perception Index.

When an employee of an Australian business acts contrary to the interests of his or her employer in exchange for some form of secret commission, financial loss – in the long term if not the short term – will be the inevitable result. The most obvious example of corruption within Australian business is corruption of the purchasing process. This can take a number of forms. It may involve accepting a secret commission in exchange for unauthorised disclosure of commercially sensitive information in connection with one or more bids; accepting substandard work performance; or accepting an inferior bid in terms of price or quality. Many Australian managers do not recognise the financial impact of corruption on their business.

In addition to the corruption of the purchasing process, other forms of corruption such as nepotism, cronyism, sale of confidential information, or extreme self-interest on the part of the board, an executive or senior manager will inevitably have a financial impact on the organisation, at least in the medium to longer term.

DETECTING FRAUD AND CORRUPTION

The most common way in which fraud and corruption is detected within Australian organisations is through colleagues of the offending employee. Experience has shown that many frauds within Australian business can continue for four, five or six years – or even longer – without being brought to the attention of senior management, even though the fraudulent conduct of the employee concerned was well known or strongly suspected by one or more of his or her workplace colleagues.

The reasons why this kind of activity has not traditionally been brought to the attention of management are worth considering. A reluctance to 'dob in' a mate, fear of reprisal, fear of not being believed and lack of alternative reporting channels are all factors in allowing fraudulent conduct to continue unabated. Studies on reprisals against whistleblowers suggest that Australian entities have performed very poorly in this area.

Fraud detection approaches fall into five main categories:

- procedures aimed at detecting fraud during the authorisation process (essentially, fraud 'prevention')
- post-transactional review as part of an internal audit program
- application of computerised techniques to analyse data held within the entity's systems (e.g. data mining)
- use of management accounts to identify indicators of fraud or corruption
- recognition of behavioural signs exhibited by people who are involved in fraudulent or corrupt conduct.

Fraud detection techniques can only be used effectively after the organisation has identified its specific risks of fraud and corruption. Having identified these risks, an entity can develop and implement a program designed specifically to look for and locate evidence of specific fraud and corruption types.

AUSTRALIAN STANDARDS

Two standards released by Standards Australia International on 23 June 2003 are aimed specifically at combatting fraud and corruption:

- AS 8001 *Fraud and Corruption Control*
- AS 8004 *Whistleblower Protection Programs for Entities.*

Copies of these standards can be obtained from Standards Australia (www.standards.org.au)

Fraud and Corruption Control

AS 8001 *Fraud and Corruption Control* provides an outline for an approach to controlling fraud and corruption across all entities. It covers a range of issues including:

- implementation of a sound ethical culture including a program for regular benchmarking
- ensuring senior management commitment to the control of fraud and corruption
- periodic risk assessment of fraud and corruption facing the entity
- management and staff awareness of fraud and how to respond
- fraud and corruption control planning
- the importance of internal control systems
- fraud detection programs
- reporting mechanisms.

The operational elements of the *Fraud and Corruption Control* standard include ten practically-based initiatives that organisations could and should adopt in the interests of mitigating the risks of fraud.

Whistleblower Protection Programs

AS 8004 *Whistleblower Protection Programs for Entities* is the first attempt in Australia to provide broad-based guidance for entities wishing to implement a whistleblower protection program.

The main principles of this standard are the active protection of whistleblowers through the development and promulgation of an appropriate policy; the appointment of a 'Whistleblower Protection Officer'; and the appointment of a 'Whistleblower Investigation Officer'. The standard aims to encourage the reporting of fraudulent and corrupt conduct by creating conditions in which employees will feel comfortable reporting matters to senior management. It also provides guidance on how an organisation might go about providing alternative channels for the reporting of fraudulent and corrupt conduct.

The importance of encouraging the organisation's own personnel to report this kind of matter to senior management cannot be overstated. As noted earlier, fraud is most commonly detected through means other than the internal control system. Providing employees with the mechanism to report detected or suspected fraudulent conduct is therefore very important.

INTERNAL CONTROLS

Internal control is essentially a system of policies and procedures developed and implemented by an entity to guide those directors, executives and employees responsible for the entity's performance. It might involve, for example: guidance on how certain types of transaction should be processed, including authorisation procedures; limitations on how much can be spent by a given cost centre during a financial year; or the way in which annual leave is to be recorded.

There are four main purposes of internal control:
- to prevent errors in the processing or recording of the entity's transactions
- to provide for accurate reporting of the entity's financial performance and financial position to interested stakeholders and external parties
- to provide for effective monitoring and management of the entity's business performance during a particular accounting period
- to prevent fraud and corruption.

Internal control is most effective if it targets risks that are of particular concern to the organisation. This implies identification of the risks, and then the structuring of the control systems in such a way that it has the maximum impact on the risks the entity seeks to manage.

When you think about internal control within your own business, it is not difficult to identity the particular risk that a given control is trying to prevent. For example, an internal control that requires authorisation of accounts-payable transactions by a person more senior than the person who requisitioned the goods is aimed at ensuring that goods ordered are necessary for the operation of the business. An internal control that requires the cost of goods purchased to be allocated to individual profit centres is aimed at ensuring that the manager responsible for that profit centre is able to monitor the expenditure incurred. An internal control that requires the person who acknowledges the receipt of goods into the organisation to be a person other than the person who authorised the purchase of those goods is aimed at preventing unauthorised purchase of goods, possibly for the personal benefit of the staff members involved.

Tip from the trenches

Practical internal control for your business should include:

- documenting all policies and procedures
- ensuring the policies and procedures actually address the organisation's risks
- ensuring that policies and procedures are adhered to
- ensuring that details of every business transaction are known by at least two people (and preferably more than two) within the business
- ensuring that all business transactions are authorised by a person other than the person initiating the transaction
- ensuring that profit/cost centre reports are issued in sufficient detail for the manager of the profit/cost centre to review large items of expenditure or significant budget variances
- retaining business records for at least seven years
- reviewing a sample of transactions after they have been processed (looking for irregular changes to transactions after the event)
- knowing your suppliers (and ensuring that new suppliers your business is dealing with for the first time actually exist)
- obtaining alternative quotations for all major purchases.

Categories of internal control

Internal controls fall into six major categories, as set out in the table below.

Category	Purpose
Policies and procedures	To ensure that policies and procedures are documented and properly communicated.
Segregation of duty	To ensure that no one person within the organisation has control of all of the processes required in order to effect a transaction.
Reconciliation	To ensure that all transactions affecting the entity recorded in one system agree with other systems used by the entity (e.g. debtor reconciliation, bank reconciliation).
Authorisation	To ensure that all transactions undertaken are for the benefit of the entity.
Recording	To ensure that transactions are accurately recorded in the entity's accounting records.
Supervision	To ensure that every person is supervised in his or her job function by at least one other person – even the CEO of the organisation should be supervised (i.e. by the board).

PHYSICAL SECURITY

Aside from an internal control system aimed, at least in part, at preventing or identifying incidence of fraud and corruption against the entity, all entities should regularly consider the effectiveness of their security systems. Experience has shown that criminals, whether they be fraudsters or criminals bent on stealing corporate assets, will attack the 'soft target' in preference to an entity that has gone to some trouble to safeguard its assets.

The table below provides a checklist of the attributes of a sound physical security regime.

Attribute	Definition
Access and egress controls	Control over physical access to any site controlled by the entity and used for business purposes. This will typically involve security at the usual points of entry onto the site including gates, guardhouse, electronic monitoring at the point of entry, card-reading devices.
Secure doors and windows	General condition and security of doors and windows, particularly after-hours. Are they sufficient to deny access to a determined trespasser?
Perimeter security	General condition of gates and fences. Are they in good repair? Do they notify people that security procedures are in place that will detect them if they enter the site?
Security lighting	General condition of after-hours lighting. Is it sufficient to illuminate all potential points of entry onto the site? If movement-activated, is this feature operational? Is it sufficient to allow any closed-circuit television (CCTV) cameras to be effective?

Car-park security	Are vehicles, including private vehicles of the entity's employees, allowed to stand adjacent to critical areas of the entity's assets (e.g. adjacent to loading bays)?
Alarms	Is there a 'back-to-base' alarm installed with 24-hour monitoring and arrangements for immediate response to the site?
CCTV cameras	Are CCTV cameras installed as appropriate to the assets controlled? Is there monitoring of activity on CCTV cameras during business hours? Is activity captured on CCTV cameras taped and stored for at least 30 days?
Security of IT area	Is the information technology (IT) area secure against physical attack or intrusion? Is at least one copy of back-up media stored off-site? Is access to IT areas restricted to those members of staff who are required to be there?
Key register	Is there a program of strict control over keys, key cards and passwords on issue? Is there a program for changing keys on a rotation basis?
Security patrols	Does a contractor provide security patrols after-hours?

SECURITY ISSUES FOR RETAILERS

Most retailers will experience 'shrinkage', i.e. loss or theft of stock and takings. The cause of shrinkage is a combination of theft by employees (35 per cent), shoplifting (45 per cent) and system errors (20 per cent). On average, retailers will experience 2–3 per cent shrinkage per annum in their business (relative to sales), so that their revenue will be 2–3 per cent lower than it should have been. For example, if a business sells $2 million worth of goods then average shrinkage would represent a loss of $60 000.

To minimise shrinkage due to stock theft, either by employees or parties external to the entity, retailers should consider the following strategies.

Mirrors Install convex mirrors in your store to give your staff a better perspective of what is happening on the premises. It is important to ensure that staff members pay attention to the mirrors as they are a valuable tool in detecting shoplifters.

Article surveillance Ensure all your goods have sensors built into their price tags so that when an item which has not been paid for is passed through the exit of your store, it triggers a central alarm to alert staff.

Training your staff It is important to train your staff to be alert to shoplifters. Make sure:
- staff are familiar with the prices of all your merchandise. This will keep them from being fooled by people who switch price tags.
- a department is never left unattended.

- staff offer assistance and keep a close eye on anyone who looks anxious or keeps watching their back.
- displays are kept neat and tidy – that way a missing item is easier to notice.

Operating systems and procedures

Consider the following systems and procedures to help minimise security risks in your retail business.

Practical procedures Some practical procedures include:

- limiting the amount of cash in the register or on the premises at any one time. The less money that you have on the premises, the less that can be stolen. Make regular trips to the bank or to a safe. You should never carry your takings home with you
- keeping valuable or easily pocketed merchandise in lockable displays
- considering the use of an armoured-car service to transfer cash to the bank
- ensuring that two employees do the banking together (not only is there a risk that a lone employee will be mugged, but they may be tempted to pretend that they were mugged)
- keeping an eye out for people who appear to be 'staking out' your shop from the outside. If they appear to be loitering, note down any identifying details and don't be afraid to call the police.

What to do in a robbery Premises which have a high turnover of cash – such as petrol stations, liquor stores and fast-food outlets – are common targets for armed robbers. It is vital that you brief your staff on how to react in a robbery. The key rules are that your staff should:

- not resist the demands of the robber

- protect themselves not the money (this is not the time for heroics)
- stay calm and avoid direct eye contact with the robber
- obey the robber's directions and answer their questions with short and simple responses
- always keep their hands in view
- not follow the robber or try to disarm them.

Employee theft in the retail environment Employee theft is rampant in the Australian retail sector and it is estimated that one in ten employees has stolen from their employer, whether it be merchandise, takings, stationery or other items of equipment such as laptops. It is easier for an employee to steal from their employer than it is for an outsider, as they have regular access and inside knowledge about the employer's security systems (or lack thereof).

While those employees who steal things often do it to take home for themselves or their family, some steal on a more professional level for on-sale to third parties. For example, an employee of a large computer wholesaler was apprehended stealing computer chips and then on-selling them, below cost, to another computer retailer who knew that the chips were stolen. Another example involved a large grocery chain where a number of employees colluded in a multi-million-dollar fraud over several years. In this case, fresh groceries were loaded onto a transport truck at one depot and shipped interstate. By the time the trucks arrived at their destination, a significant portion of the groceries had been unloaded and sold to high-street retailers below cost.

You should run regular and random checks of cash takings and stock at hand, and also carefully monitor any wastage reported. If your employees know that you are serious about security and that you have checks in place, they are less likely to attempt theft. Always split responsibility for cash-handling between different people.

Be upfront with your employees about what the rules are on employee discounts or 'freebies'. Indifference by management, or over-generosity, can create an atmosphere ripe for abuse. If you allow staff to take home merchandise indiscriminately or give special preference to individual staff members, you may be seen to be condoning theft (the other staff will think that 'what is good for one should be good for all'). On the other hand, running your business like an army camp is not good for morale, and high morale should lessen the chances of fraud.

One way of minimising security risk in your business is to maintain a regular presence and to be involved in its day-to-day running. If you are an anonymous figurehead then your employees will care less about stealing from you; if you are actively involved, you will get to know your staff better.

Another way of minimising the risk of employee theft is to encourage an environment of staff and/or clients reporting theft or fraud. The reporting system can include an anonymous complaints system, such as a suggestions box. If one of your staff members starts to live beyond their means, it may be that they are doing so at the business's expense. Staff who have problems with gambling, alcohol or drugs may resort to fraud or theft to finance their problems.

Concealing an ongoing fraud will never be easy and stress may be a symptom of a staff member's attempt to cover up their crime. Staff who never take their holidays may be trying to avoid the risk of replacement staff uncovering fraudulent activities.

You may be able to protect yourself by taking out fidelity

insurance (see chapter fifteen). Other controls which can be put in place to reduce the risk of employee fraud include:

- ensuring employees take allocated holidays
- conducting reconciliations between cash and stock
- ensuring separation of duties and staff rotation on a periodic basis.

You should ensure that employees are trained with respect to your systems and procedures as soon as they join your business; if you have a relaxed attitude to security, you cannot expect any more of your staff.

Cash registers If your company deals predominately with cash and you do not use a cash register, it will be extremely difficult to track your cashflow position. It may take quite some time to uncover theft of takings, by which time the employee may well have resigned from your business – particularly in the retail sector, where employees are often transient (and therefore less committed to their employers).

A cash register gives you the ability to 'check and balance' the amount at the end of the day's trading against the amount in the register at the beginning of the day. In other words, if you add your cash float to the day's takings it should equal the figure shown on your cash-register roll. If it does not, you have the right to ask questions of the people in charge of the register.

It is important to bear in mind, however, that your employees might still find ways of taking cash, even if you use a cash register. You will still need to conduct random audits of the register to demonstrate to your staff that you are monitoring how much money is in the till. You should also install a security camera above the cash register. If a customer presents cash, the camera will pick up whether it lands in a staff member's pocket or in the register. Obviously, if a sale is not rung up on the cash register, there is no evidence that the sale was ever made.

Refunds Another problem area occurs when employees claim illegitimate cash refunds by filling in a cash-refund form and pocketing the money. The best way of managing this risk is to only allow cash refunds to customers who can display a receipt for the original purchase. Ensure that all employees staple the receipt to the refund docket and take a record of the customer's name, telephone number and licence number. The form should also clearly display the employee who administered the return. At the end of each week or fortnight you can randomly call customers whose names appear on the docket to find out if they actually returned a product.

Discounts Ensure that you do not allow staff to give customer discounts indiscriminately. Staff need to understand your margins and to be given a range within which they can discount certain items. If they give a discount within the range, they should mark it in a transaction register book. A problem commonly occurs when businesses promise to match discounts given by competitors. Staff should always verify the prices by sighting a brochure or advertisement, or by phoning that competitor.

CHECKLIST FOR FRAUD AND THEFT PREVENTION

Australian business does not need to suffer fraud. Most cases of fraud are preventable if some basic, and relatively inexpensive, precautionary measures are taken.

The following ten steps can be implemented in most

organisations in most industries to help reduce the risk of fraud and corruption:

1. Implement a fraud and corruption control plan based on AS 8001.
2. Implement a whistleblower protection program as outlined in AS 8004.
3. Ensure that executives and senior management are aware of, and committed to, the need to control the risks of fraud and corruption.
4. Conduct a regular program of fraud and corruption risk assessment.
5. Consider the adequacy of the entity's code of conduct/ code of ethics and, where necessary, ensure that it is regularly updated.
6. Conduct regular benchmark testing of ethics and integrity within the organisation.
7. Train all staff in how to recognise fraud or corruption and what to do if it is detected or suspected.
8. Ensure that internal controls are properly documented, updated and enforced, and that there are sufficient resources to enable internal controls to be enforced.
9. Implement a fraud and corruption detection program aimed at identifying early warning indicators of fraud or corruption.
10. Implement a pre-employment screening program for all prospective employees in order to identify those with a criminal record or those who have been terminated from previous employment because of dishonest behaviour.

23. WHERE TO GET HELP

- **State and territory assistance**
- **Other resources**

STATE AND TERRITORY ASSISTANCE

The state and territory governments are responsible for the provision of the following services to small business operators through their small business agencies:

- booklets and reference publications
- video tapes, audio tapes and training packages
- management training and education
- telephone information and advice
- in-depth counselling and management advice
- information and resources databases
- referrals to other government departments
- business licensing
- referrals to specialist consultants
- direct and indirect financial assistance.

State and territory contact details

Australian Capital Territory: (02) 6283 5200
   www.actchamber.com.au
New South Wales: (02) 9338 6600 or toll-free 13 11 45
   www.business.nsw.gov.au
Northern Territory: (08) 8982 1700 or toll-free 1800 193 111
   www.tbc.nt.gov.au

Queensland: (07) 3001 6359 or toll-free 1300 363 711
   www.sdi.qld.gov.au
South Australia: (08) 8303 2400
   www.southaustralia.biz
Tasmania: (03) 6233 5888 or toll-free 1800 030 688
   www.development.tas.gov.au
Victoria: (03) 9651 7596 or toll-free 13 22 15
   www.businessaccess.vic.gov.au
Western Australia: (08) 9220 0222 or toll-free 1800 199 125
   www.sbdc.com.au

OTHER RESOURCES

The following table lists a number of organisations that can also assist your small business.

RESOURCES FOR SMALL BUSINESSES

Name	Description	Web site address/phone number
ASIC	Australian Securities and Investments Commission	www.asic.gov.au
ASX	Australian Stock Exchange	www.asx.com.au
Australian Bureau of Statistics	The Australian Bureau of Statistics (ABS) collects statistical information on a wide variety of social and economic activities. It publishes a large number of reports including: • demographic statistics and trends • manufacturing and wholesale businesses • census of population and housing • household expenditure survey • census of retail businesses and selected service businesses.	Phone: 1300 135 070 www.abs.gov.au
Australian Business Limited	Provides advice on making business decisions and staying competitive.	www.australianbusiness.com.au

Australian Franchise Opportunities Exchange	Exchange service which lists opportunities in the franchise sector.	www.franchisedirectory.com.au
Australian Government Publishing Service	The Australian Government Publishing Service (AGPS) publishes a wide range of publications for small businesses on behalf of the Commonwealth Government. You can purchase AGPS publications over the counter from Government Info Shops or by contacting AGPS Mail Order Sales in Canberra. Ask for a copy of the *Business Publications* catalogue for a full listing.	www.publications.gov.au
Australian Taxation Office	Provides a wealth of tax information for businesses and individuals, including employer obligations, a small business guide and details of expense claims.	www.ato.gov.au
Australian Venture Capital Association	The industry body which represents the venture capital industry. Its web site contains a very useful listing of its members.	www.avcal.com.au

Name	Description	Web site address/phone number
Chambers of commerce	There is a chamber of commerce in most communities which offers legal and financial advice, economic and taxation advice, business information, import/export information, and a reference library.	These can be accessed at www.business.gov.au
Franchisenet	Offers news on franchising, a directory of franchising opportunities and a search facility.	www.franchise.net.au
QCCI	Queensland Chamber of Commerce and Industry	www.qcci.com.au
Small Business Centre	Provides information, resources and tutorials for small and home-based businesses.	www.ozemail.com.au/sbguide (click on 'Your business')
Small Business Institute of WA	Offers courses and programs, or search the institute's database for documents and offer your opinions.	www.wa.gov.au
Small Business Support Network	Provides local and international networking and promotional opportunities.	www.ozsmallbiz.net

State and Regional Development NSW	Provides information, advice and assistance to foster business growth in NSW.	www.business.nsw.gov.au
Venture Capital Marketplace	Provides a current list of direct investment opportunities.	www.v-capital.com.au
WA Chamber of Commerce and Industry		www.cciwa.com

GLOSSARY

A

Account – a record of a business transaction. When you buy something on credit, the company you are dealing with sets up an account – a record of what you buy and pay. You will do the same thing with any customers to whom you extend credit.

Account payee only – words often written on crossed cheques directing the bank to pay the cheque only to the bank account of the payee.

Accountant – a person skilled in keeping business financial records. Commonly refers to a trained professional rather than someone who keeps books of account.

Accounts payable – money owed to suppliers and other business creditors as a result of purchases of stock and other expenses such as overheads and taxes.

Accounts receivable – a record of what is owed to you. The records of what each customer owes you are your accounts receivable.

Amortisation – the gradual process of writing off the cost of an asset (typically an intangible asset such as goodwill), or of paying off a liability by means of a sinking fund, over a period of time.

Asset – anything of worth that is owned or controlled by a business, including cash at bank, accounts receivable, property or buildings, and intangible assets such as trademarks or designs.

ASX – Australian Stock Exchange.

Audit – a detailed inspection of the financial records of a business by an independent qualified person (auditor) to confirm their correctness or to detect errors or fraud.

Australian Business Number (ABN) – an identifier for dealings with the Australian Taxation Office and for future dealings with other government departments and agencies.

Award – an agreement with legal enforceability which sets out working conditions and wages for certain types of employment.

B

Bad debts – money owed to you (i.e. accounts receivable) that you cannot collect.

Balance – the amount of money remaining in an account. The total amount of your money in the bank after accounting for all transactions (deposits and withdrawals) is called a balance.

Balance sheet – an important business document that shows what a business owns and what it owes as of the date shown. Essentially it is a list of business assets and their historical cost on one side, and a list of liabilities and owners' equity (investment in the business) on the other.

Bank reconciliation – a comparison between the bank's record of transactions and the record of the firm's cashbook. The two records should show an identical balance after taking into account items such as unpresented cheques, bank charges, etc.

Bankrupt – a debtor who has volunteered or been forced to appear before a bankruptcy court and been judged insolvent because they have insufficient assets to meet the demands of all creditors.

Benchmarking – comparing different companies in the same industry based on the same criteria (for example, mobile-phone businesses could be compared on average number of months before a customer terminates their contract).

Bond – payment by a tenant to a landlord before the tenant takes over the premises. The landlord may deduct arrears and costs of remedying any damage from the bond.

Bookkeeping – the process of recording business transactions in the accounting records.

Break-even point – the point at which volume of sales is sufficient to cover all costs.

Bridging loan – a loan to provide short-term finance, usually to buy property or land, where the loan is to be cleared by longer-term borrowing or the sale of assets.

Budget – a plan of revenues and expenses for the future (generally twelve months), expressed in monetary terms.

Business Activity Statement (BAS) – a single form used to report your business tax entitlements and obligations, including the amount of GST payable and your input tax credits.

Business name – the name under which a business trades. Generally must be registered in each state where the business trades in a register of business names.

C

Capital – the total owned and borrowed funds in a business.

Capital gain – a financial gain made from selling fixed assets such as land, buildings or shares at a profit over the historic value.

Capital requirement – a list of expenses that must be met to establish a business. Even before a business is started, the owner should begin to keep records.

Cash – includes all money in the bank, in the cash drawer and in petty cash. Banknotes, coins, bills and negotiable securities (like cheques), and money you can draw on demand (bank accounts or savings accounts) are all classified as cash.

Cash flow – the flow of internal funds generated within a business as a result of receipts from debtors, payments to creditors, drawings and cash sales.

Caveat emptor – let the buyer beware. The condition of sale is that the purchase is at the buyer's risk.

Collateral – security provided by a borrower to the lender to cover the possibility that the loan will not be repaid.

Consumer price index (CPI) – a measure of the aggregate rises or falls in prices of commonly used goods and services. It is published by the Commonwealth Government to be used as a foundation for deciding what general increases should be made to wages and salaries (among other things).

Contingent liability – a liability which may arise depending upon the occurrence of a certain event (for example, the guarantor of a loan being asked to honour the guarantee if the borrower defaults).

Contract – a legally binding agreement between two or more parties.

Copyright – a type of intellectual property right preventing the expression of ideas (such as literary or dramatic works, television productions, drawings, etc.) from being used for commercial gain without permission of the copyright owner. Registration is not a prerequisite for protection.

Cost of goods sold – the total cost to a business of the goods sold during an accounting period. In its simplest form this is the sum of the opening stock plus all purchases, less the closing stock.

Cover note – a temporary certificate of insurance issued by an insurance company to give immediate insurance cover until a formal document is prepared and issued.

Credit – an entry made on the right-hand side of an account and indicating a gain to a liability, owners' equity or revenue account.

Credit application – a form to be completed by an applicant for a credit account, giving sufficient details to allow the lender to establish the applicant's creditworthiness.

Creditor – a person or business to whom money is owed by your business.

Crossed cheque – a cheque across which two parallel lines have been drawn. This indicates to the bank that the cheque must be paid into an account and cannot be cashed.

Current assets – includes cash, short-term deposits, accounts receivable, trading stock, or any other assets that will be converted into cash during the normal course of business, within a year of the date of the balance sheet.

Current liabilities – short-term debts such as bank overdrafts, trade creditors and provisions set aside to pay taxation and other commitments (for example, holiday or long-service leave), and expected to come due within one year of the date of the balance sheet.

D

Debit – to place an entry on the left-hand side of an account. A debit in a liability account makes it smaller. A debit in an asset account makes it larger.

Debt – money which is owed to another party. If you borrow money, buy something on credit or receive more money on an account than is owed, you have a debt.

Debtor – a person or business who owes money to your business.

Depreciation expense – the gradual reduction of the value of a fixed asset and the gradual application of this cost to the expenses of a business over the useful life of the asset.

Depreciation schedule – a table showing depreciable assets and the year in which each was purchased, its cost, the percentage by which it is depreciated each year and its written-down current value.

Direct costs – in addition to fixed costs, these are the costs incurred as a result of manufacturing a product or providing a service. Direct costs are made up of direct material, direct labour and direct manufacturing or servicing costs.

Director's guarantee – a personal guarantee given by a director of a company that they will be personally responsible for a debt or other liability of the company. Usually requested in credit applications, leases, loans and hire-purchase agreements.

Disbursements – money paid out of a business in settlement of obligations.

Dishonoured – used to describe a cheque which the bank will not pay because of a lack of sufficient funds in the customer's account.

Dividend – a distribution of the profits of a company among its members or shareholders.

Drawer – the person who writes a cheque in payment for goods or services.

Drawings – withdrawals of assets (usually cash) from a business by a sole proprietor or a partner.

E

Entity – an individual (sole trader), partnership, body corporate, corporation, incorporated association or body of persons, trust or superannuation fund.

Entrepreneur – generally applied to managers or organisers of a business displaying outstanding ability and creativity in launching and succeeding with new business ventures.

Equities – stocks and shares invested in a business, entitled to a proportionate share of the profit and not generally bearing fixed interest or a right to repayment.

Equity capital – money provided by the business owner/s to finance the business.

Excess – in an insurance policy, excess clauses specify that the policyholder will be responsible for a portion of claims under certain conditions.

Expenses – costs incurred by a business in earning income – for example, rent, advertising, wages, etc.

F

Factoring – the process of selling your accounts receivable to a 'factor' at a discount. The factoring company then collects the invoiced amounts from the business's customers. Factoring is undertaken when a business needs immediate cash.

Financial statements – formal reports prepared from accounting records and describing the financial position and performance of a business.

Financial year – an accounting period of twelve months, usually 1 July to 30 June.

Fixed assets – the land, buildings, vehicles, materials and equipment owned by a business, which are used to earn revenue instead of being for sale.

Fixed costs – costs incurred by a business, whether it is operating to generate income or not. They are unaffected by the volume of production. Rent, for example, must be paid whether or not any business is accomplished.

Franchise – a business arrangement in which knowledge, expertise and often a trademark or trade name, are all licensed to an operator, generally for an initial fee and a yearly payment.

Franchisee – the purchaser of a franchise licence who operates one or more outlets of the franchise business.

Franchisor – the owner of a franchise system.

G

Gearing – the ratio between a business's debt and equity finance.

Goodwill – the excess price asked for the sale of a business, above the value of its physical assets, representing a payment for the existing client base and future profits. Goodwill is an intangible asset.

Gross profit – the excess of net sales over cost of goods sold, usually expressed as a percentage.

GST-free – some supplies are GST-free, which means you do not charge GST for them, but you are entitled to claim input tax credits for anything acquired or imported to use in your business.

H

Hire purchase – a system for financing the purchase of plant and equipment. The borrower places a deposit and makes periodic payments (usually monthly) at a flat rate of interest and, upon the final payment, ownership is transferred from the lender to the borrower.

I

Indemnity insurance – risk protection for actions for which a business is liable. A business carries indemnity insurance to cover the possibility of loss from a lawsuit in the event that the business or its agents are found at fault if an action occurs.

Industry ratio – the standard or 'average' percentage of expenses spent by firms in a similar type of business.

Input tax credits – you are entitled to an input tax credit for the GST included in the price you pay for an acquisition, or the GST paid for an importation, if it is for use in your enterprise.

Input taxed – some supplies are input taxed, which means you do not charge GST for them, but neither are you entitled to input tax credits for anything acquired or imported to make the supply.

Intangible assets – those assets of a business which cannot be assigned a definite, fixed value (e.g. leases, franchises, trademarks, goodwill, patent rights).

Interest – the cost of borrowing money.

Inventory – the value of all the stock of physical items that a business uses in its production process or for sale in the ordinary course of doing business. Also known as stock in trade or trading stock.

Investment – money used to purchase any capital items for a business which are expected to yield an income.

Invoice – document that shows the customer charges for goods delivered or work done.

L

Lease – a legal contract covering the possession and use of property, plant or equipment between the owner (lessor) and another person (lessee) at a specified rent for a certain period of time (such as two years).

Leasing finance – a method of acquiring business equipment without capital outlay. The lender buys the equipment and leases it to the customer, in return for regular rental payments for the duration of the lease period.

Lessee – the party to a lease who is the user of the land, buildings, plant or equipment.

Lessor – the party to a lease (owner) who allows his/her land, buildings, plant or equipment to be used under a lease contract.

Liquidator – a qualified person appointed by a court to close down a business that is a proprietary company, and to sell and distribute its assets in payment of its liabilities.

Liquidity ratio – current assets divided by current liabilities.

Loan – money lent at interest. A lender makes a loan with the idea that it will be paid back as agreed and that interest will be paid for the use of the money.

Loss of profits insurance – insurance to cover loss of profits incurred by the policyholder in the event of some catastrophe overtaking the policyholder's business, with the result that trading is interrupted.

M

Margin – the difference between the selling price and the purchase price of an item, generally expressed as a percentage of the selling price.

Market segmentation – the splitting of a market into segments. Each segment consists of a group of consumers with similar requirements, distinguishable from the requirements of other consumers in the market. There will be slight, but distinct, differences between the goods and services needed to meet the requirements of each segment.

Mark-up – the price increase between buying at wholesale and selling at retail, often expressed as a percentage of the wholesale or cost price.

Merchandise – goods that may be sold or traded.

Merchandising – trading in and promoting a range of goods that are sold in a business.

Mortgage – the transfer of right of ownership of a property from a debtor to a creditor as security for a debt, with the proviso that once the debt is paid ownership is transferred back.

Mortgagee – the organisation or person to whom a property is mortgaged. In the case of a bank loan, the organisation is usually the bank.

Mortgagor – a person who mortgages a property.

N

Negative gearing – occurs where an investment is purchased with the assistance of borrowed funds and the income from that investment (after the deduction of expenses) is less than the interest commitment in the course of a year.

Net profit – the remainder after all expenses of an accounting period are deducted from all revenue of the same period.

Net worth – the owner's (or owners') interest in a business, calculated by subtracting all liabilities from the assets of the business.

Niche – a small, specialised portion of a total market, which is viable for a small business.

O

Operating expense – all the expenses normally incurred in operating a business during an accounting period, excluding the cost of goods sold.

Option – an agreement permitting the purchase or sale of something within a specified time, in accordance with the terms of the agreement. For example, a right by a tenant to take up a further lease of premises, usually under conditions outlined in the original lease.

Overdraft – a form of loan by which a person with a trading bank current account is given permission to continue making drawings on the account up to an agreed limit, after the balance has been reduced to nil.

Overheads – expenses which are incurred in producing a commodity or rendering a service, but which cannot easily be attributed to individual units of production or service (such as heating or lighting).

P

Paid-up capital – the total capital of a company comprising of both shares issued for cash and for acquisition of assets, and bonus shares.

Partnership – a legal business relationship of two or more people who share responsibilities, resources, profits and liabilities.

Patent – monopoly rights granted by a government to the owner of an invention to manufacture and sell it for a certain number of years, conditional on the owner being willing to immediately reveal the ideas incorporated in the invention so that they can be published for the advancement of knowledge of the general public.

Pay As You Go (PAYG) instalments – the amounts you pay directly to the Commissioner of Taxation to meet your income tax and other liabilities. Usually paid each quarter.

Payee – person to whom money is paid.

Personal assets – the money you have in the bank, whatever is owed to you, any securities (shares), property, furniture and appliances you own, plus any other miscellaneous items that you personally own.

Petty cash – a small amount of money kept for minor purchases (not large enough to justify writing a cheque) for the business.

Power of attorney – the power to act on behalf of another person for specified purposes.

Premium – the amount paid for an insurance policy.

Principal – the actual amount borrowed and, in the case of a loan, on which interest is paid.

Profit – total revenue less total expenses for a period of time, calculated in accordance with generally accepted accounting principles.

Profit and loss statement – a statement of revenue and expenses showing the profit or loss for a certain period of time.

Profit margin – the amount by which the price of a product or service is raised above its cost in order to provide a gross profit.

Pro-forma invoice – a document giving all the details of a proposed transaction, but not committing either the sender or recipient until the recipient pays the sender the amount shown. Commonly used by wholesalers for the first transaction with new customers.

Projection – a forecast of future trends in the operation of a business.

Proprietary company – a business which is owned by not less than two, and not more than fifty, persons and which restricts the right of the shareholders to transfer shares. Such a business is a separate legal entity and must use the words Proprietary Limited (Pty Ltd) after its name.

R

Receipt – documentary evidence provided by a person or business that goods/money have been received by them.

Receivership – the legal condition of a company when an official receiver is appointed to investigate and manage its affairs.

Residual – the pre-agreed estimated value at the end of a leasing period of an item subject to a leasing agreement.

Retail – selling directly to the consumer, usually in small quantities in comparison with the total level of sales.

Return on investment (ROI) – net profit after income tax, over owners' equity (commonly expressed as a percentage).

S

Sales – the total value of goods sold or revenue from services rendered.

Secured – protected or guaranteed, as in the case of a loan where the lender holds the title of some asset until the borrower has fully repaid the loan.

Sole trader – a person who trades by himself/herself without the use of a company structure or partners, and who is solely responsible for the actions of the business.

Solvent – the condition of a business when all debts can be paid as they fall due.

Stock – physical items that a business uses in its production process or has for sale in the ordinary course of doing business.

Stock at valuation (SAV) – stock valued at wholesale or cost price.

Stock control – the process of determining how much stock should be held, and how much needs to be reordered and when. The goal is to control stock holding costs whilst maintaining the operational efficiency of the business.

Stock turnover – the cost of goods sold to average stock (at cost). This ratio indicates how many times, on average, the entire inventory (stock) was sold and replaced during the year.

T

Tangible asset – something substantial or real that is capable of being given an actual or approximate value, such as land and buildings.

Tender – an offer in writing to carry out work specified by another person. It quotes the fixed price to be charged for carrying out the work.

Term loan – a loan for a fixed period of more than one year, repayable by regular instalments.

Trade credit – an arrangement to buy goods or services on account without making immediate cash payment.

Trade discount – an allowance made by a seller to a buyer at the time of purchase, for the deduction of a percentage of the price (provided the payment is made within the agreed terms).

Trademark – a name, symbol, figure, letter, word or other mark used to distinguish goods as the produce of a particular manufacturer.

U

Undercapitalisation – insufficient investment of funds in a business.

Unsecured loan – a loan made without any guarantee that the lender will be repaid.

V

Valuation – the process of appraising the worth of property according to some established criteria.

Variable costs – the costs, additional to fixed costs, of running a business.

Vendor – a seller of goods or of a business.

Venture capital – capital invested into a high-growth business, generally structured as an equity investment.

W

Walk-in, walk-out (WIWO) – indicates that a business is for sale as a going concern (with all the fittings, stock, etc. included) and may be purchased without interruption to trading.

Wholesale – selling in large quantities to businesses, which will then resell to consumers in smaller quantities.

Workers' compensation – money paid to an employee to compensate for injuries received in connection with their work. All employers must insure against claims for this kind of compensation.

Working capital – the excess of current assets over current liabilities of any business at any time.

INDEX

The Penguin Australian Home Buyer's Guide
Nicholas Humphrey

Whether you're a newcomer to home ownership or a seasoned investor, buying property is likely to be the biggest investment decision you'll ever make.

The Penguin Australian Home Buyer's Guide is THE guide to finding, financing and buying a home or investment property. It explains in plain English the key legal and financial issues in property purchase and provides an up-to-date, Australia-wide analysis of the property market. This practical guide contains advice on everything you need to know about property investment, such as:

- when and where you should buy
- what you can afford to borrow
- how to use the Net to find the right property
- how the GST impacts on new home buyers
- how to apply for your first-home-buyer's grant
- what to expect in transaction costs
- how to save on your mortgage.

Fully revised and updated, this book equips first-home buyers, property investors and vendors to make informed, profitable investment decisions.

'All you need to know about the biggest investment you'll make.'
Better Homes and Gardens